VIETNAM WAR STORIES

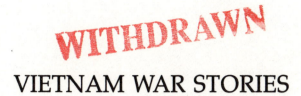

Almost two decades after the end of hostilities, the Vietnam War remains a dominant moral, political, and military touchstone in American cultural consciousness.

Vietnam War Stories provides a comprehensive critical framework for understanding the Vietnam experience, Vietnam narratives, and modern war literature. The narratives examined – personal accounts as well as novels – portray a soldier's and a country's journey from pre-war innocence, through battlefield experience and consideration, to a difficult post-war adjustment. Tobey Herzog places these narratives within the context of important cultural and literary themes, including inherent ironies of war, the "John Wayne syndrome" of pre-war innocence, and the "heavy Heart-of-Darkness trip" of the conflict itself.

Vietnam War Stories will be essential reading for various literature courses, as well as a useful supplementary text for courses in cultural and media studies, American studies, political science, and military history. Accessibly written, it will also appeal to general readers interested in America's loss of innocence on the Vietnam battlefield.

Tobey Herzog is Associate Professor of English at Wabash College, Indiana, and a Vietnam veteran. For the past twelve years he has taught courses on American and modern war literature, and on film emerging from the Vietnam War. He has also published a number of articles in this field.

Vietnam War Stories

INNOCENCE LOST

TOBEY C. HERZOG

London and New York

First published in 1992
by Routledge
11 New Fetter Lane, London EC4P 4EE

Simultaneously published in the USA and Canada
by Routledge
a division of Routledge, Chapman and Hall Inc.
29 West 35th Street, New York, NY 10001

Typeset by Falcon Typographic Art Ltd,
Edinburgh
Printed and bound in Great Britain

British Library Cataloguing in Publication Data
A catalogue record for this book is
available from the British Library

Library of Congress Cataloging in Publication Data
Herzog, Tobey C.
Vietnam war stories: innocence lost / Tobey C. Herzog.
p. cm.
Includes bibliographical references and index.
1. Vietnamese Conflict, 1961–1975 – Literature and the conflict.
2. American literature – 20th century – History and criticism.
3. War stories, American – History and criticism. 4. Innocence in
literature. I. Title.
PS228.V5H4   1992
813'.5409358 – dc20   91–41795   CIP

ISBN 0–415–07630–7 (hbk)
ISBN 0–415–07631–5 (pbk)

This book is dedicated to
my wife, Peggy
my sons, Rob and Joe
my mother, Ann
my father, First Sergeant Robert F. Herzog

Contents

Acknowledgements

I was able to complete this book because of the generous financial support of Wabash College through its McLain–McTurnan–Arnold Research Grants for faculty. Several individuals made this project much easier by contributing their time, talents, advice, and friendship. Staff at the American School in London and Debbie Wagers helped with manuscript preparation; David Schulz assisted with initial research; Wabash student-intern David Stone provided invaluable research and background information and served as a helpful reader; and Professor William J. Searle, friend and fellow Vietnam veteran, gave advice and support. Most of all, Wabash students in my Vietnam Tutorial and Modern War Literature course contributed questions, insights, and enthusiastic encouragement. Finally, my deepest gratitude goes to friend and colleague Donald W. Baker, who has taught me about war through his poetry and his conversation.

The author also wishes to thank the following who have kindly given permission for the use of copyright material:

Parts of Chapter 1 are based on previously published material by the author which appeared in *Search and Clear: Critical Responses to Selected Literature and Films of the Vietnam War*, edited by William J. Searle 1988. Copyright © 1988 by the Bowling Green State University Popular Press, Bowling Green, Ohio 43403. Reprinted with permission.

Parts of Chapter 4 are based on previously published material by the author which appeared in *Critique: Studies in Modern Fiction*, volume 24, pages 88–96, Winter 1983. Copyright © 1983.

ACKNOWLEDGEMENTS

Published by Heldref Publications, 4000 Albermarle Street, NW, Washington, DC, 20016. Reprinted with permission of the Helen Dwight Reid Educational Foundation.

Excerpts from the book *Dispatches* by Michael Herr, 1977. Copyright © 1968, 1969, 1970, 1977 by Michael Herr. Reprinted by permission of Alfred A. Knopf, Inc., and Picador.

Excerpts from the book *Fields of Fire* by James Webb. Copyright © 1978 by James Webb. Used by permission of the publisher, Prentice Hall, a division of Simon & Schuster, Englewood Cliffs, NJ.

Excerpts from the book *Going After Cacciato* by Tim O'Brien. Copyright © 1975, 1976, 1977, 1978 by Tim O'Brien. Used by permission of Delacorte Press/Seymour Lawrence, a division of Bantam Doubleday Dell Publishing Group, Inc.

Excerpts from the book *If I Die in a Combat Zone* by Tim O'Brien. Copyright © 1973 by Tim O'Brien. Used by permission of Delacorte Press/Seymour Lawrence, a division of Bantam Doubleday Dell Publishing Group, Inc.

Excerpts from the book *Indian Country* by Philip Caputo. Copyright © 1987 by Philip Caputo. Used by permission of Bantam Books, a division of Bantam Doubleday Dell Publishing Group, Inc.

Excerpts from the book *The 13th Valley* by John Del Vecchio. Copyright © 1982 by John M. Del Vecchio. Used by permission of Bantam Books, a division of Bantam Doubleday Dell Publishing Group, Inc.

Excerpts from the book *A Rumor of War* by Philip Caputo. Copyright © 1977 by Philip Caputo. Reprinted by permission of Henry Holt and Company, Inc., and the author.

My Subject is War, and the pity of War.
Wilfred Owen
"Preface" to his World War I poetry

Look, sure Vietnam's a terrible, horrible war, and we've lost a helluva lot of good men over there, but . . . but everything is not black about Vietnam and everybody who participated is not a . . . a double-headed ogre! It's misconceptions, distortions, blanket condemnations of anyone and everyone involved with Vietnam that I disagree with so vehemently.

H. Norman Schwarzkopf
LTC, US Army Infantry
November 1971
(C. D. B. Bryan, *Friendly Fire*, 1976, 317)

Introduction

Can the foot soldier teach anything important about war, merely for having been there? I think not. He can tell war stories.

Tim O'Brien, *If I Die in a Combat Zone*

War stories are nothing more than stories about people.

Michael Herr, *Dispatches*

As rhetoric and events of the recent Gulf War and its aftermath pointedly illustrate, for Americans, the word "Vietnam" is much more than the name of a country or of a war fought years ago. In fact, American film director Oliver Stone (*Platoon* and *Born on the Fourth of July*) observed, that Vietnam is a "state of mind": a moral, political, emotional, and even artistic touchstone for people living through the Vietnam experience in the 1960s and 1970s, at home or on the battlefield. For these "veterans" the word evokes names (Kennedy, Nixon, Ellsberg, Westmoreland, Ho Chi Minh, General Nguyen Giap, Jane Fonda), events (My Lai, 1968 Tet Offensive, 1968 Democratic Convention, the return of America's POWs in 1973), and powerful emotions (anger, patriotism, confusion, grief, sympathy). For a new generation of Americans not yet born during the Vietnam era or too young to remember the events, the word summons myths, an intense fascination, and many questions. This generation connects with the war often through the numerous Vietnam War movies, survivors' war stories, continued controversies about Agent Orange and Post-Traumatic Stress Disorder, and belated outpourings of support for Vietnam veterans – homecoming

1

parades and pilgrimages to the Vietnam Veterans Memorial in Washington, DC.

Increasingly these young people and the participants who lived through the experience have turned to the astonishing amount of literature dealing with the conflict (histories, memoirs, poetry, drama, nonfiction, and fiction) for entertainment, information, catharsis, or analysis of this enigmatic experience.[1] In fact, because of widespread interest in the Vietnam era, American literature about the war has attained commercial success. Even Danielle Steel, one of America's most popular and prolific romantic novelists, gratuitously uses the Vietnam War as a setting for her recent bestseller *Message from Nam*. Furthermore, just as many military veterans, male and female, now feel comfortable discussing their service in Vietnam, or just as some baby-boomers now regret their Vietnam-era draft deferments, so it is *de rigueur* for people to boast that they are serious readers of Vietnam War literature. Such literary journeys into this "modern Heart of Darkness" frequently occur independently or within the boundaries of the growing number of college courses (political science, sociology, history, and literature) or reading groups exploring the Vietnam era. For these readers – those traveling alone or with others – this book introduces selected works from this body of Vietnam narratives (nonfiction and fiction). It also broadens critical perspectives of these narratives by presenting some overarching cultural and literary themes, along with basic critical, historical, and biographical commentary to aid readers in understanding and evaluating these books.

Simply stated, this critical study examines literary war stories, specifically American soldier–authors' narratives from the Vietnam War, and it does so influenced by two basic observations. First, notwithstanding the apparent insignificance Tim O'Brien attaches to such tales, and despite a comment in his latest novel, *The Things They Carried*, that "a true war story is never moral" (1990, 76), the best war stories, fiction and nonfiction, contain important lessons about war – if readers pay attention. More important, as Herr notes, these stories tell readers a lot about people, including the storytellers. The best tales, whether told by participants and observers remembering war or by artists imagining the experiences, cut through ideological

2

cant and battlefield action to explore the often disturbing, ambiguous, and complex elements of war, human behavior, and life. They tell of courage, fear, cowardice, self-sacrifice, evil, life, death, and war's obscenity, as well as its attraction. A few of these stories contain occasional humorous anecdotes about war. Others are confessionals, as storytellers pour out their exhilaration, physical pain, emotional suffering, or guilt related to the experience. Most reduce war to basic issues: participants instinctively struggling to kill and survive and in the process sinking to ignominious depths of evil; rising to glorious moments of self-sacrifice, compassion, and honor; or routinely existing on the battlefield. The result is a fundamental sympathy for combat soldiers as fallible human beings living within the crucible of war. Finally, these war stories strive for a higher level of literary truth that Joseph Conrad describes in his preface to *The Nigger of the "Narcissus"* "as a single-minded attempt to render the highest kind of justice to the visible universe, by bringing to light the truth, manifold and one, underlying its every aspect." Tim O'Brien (1990, 203) says this more simply: "Story truth is truer sometimes than happening truth."

The second observation is that, in spite of obvious differences involving the nature, conduct, and perceptions of the Vietnam War and other modern wars, the best stories from these conflicts suggest a fundamental universality among wars: emotions, combat experiences, battlefield rituals, and changes soldiers undergo. In other words, to understand Vietnam narratives, readers should know something about events and people from other wars. Thus, seeing the images and hearing the words of civilians and soldiers in Ken Burns's 1990 film documentary *The Civil War* confirms these connections, especially the recurring tedium and terror in a soldier's battlefield existence. Or the following quote from Tim O'Brien's Vietnam memoir, *If I Die in a Combat Zone,* suggests this historical and human continuity:

> The night was clear. We ate C rations and drank some beer. Then the guard started, the ritual come alive from our pagan past – Thucydides and Polybius and Julius Caesar, tales of encampment, tales of night terror – the long silent stare into an opaque shell of shadows and dark. ([1973] 1979, 132)

And another example of such bonds emerges from media coverage of America's military action in Panama in December 1989. A story in the *Chicago Tribune* (23 December 1989, p. 4) headlined "For paratrooper, a startling reality: Combat changes ideas of soldier 19" reiterates a familiar theme – a young soldier's loss of innocence and romantic illusions on the battlefield. In this article about an American army private wounded during the initial military assault, the soldier describes himself before combat as a typical "'gung-ho paratrooper who had seen every movie and read every book on the Vietnam War . . . and couldn't wait to experience combat firsthand.'" His mother, interviewed at the military hospital in the USA where her son later had been evacuated, observes that now "'he's scared. He said it was nothing like any of the war movies he'd seen. . . . He's changed.'" Such reactions are typical as soldiers, usually young and frequently from diverse backgrounds, enter war with this sense of adventure and innocence shaped by cultural myths, an older generation's war stories, and society's beliefs about war as a rite of passage and a test of character and courage. But, for many real and fictional warriors, the realities and ironies of combat forever destroy their naïveté and lead them to crucial insights about human nature and war. Some soldiers submit to this spiritual and psychological journey; others resist as they hold on to civilization's trappings, saving illusions, or surface details.

Because of these similarities among soldiers' experiences, literary war stories, across time, wars, continents, and cultures, have common elements: narrative patterns, images, characters, themes, inner conflicts, and an overall ironic perspective. Philip Caputo in *A Rumor of War* describes these timeless tales as basically stories of "what men do in war and what war does to them" ([1977] 1978, xiii). Such formal and thematic connections within the war genre suggest one significant literary context for reading Vietnam war stories. Modern war literature from America's Civil War, World War I, and World War II become helpful introductions to Vietnam narratives. This book critically examines a particular group of these literary war stories and their characters – specifically stories about foot soldiers, or grunts. For the most part, the narratives involve American infantry soldiers in the Vietnam War, but also include foot soldiers from other wars who together form a timeless brotherhood of warriors. Within this collection, we find individuals who are naïve or cynical, intuitive or unthinking, powerful or powerless, civilized or uncivilized, callous or compassionate, cowardly or courageous. This book surveys their language, actions, humor, doubts, fears, rituals, attitudes, courage, bravery, cowardice, and unspeakable acts. Most of all, this book chronicles quests – quests by characters and authors to achieve some understanding of themselves and their war experiences and quests to find a spiritual home once they return from the battlefield. As Peter G. Jones notes in *War and the Novelist*, in the most thoughtful war literature "the predicament of war drives the protagonist deep into his own resources, forcing him to face himself and to examine his principles with unprecedented scrutiny" (1976, 3). Thus, this book studies what Philip D. Beidler in *American Literature and the Experience of Vietnam* calls "literary sense making," an attempt by authors, characters, and even readers to arrive at individual and collective meaning in the midst of the befuddlement, confusion, and chaos of combat. Indirectly, it also explores emotional catharsis as soldier–authors and a nation work through their war experiences – recalling, shaping, altering, purging, and understanding their feelings and memories.

In fact, as indicated by the label "soldier–authors," nine of the ten Vietnam books discussed in detail were written by people who experienced war firsthand, either as combatants or as war correspondents. (The one exception is Bobbie Ann Mason's *In Country*.) The voices of these soldier–authors present an important perspective of war, one counterbalancing the views of media, historians, the military hierarchy, government, and people at home. Sometimes, as in Philip Caputo's *A Rumor of War*, Michael Herr's *Dispatches*, or Tim O'Brien's *If I Die in a Combat Zone*, the perspective is strongly rooted in the authors' personal experiences – eyewitness accounts filtered through memory and shaped by literary devices. These stories, structured to develop personal and moral conflicts, as well as the ironies of war, have the feel of experiential truth as their authors re-create for readers the sights, sounds, smells, feelings, language, and strategies of war. In contrast, the other narratives progress beyond this level of factual realism into a realm where memory and invention transmute raw materials into a fictional treatment of war experiences (Larry Heinemann's *Close Quarters*, James Webb's *Fields of Fire*, John Del Vecchio's *The 13th Valley*, O'Brien's *Going After Cacciato*, Caputo's *Indian Country*, and Heinemann's *Paco's Story*). These soldier-authors become much more than recorders as they grapple with creative tensions between memories of their own war experiences and the transforming power of the imagination, which allows for greater interpretation and Conrad's higher order of truth. They portray lives and events clearly not their own but ones closely allied with their own Vietnam experiences. O'Brien in *The Things They Carried* describes this creative process:

> You take the material where you find it, which is in your life, at the intersection of past and present. The memory-traffic feeds into a rotary up in your head, where it goes in circles for a while, then pretty soon imagination flows in and the traffic merges and shoots off down a thousand different streets. (1990, 38)

What unites all these nonfiction and fiction books, including those briefly discussed from previous wars, is that, for the most part, they do not celebrate war. Certainly battlefield camaraderie, noble sacrifices, courageous acts, and the exhilaration of performing well in combat surface in many of the stories. But these war stories repeatedly illustrate Paul Fussell's observation in *The Great War and Modern Memory* that wars are ironic because they are always "worse than expected." Nevertheless, the Vietnam narratives do not become politically charged pro- or anti-Vietnam War propaganda portraying the soldiers as mere agents of a government's political, social, and economic policies. The authors, like British soldier-poet Wilfred Owen, broadly examine the underlying truths about conflict, the changes participants undergo, and the human toll of war:

> My Subject is War, and the pity of War.
> The Poetry is in the pity.
> Yet these elegies are to this generation in no sense consolatory. They may be to the next. All a poet can do today is warn. That is why the true Poets must be truthful. (Owen, "Preface")

If indeed any consolations occur, they appear when authors marvel at the variety, mystery, power, adaptability, and even darkness of the human spirit within the crucible of war.

The difficult task of selecting specific works of American literature from the Vietnam War to include in this critical study raises unavoidable questions about literary merit and the existence of an emerging "Vietnam canon." In comparing war novels emerging from World War II with critically acclaimed fiction from World War I (Dos Passos' *Three Soldiers*, Hemingway's *In Our Time* and *A Farewell to Arms*, and Cummings's *The Enormous Room*), Chester Eisinger comments about books from World War II: "Everyone – everyone and his brother, one is tempted to say – wrote a war novel. Some of these books were dull but a great many were competent. . . . Many were written by men who had not before published a novel and have not since" (1963, 21). This critical assessment rings true for American Vietnam narratives written by combat correspondents, officers, and enlisted personnel – many of whom wrote one book and disappeared from the literary scene. Within this growing collection of war literature, both fiction and nonfiction, readers find books that are indeed dull memoirs, propaganda (for or against the war), daily journals in book form, or recycled adventure stories. They also discover, however, significant works that will survive the current fascination with the Vietnam War and will continue to be read for their literary merit and for their contributions to the broader category of modern war literature. These books, transcending immediate experiences, explore the broad continuum of life and war.

Vietnam War Stories: Innocence Lost examines this latter category of war stories written by Vietnam soldier–authors and civilians who also continued on the literary scene after publishing one book. These authors treat serious themes of the Vietnam War in a sophisticated, artistic, and honest fashion. For the most part, they instinctively perceive people and events, dramatically and coherently tell their stories, and combine depth with subtlety in portraying characters' feelings and thoughts. Some of the works, such as *Dispatches, Going After Cacciato*, and *Paco's Story*, also extend the content or form of war literature. All treat universal themes of the war genre from an interesting perspective; and all realistically and perceptively define the age, the war, and the people who participated in the Vietnam experience. In addition to satisfying these critical criteria, the ten Vietnam narratives under discussion also represent a larger body of important Vietnam texts. Therefore, in their form and content they constitute a critical framework for studying other Vietnam war stories, current or future. Furthermore, the ten books have intriguing thematic and authorial relationships as three of the writers (Caputo, Heinemann, and O'Brien) are represented by two works each. This feature allows readers to trace these authors' literary development and their treatment of fundamental themes from changing perspectives and within different narrative structures.

What follows, then, is a reader's guide to ten Vietnam narratives about American foot soldiers. Missing from the list, because of the arbitrary criteria I have used for choosing the books, are other significant Vietnam war stories, as well as eloquent minority voices heard, for example, in the oral histories collected in Wallace Terry's *Bloods* or Al Santoli's *Everything We Had*. Also missing are significant books written by some of the approximately 8,000 women who served as military nurses and support staff in Vietnam.[2] But, for those works selected, I begin this study with a chapter describing five thematic contexts affording significant entry-points for most American literature about the Vietnam War: (1) "The Ironic Spirit" (a theme of expectation versus reality leading to a recurring three-part structure in war literature of innocence, experience, and consideration); (2) "The John Wayne Syndrome" (John Wayne's influence on American soldiers' and on the public's expectations for the ideal soldier in an ideal war); (3) "A Heavy Heart-of-Darkness Trip" (soldiers' insights and self-discovery acquired in an alien, chaotic, and threatening environment); (4) "Voices from the Past" (soldiers' feelings of insignificance and helplessness described in modern war literature and in Vietnam texts); and (5) "A Different War" (special features of the Vietnam War influencing soldiers' and authors' literary perceptions of war experiences). Along with illustrating these themes, the remaining four chapters trace the natural progression of soldiers engaged in an archetypal journey from prewar innocence (*A Rumor of War* and *Dispatches*), through battlefield experiences (*Close Quarters, Fields of Fire,* and *The 13th*

Valley), to intense consideration of events and feelings (*If I Die in a Combat Zone* and *Going After Cacciato*), and ending with their difficult adjustments to a postwar existence (*Indian Country*, *Paco's Story*, and *In Country*). Scattered throughout these chapters are references to other prominent Vietnam narratives. And, as another important literary context for Chapters 2 through 5, I briefly discuss appropriate selections of modern war literature (*All Quiet on the Western Front*, *The Naked and the Dead*, *The Thin Red Line*, *The Red Badge of Courage*, Wilfred Owen's poetry, and Hemingway's "Big Two-Hearted River") that illuminate the Vietnam works. As a whole these war stories from different times and places form a panegyric for the common soldier and confirm Philip Caputo's observation that "every generation is doomed to fight its war, to endure the same old experiences, suffer the loss of the same old illusions, and learn the same old lessons on its own" ([1977] 1978, 77). They also validate O'Brien's sense that a "true war story, if truly told, makes the stomach believe" (1990, 84).

1

Thematic Contexts

There's nothing new to tell about Vietnam; I'm saying it
was just a war like every war.

Tim O'Brien, *Going After Cacciato*

Paul Fussell, John Wayne, *Heart of Darkness*, *The Naked and
the Dead*, and Post-Traumatic Stress Disorder – what do these
people, books, and a psychological disorder have in common with American literature about the Vietnam War? The
answer: each represents a thematic context (a war theme) to aid
readers in understanding and evaluating Vietnam war stories
by connecting them to historical events, other modern war
literature, and American culture. This chapter introduces five
of these contexts, ones that significantly help readers appreciate
these narratives. Such contextual approaches to reading these
works counteract the tendency of inexperienced readers of
war literature to approach Vietnam narratives in a vacuum.
Immersed in this popular contemporary literature, these readers
often are unaware of the literary, cultural, and historical connections directly or indirectly influencing the purpose, content, and
form of Vietnam war stories. Were the combat experiences of
Americans in Vietnam unique among wars; or is the epigraph
from Tim O'Brien's *Going After Cacciato* about the sameness
of wars also accurate? Compared to soldier-authors writing
about other wars, do Vietnam veterans view their experiences
differently and present war stories in distinct forms? Or is
there a continuity among themes, characters, and narrative
strategies throughout modern war literature? These are some
of the questions addressed in this chapter on contexts.

Certainly, the critic's goal to explore such connections within war stories shapes four current studies of Vietnam narratives and American society during the war: Philip D. Beidler's *American Literature and the Experience of Vietnam,* John Hellmann's *American Myth and the Legacy of Vietnam,* Thomas Myers's *Walking Point: American Narratives of Vietnam,* and Loren Baritz's *Backfire.* Each critic establishes historical, cultural, or literary connections, perhaps as an antidote to what James C. Wilson calls the inability of Vietnam soldiers and some authors to see their war in political, moral, and historical context (1982, 52). Each of these critics suggests that in the Vietnam narratives, fiction and nonfiction, readers find literary or mythic visions that Beidler labels "prophecy and context." Thus, using old and new literary conventions, authors consciously or unconsciously combine new visions with traditional myths and thematic patterns. In short, as Beidler notes, they mix old and new experiences:

American writing about Vietnam, for all one's sense of the new and even unprecedented character of the experience it describes, often turns out to be very much in context . . . with regard to our national traditions of literature and popular myth-making at large. (1982, 19)

Accordingly, for Beidler the literary Vietnam experience is prefigured in works by American authors such as James Fenimore Cooper, Mark Twain, and Herman Melville; the historical documents of exploration and settlement written by the first colonists; and the later mythology surrounding the settlement of the American West.

Hellmann explores in much greater detail the context of American myths shaping Vietnam War literature, specifically the thematic influence of mythic heroes, values, and actions associated with the American frontier. These were resurrected during our early involvement in Vietnam through President Kennedy's "New Frontier" and his close identification with the Green Berets: "Above all the Green Berets symbolized the rededication to the American errand, the reassertion of the virtues and imperatives of America's frontier mythos" (1986, 37–8). Thus, Hellmann notes that Vietnam narratives often portray Americans' expectations that this war will be an opportunity to regenerate our traditional frontier values of self-reliance, democratic idealism, ingenuity, practicality, and generosity while bringing democracy to Southeast Asia. However, much of this war literature also undercuts these frontier myths, suggesting that instead of following the romantic plot of a traditional John Wayne western the unconventional movie script for Vietnam seems more appropriate for a surrealistic foreign film.

In *Walking Point: American Narratives of Vietnam*, Thomas Myers also proposes contexts for understanding the form and content of Vietnam narratives. He examines the American character (myths and beliefs) and literary traditions, particularly those of the historical novel and war genre, influencing these books. Echoing Beidler, he suggests that the best works about Vietnam are those that move beyond battlefield realism and incorporate or play against historical, experiential, cultural, and literary connections – previous wars, popular myths, and American historical novels:

> In regard to specific narrative inevitabilities, the Vietnam War was, despite its claims to difference, the extension and evolution of a number of deeply rooted American traditions, a crucial national experience requiring both text and context. (1988, 5)

Finally, social historian Loren Baritz in *Backfire* presents a broad context for understanding the war and its literature: an overriding tension between the realities of the war and America's moral and political beliefs. As a result, in Vietnam Americans conducted "an American way of war congruent with the American way of life, with American culture" (1986, viii). At the heart of this American way is a vision characterized by John Winthrop's admonition in 1630 to his Puritan followers to establish a "City upon a Hill," a chosen people becoming a moral and political example to the rest of the world. This point of view results in a political and moral idealism that, according to Baritz, underlies the Government's and military's conduct of the Vietnam War; surfaces as an important theme in soldiers' memoirs; and crumbles under the political, moral, cultural, and military realities of Vietnam.

The Ironic Spirit: War is Hell

My own search for connections partially arises from the contexts described in these four critical studies, but moves into five other areas, ones rooted primarily in literary contexts but also containing cultural and historical elements. The first of these springs from Paul Fussell's seminal book *The Great War and Modern Memory*. This accessible critical study, written by an American combat veteran of World War II and well-known literary critic, examines British literature (memoir, fiction, and poetry) emanating from World War I. It is a model for readers and critics exploring themes and structures in modern war literature, including works about Vietnam. Fussell's book explores the soldier-authors' uses of memory and imagination in recalling, re-creating, and mythologizing war experiences. More precisely, he examines patterns in this body of literature to demonstrate how the soldier-author recalls the war (content) and orders these recollections (form).

Among the various thematic and structural patterns Fussell discusses, he notes the ironic spirit pervading the most thoughtful and revealing pieces of World War I literature written by Wilfred Owen, Siegfried Sassoon, Robert Graves, Edmund Blunden, and others. A simple reality shapes these British soldier-authors' perceptions of their war experiences: "Every war is ironic because every war is worse than expected" ([1975] 1981, 7). This tension between the soldier's romantic expectations of war and the harsh realities of the battlefield influences the World War I authors as they recall their experiences. Such a familiar archetypal pattern of "hope abridged" becomes an important theme and also an ordering device – a way of shaping and dramatically heightening war stories.

According to Fussell, "the fuel of hope is innocence" (p. 18). British soldiers entered World War I with unrealistic notions of war engendered by the language, popular myths, and chivalrous conduct found in popular "male romances" and more literate works by Alfred Tennyson, William Morris, and Rupert Brooke (p. 21). With this idealism, visions of courage and heroism, a secure sense of purpose and control of their destiny, and an almost "sporting" view of the war, they expected to make quick work of the Germans. Fussell quotes A. J. P. Taylor as

13

saying, "No man in the prime of life knew what war was like. All imagined that it would be an affair of great marches and great battles quickly decided" (p. 21). But as Fussell notes, "Irony is the attendant of hope ..." (p. 18), and the British soldiers encountered neither a "sporting" war nor a quick end to the conflict. The horrors of protracted trench warfare, deadly gas, frequent artillery barrages, and the killing efficiency of the machine-gun quickly destroyed innocence. How could glorious illusions remain after 60,000 British soldiers lost their lives in one day of fighting at the Somme on 1 July 1916? Soldiers quickly realized how far removed from normal patterns of life and moral conduct were the realities of the battlefield. Their unshaken beliefs in purpose and destiny waned.

Such an ironic vision of these experiences also influenced the soldier-author's telling of these events. The result, according to Fussell, is an underlying three-part structure in the paradigmatic British World War I memoir and even in some of the poetry:

> first, the sinister or absurd or even farcical preparation [for battle]; second, the unmanning experience of battle; and third, the retirement from the line to a contrasting (usually pastoral) scene, where there is time and quiet for consideration, meditation, and reconstruction. The middle stage is always characterized by disenchantment and loss of innocence.... (p. 130)

The third stage, a more open-ended period of contemplation, begins on the battlefield, but may continue long after the war has ended and the soldiers have returned home. It may even extend into a fourth stage, one that Fussell does not identify, where soldiers not only continue to reflect on their war experiences but also struggle to adjust to civilian life. Obviously, Fussell's tripartite pattern of innocence, experience, and consideration has archetypal connections, and in various forms shapes much of the general *Bildungsroman*, or rite-of-passage, literature focusing on the education, spiritual growth, or mythic quest of a central character. Since so many war narratives are typically a form of this initiation literature, Fussell's structure of irony and evolution, especially stages one and two, underlies many of the best pieces of modern war writing: Crane's *The Red Badge of Courage*, Remarque's *All Quiet on the Western Front*, Hemingway's *A Farewell to Arms*, Jones's *The Thin Red Line*, and even portions of Joseph Heller's *Catch-22*.

Moving to the Vietnam narratives, we find this ironic spirit and structure also present. For example, Caputo's war memoir, *A Rumor of War*, best illustrates the content, style and tripartite structure of Fussell's paradigm.[1] Caputo describes his movement from the innocent and patriotic Marine officer in basic training to the hardened combat veteran, to the chastened officer on trial for his part in a war atrocity. This progression through innocence, experience, and reflection is also an important structural device in two other nonfiction works – Michael Herr's *Dispatches* and Ron Kovic's *Born on the Fourth of July* – and in Tim O'Brien's novel *Going After Cacciato*. But Fussell's way of looking at war literature is also helpful with those works containing only two of the stages (innocence and experience) – Gustav Hasford's *The Short-Timers* for instance – or with works focusing on one or more characters moving through stages of innocence and battlefield disillusionment. The experiences of Lieutenant Anderson in David Halberstam's *One Very Hot Day*, Corporal Chelini in John Del Vecchio's *The 13th Valley*, and Lieutenant Hodges in James Webb's *Fields of Fire* are examples of this thematic pattern shaping individual characterization rather than the overall structure of the book.

Perhaps most significant, Fussell's observations about the three-part theme and structure guide readers and critics evaluating the quality of many war books. The least successful works, usually promoting an upbeat, romantic view of war, are centered in one of the categories. Characters maintain the youthful innocence and idealism throughout their entire war experiences, or the book focuses on the experience section at the expense of others. In the latter category, authors make realism the ultimate goal of their re-creation. As a result, these books, whether nonfiction or fiction, are merely battlefield diaries or warfare manuals. Authors emphasize experience while excluding truths, internal conflict, moral dilemmas, or character development. More sophisticated war literature, however, moves beyond innocence and battlefield experiences into Fussell's third category as the soldiers attempt to order and understand their experiences. This third stage of memory, reconstruction, and consideration may result in repudiation or affirmation of the war, insight about the ironies of war, self-awareness, nostalgia for the war environment and battlefield friends, or social estrangement. Such moments can occur in the war environment – for example, Paul Berlin's night of consideration in *Going After Cacciato* – or this reflection may primarily occur on a return to the States, as in Herr's *Dispatches*.

The John Wayne Syndrome: The Ideal Soldier

Picture this final scene in *The Green Berets*, Hollywood's and John Wayne's 1967 version of the Vietnam War. Colonel Kirby (John Wayne) has his arm around the young Vietnamese orphan, Hamchung, whose American benefactor, a Green Beret, has been killed by a Vietcong booby-trap. As they walk into the sunset (with the sun inexplicably setting in the east), Hamchung asks Kirby what will happen to him now that his friend is dead. Kirby turns to the boy and says: "You let me worry about that, Green Beret; you're what this war is all about." It's a scene right out of an American western movie updated for Vietnam. It's also a scene introducing a second thematic context for understanding the Vietnam works – the John Wayne Syndrome. Suggested by this dialogue is Hollywood's, and especially John Wayne's, connection to the complicated process of shaping American soldiers' views of Vietnam prior to their involvement in combat and of creating society's expectations for the ideal warrior. If, as Fussell suggests, innocence, idealism, and unrealistic expectations are customary baggage for young soldiers going off to war, the question becomes who or what are the sources for these illusions and myths? For the large number of literate British soldiers fighting as common soldiers in World War I, Fussell notes that their sources of images, beliefs, and values about war frequently came from literary romances – specifically Bunyan's *Pilgrim's Progress* (1673) and the "Victorian pseudo-medieval romances" of Tennyson's poetry and the prose romances of William Morris ([1975] 1981, 135).

But neither literature nor medieval knights are the principal cultural influences for American soldiers fighting in Vietnam. Granted the fictional character Alden Pyle in Graham Greene's *The Quiet American* has his idealism and illusions about Vietnam of the early 1950s shaped by the books of the fictional author York Harding. But as a key influence for many Americans, soldiers and civilians, Hellmann cites political figures and their rhetoric, principally President Kennedy's mythic frontier values and symbolic call to action embodied in his "New Frontier" (1986, 36). Lloyd B. Lewis in *The Tainted War: Culture and Identity in Vietnam War Narratives* comments that, as was true for combatants in previous wars, family (especially fathers) and the military influenced these young soldiers. He goes on to say that for this first true electronic-media generation,

> [m]ore than any other single factor cited in the Vietnam War literature, the media (especially motion pictures) served to initiate young American males into the mysteries of making war, the purposes war is intended to accomplish, and the role one is expected to adopt within that war. (1985, 22)

And Julian Smith, in *Looking Away: Hollywood and Vietnam*, labels Vietnam "America's first film-generated war ... the first ... war to grow out of attitudes supported, perhaps even created, by a generation of [World War II] movies depicting America's military omnipotence" (1975, 4). The values, purposes, and nature of war portrayed in these films suggested for Americans in the 1960s that the Vietnam War should be modelled after World War II, "the Big One" as television-character Archie Bunker always labeled it. The irony of such a naïve view of World War II is that this war had also been romanticized by authors, historians, veterans, and filmmakers. As Fussell notes in his recent book on World War II, *Wartime: Understanding and Behavior in the Second World War*, "For the past fifty years the Allied war has been sanitized and romanticized almost beyond recognition by the sentimental, the loony patriotic, the ignorant, and the bloodthirsty" (1989, ix).

Several Vietnam authors and characters readily cite the media's influence on their expectations for the war and their image of the ideal soldier. For example, Jamie Hawkins, the narrator in Charles Durden's *No Bugles, No Drums*, observes that "like it 'r not, we'd all been raised on late-night TV movies that glamourized Americans wadin' ashore under an umbrella of palm fronds 'n' 40mm cannon fire from the fleet. And the only guys who got killed were extras" (1976, 3). Ron Kovic also recalls his fascination with World War II movies:

> I'll never forget Audie Murphy in *To Hell and Back*. At the end he jumps on top of a flaming tank that's just about to explode and grabs the machine gun blasting it into the German lines. He was so brave I had chills running up and down my back, wishing it were me up there. . . . It was the greatest movie I ever saw in my life. ([1976] 1977, 54)

Finally, several soldier-authors demonstrate their film literacy by using movie metaphors to explain their narrative strategies: "I can recall only snatches of that time; fragmentary scenes flicker across my mental screen like excerpts from a film . . ." (Caputo [1977] 1978, 295).

If movies were indeed the principal introduction to war for young Americans going off to Vietnam, then one movie figure, perhaps, did more than anyone else, even Audie Murphy (a World War II hero and later a movie actor), to develop Americans' expectations about this war and the people fighting it. That person was, as Lewis and others have noted, John Wayne. In the early 1960s, as President Kennedy was influencing young Americans with his calls to action and his visions for an expanded role of the Green Berets in Vietnam, another prominent American and popular mythmaker was waging his own campaign to revive sagging American patriotism and to restore America's role as "a City upon a Hill." In 1960, Wayne produced, directed, and starred in *The Alamo*, a movie affirming the indomitable American spirit and promoting the same principles of nation-building and adventure underlying Kennedy's "New Frontier." Regarding this unlikely alliance, Julian Smith observes that, despite their markedly different political views, "John Wayne and John Kennedy were not so terribly far apart. Both were trying to awaken their countrymen from lethargy, to inspire them with tales of courage, to make them feel . . . more energetic" (1975, 92). Of course, Wayne and Hollywood had been at this task much longer than the new President, and with greater success. Wayne's young audiences were growing up on a steady diet of his westerns and World War II movies. The result, as depicted by many soldier-authors of Vietnam narratives, was the John Wayne Syndrome: Wayne's widespread role in shaping the romantic illusions about Vietnam embraced by the young American combat soldiers entering the conflict.

But exactly how did this John Wayne Syndrome emerge, and what was the content of its romantic portrait of war? By the early 1960s, "the Duke," through his movies and political stands, had already approached his present status as a cultural icon representing traditional American values of patriotism, courage, confidence, and leadership. Over the years, the man and his screen character had become one and the same – a mythical figure. The name of John Wayne was invoked as a verbal shorthand to describe the larger-than-life character of the American warrior-gentleman and to represent for young males the elements of manhood. The name John Wayne also entered our war vocabulary in other ways. For soldiers, it became a noun phrase, such as "we did John Waynes," or a verb, as in "he John Wayned it." Both uses refer to some grand heroic action, such as a soldier pulling out the pin of a hand grenade with his teeth or charging a heavily fortified enemy bunker complex firing his rifle from his hip and simultaneously lobbing grenades. Or a soldier routinely found himself comparing battlefield reality with a John Wayne movie. For example, in James Jones's *The Thin Red Line*, a World War II novel published in 1962, the following description appears, suggesting that even for American soldiers in World War II, Hollywood influenced their images of combat:

> It had no reality to Welsh. Tella was dying, maybe it was real to Tella, but to Welsh it wasn't real . . . it had no more reality for Welsh than a movie. He was John Wayne and Tella was John Agar. (1962, 242)

By the early 1960s American movie and television audiences had seen Wayne as a cavalry officer, cowboy, soldier, sailor, pilot, Seabee, and in 1960 as Davy Crockett – frontier hero. Basically the roles and images were the same. As Baritz notes:

The traditional American male, as John Wayne personified him in scores of movies, performs, delivers the goods, is a loner, has the equipment, usually a six-shooter or a superior rifle, to beat the bad guys, and he knows what he is doing. He does not need to depend on others because he can perform, can deliver, and can bring home the bacon. He is also very good. ([1985] 1986, 37)

Out of these values and conduct emerged widely accepted stereotypes of masculinity, the hero, conflict, and even America's foreign policy – whether dealing with Native Americans or foreign enemies: American heroes, while engaged in a simple and ordered conflict, firmly control their own fate and others' destiny.

In his book *Home from the War*, psychiatrist Robert Jay Lifton documents the pronounced impact of the John Wayne Syndrome on American soldiers in Vietnam. He describes rap groups in which veterans struggled to free themselves from the "John Wayne thing":

We have seen the John Wayne thing to be many things, including quiet courage, unquestioning loyalty, the idea of noble contest, and a certain kind of male mystique. . . . But its combat version, as far as the men in the rap group were concerned, meant military pride, lust for battle, fearless exposure to danger, and prowess in killing. ([1973] 1985, 219)

As further evidence of this phenomenon, William Ehrhart, a Vietnam veteran and war poet, writes in a short memoir about his early combat experience that "I had also at the time a rather unrealistic perception of what it meant to be in the service and fight a war. . . . I'd grown up on John Wayne, Audie Murphy, and William Holden" (1980, 26).

In light of Baritz's, Lifton's, and Ehrhart's observations, it is not surprising, then, that direct and indirect references to the John Wayne–Hollywood initiation into war and to soldiers' imitations of the movie images appear in many Vietnam narratives, both fiction and nonfiction. Thus, authors transform the John Wayne Syndrome into a literary theme involving the inherent ironies of an ideal soldier going off to fight in an ideal war. For example, the narrator in Larry Heinemann's novel *Close Quarters* gives instructions on using a grenade: "You just set it down in your lap, and everything is right there and ready, except the bang. Why, you can even John Wayne it and pull the son of a bitch with your fucken eyetooth" ([1977] 1986, 38). Kovic writes about his admiration for sports heroes, war, and John Wayne: "Like Mickey Mantle and the fabulous New York Yankees, John Wayne in the *Sands of Iwo Jima* became one of my heroes" ([1976] 1977, 55). Philip Caputo in *A Rumor of War* also mentions Wayne's influence on his romantic illusions about war and his performance in it: "Already I saw myself charging up some distant beachhead, like John Wayne in the *Sands of Iwo Jima*, and then coming home a suntanned warrior with medals on my chest" ([1977] 1978, 6). African-American soldiers in Wallace Terry's oral history *Bloods* also cite the Wayne syndrome: "I was brought up on the Robin Hood ethic, and John Wayne came to save people" ([1984] 1985, 4); or "We were so in the spirit that we hurt ourselves. Guys would want to look like John Wayne. The dudes would just get in the country and say, 'I want a .45. I want eight grenades. I want a bandoleer'" (p. 35). Finally, journalist Michael Herr uses a John Wayne reference to describe the attraction of war: "But somewhere all the mythic tracks intersected, from the lowest John Wayne wetdream to the most aggravated soldier-poet fantasy, and . . . every one of us there a true volunteer" (1977, 20).

Indeed, if many American soldiers in Fussell's first stage of innocence went to Vietnam influenced by these Wayne–Hollywood popular myths, exactly what illusions, values, and images did they bring with them about this war, heroism, the Vietnamese, and the enemy? Perhaps the most appropriate way to answer this question and to describe the Vietnam version of this John Wayne Syndrome is briefly to examine the 1967 film version of *The Green Berets* for which Wayne is star and co-director. As Lloyd B. Lewis suggests, the media in general and this film in particular, with help from the US government, attempted to manipulate public opinion to view the Green Berets and the Vietnam War in a "noble and glamorous" light.

The Green Berets were the living embodiment of the John

Wayne Wet Dream. The emphasis on the romantic aspects of that dream obscured the reality of a war that would not conform to what one soldier recognized as "our Hollywood fantasies." (1985, 40)

In this film, elements of myth, romance, and propaganda come together. Incidents from Robin Moore's 1965 novel with the same title are conveniently altered to fit Kennedy's ideals for the Green Berets, Hollywood's traditional views of war, and Wayne's and the Defense Department's attempts to rally the American people behind the war effort in Vietnam. The result is a film that in Hellmann's terms did symbolize the "reassertion of the virtues and imperatives of America's frontier mythos" (1986, 38). The result, according to movie critics, is a film filled with cliché, absurd caricatures, propaganda, unintentional humor, and the plot of many previous John Wayne westerns and World War II movies. As Michael Herr says in typically cryptic fashion, "That [*The Green Berets*] wasn't really about Vietnam, it was about Santa Monica" (1977, 188).

What audiences find in the film is that Sergeant Stryker, Wayne's character from *Sands of Iwo Jima*, has been resurrected, had his domestic problems eliminated, and is now Colonel Kirby fighting with the Green Berets in Vietnam. The setting is different from Wayne's other war movies, and the Vietcong have replaced the Japanese as the enemy. But the message, characters, and portrait of conflict remain the same. This film promoting a patriotic, simplistic view of a complex war contains clear distinctions between right and wrong, "good guys versus bad guys," and humanitarian acts contrasted with brutal atrocities directed against civilians. Absent, for the most part, is an honest attempt to probe the realities and ironies of war in general and Vietnam in particular. Perhaps this misleading view is best epitomized by one soldier's naïve assessment of the war, "kill stinking Cong and go home."

The American soldiers in the movie do not question their purpose of fighting to preserve democracy at home and in Southeast Asia. The South Vietnamese, as worthy allies, welcome our involvement, look to us for protection, but also take an active and dedicated role in their own defense – a view of the South Vietnamese military and civilians that many

Vietnam narratives do not support.[2] Within such a purposeful context, the good guys – Americans and Vietnamese – are eager, confident, and heroic. The Americans in particular approach the war with loyalty, teamwork, and missionary zeal as they bring technology, democracy, and civilization to the country. Their sense of mission might be best described by the following quote from Caputo's *A Rumor of War* describing the mission of his own Expeditionary Brigade entering Vietnam in early 1965: "American lives and property had to be protected, a beleaguered ally helped, and a foreign enemy taught that the US meant business" ([1977] 1978, 44) – words right out of John Wayne's mouth. A similar sense of purpose and commitment leads the soldiers in *The Green Berets* to view death in combat as meaningful and heroic. Thus, after a Vietcong attack on the Green Berets' forward camp ("Dodge City"), an American soldier, describing the death of the Vietnamese Captain Nimh, notes that Nimh "bought the farm, but he took a lot of them [Vietcong] with him" – American and Hollywood praise of the highest order.

Of course, dominating the action and spirit of this film, as he had in his previous war movies and westerns, is John Wayne – the man and the myth. The roles and settings change from movie to movie, but the character remains basically the same – a character shaping the American male's image of toughness, courage, patriotic duty, honor, and glory. Above all, in his posture, movements, tone of voice, and commands, he exudes a pervasive sense of immortality and control – control of his destiny and the fate of those around him. In a difficult situation in *Sands of Iwo Jima*, Stryker calmed the fears of his squad with a simple "I'll be the mastermind here." In *The Green Berets* this self-assuredness and control also emerge in simple statements such as "Move out"; "The Mike Force is on the way"; and "We can move in there tomorrow: God willing and the river don't rise." Colonel Kirby reduces the war to simple terms (good versus evil), analyzes what needs to be done, and achieves his goals. His war is one that has definite winners and losers, logic, progress, and even immortality. For example, when his helicopter and later an observation tower are shot out from under him, just like in the westerns, he brushes himself off and returns to the fight. Fear, doubt, guilt, or even self-revelation have no part in this conflict.

The Green Berets as a typical John Wayne–Hollywood portrait of war underscores the fundamental implications of the John Wayne Syndrome as a false initiation of American soldiers into the values, purposes, and nature of the Vietnam conflict. Missing from this view of war are the difficult moral issues involved with war; the moments of self-revelation on the battlefield; the confessions of fear, brutal instincts, and frustrations; and the questions of personal responsibility for violent actions. As Herr comments about this skewed John Wayne initiation, "I keep thinking about all the kids who got wiped out by seventeen years of war movies before coming to Vietnam to get wiped out for good" (1977, 209). Not surprising, in some Vietnam narratives a few authors and characters never lose this superficial John Wayne–Hollywood view of war. They are not changed by their experiences and have not moved beyond Fussell's first stage of innocence into a serious consideration of their experiences. On the other hand, the best of the Vietnam war stories portray characters who move beyond the first stage of romance, happy-warrior mentality, and jingoistic spirit left over from the John Wayne films. They in turn confront the horrors of war, self-doubts, guilt, and feelings of helplessness. In these works, gone are the grandiose dreams of John Wayne heroism and sacrifice; replacing them are overriding concerns of survival. Gone, too, is the milieu of order, control, and progress present in Wayne's films; as Caputo notes, "[I]n the bush, nothing ever happens according to plan. Things just happen, randomly, like automobile accidents" ([1977] 1978, 100). The depth and manner in which individuals respond to these realities become important touchstones for judging characters and quality of writing. Such responses also thematically connect these works to previous literature dealing with war and man's savage instincts.

A Heavy Heart-of-Darkness Trip: The Horror! The Horror!

For many of the Vietnam soldier-authors, the Wayne-induced illusions described in poignant ways in their books are a starting-point for Fussell's tripartite journey culminating in an agonizing consideration of the realities and ironies of war. For some it's a journey into temporary madness; for others it's a confrontation with the self and with the horrors of war. Herr labels this process "some heavy heart-of-darkness trip" (1977, 8). Instead of following the melodramatic plot of a John Wayne movie, several of the Vietnam narratives chronicle soldiers' journeys into the moral, emotional, and psychological ambiguities of a war fought in an alien environment and culture against an often unseen enemy. The books become moral explorations of individuals, stripped of civilization's restraints, confronting evil, primal emotions, chaos, and savagery – the literal and metaphysical darkness of the jungle, the horrors of conflict, and the soul. These intended, or unintended, echoes of thematic patterns found in Joseph Conrad's *Heart of Darkness*, a selective indictment of late nineteenth-century imperialism in Africa, suggest that this novella is another significant thematic context for examining the Vietnam narratives.[3] Conrad's key questions – what spiritual darkness resides in our hearts and minds? and what do we possess to hold off this darkness? – become fundamental issues in modern war literature.

This reference to *Heart of Darkness* may seem obvious in light of the book's acknowledged connections to the Vietnam War film *Apocalypse Now* (1979),[4] but the film's superficial treatment of the book only hints at the striking fundamental relationships between the topographical and psychological landscapes of Conrad's story and those found in Vietnam narratives. In fact Ward Just has commented that *"Heart of Darkness* is Vietnam" (1979, 64). Although Conrad's war story of a different sort is not set in a typical war environment, the jungle setting, moral questions, internal conflicts, and characters' physical, spiritual, and psychological odysseys parallel elements found in war narratives. Like these war stories, *Heart of Darkness* deals with conflicts between moral freedom and restraint, chaos and control, idealism and reality, truth and lies, technology and primitive culture. As a piece of initiation literature following Fussell's three stages, it examines questions of self-knowledge, saving illusions, and inner character. Most of all it is a book about physical and metaphysical darkness: violence, hatred, vengeance, power, lust, and chaos. Within *Heart of Darkness* and Vietnam narratives, the crucibles for testing characters –

imperialism in the African jungle and war in the Vietnam jungle – may on the surface differ, but the physical and psychological influences of the environments on the participants are similar.

Conrad's narrative within a narrative, which is semi-autobiographical, has as its two central characters Marlow (the principal narrator) and Kurtz. Although most of the narrative detail focuses on Kurtz, the book is basically about Marlow: what he, as observer and participant, discovers about evil, himself, and human nature as he grapples with the dark truths of Kurtz's "outlaw soul" and with his own motives for lying to Kurtz's fiancée about the circumstances surrounding Kurtz's death.[5] Marlow, a British seaman seeking adventure, secures a job as a ship's captain with a European trading company exporting ivory from the Belgian Congo in Africa. After reaching the company's Central Station in the heart of the "dark continent," Marlow's first task is to restore the company's ship, resurrected from the bottom of the Congo River. Then, aided by a crew of cannibals, he is to journey up the river into the heart of the jungle to bring back the company's Chief of the Inner Station and most productive ivory-trader, Mister Kurtz. The latter came to Africa as an innocent European full of idealism and moral ideas and motivated to bring civilization to the natives: "Each station should be like a beacon on the road toward better things, a centre for trade of course, but also for humanizing, improving, instructing" ([1902] 1975, 47).

The river journey becomes for Marlow, also an innocent, a symbolic psychic journey into truth and self-understanding as he learns more about the realities of Kurtz's abhorrent conduct in the jungle and as he responds to these facts and the jungle environment. What Marlow eventually learns about Kurtz is that the jungle has "consumed his flesh and sealed his soul." Overwhelmed by the fascinating evil, monstrous passions, brutal instincts, and various lusts – ivory, power, murder, unspeakable rites – Kurtz has changed from an emissary of light for the natives to a denizen of darkness who does not want to return to civilization. His thoughts have turned from noble instincts to savage impulses – "exterminate the brutes." But as the dying Kurtz utters his final ambiguous words – "The horror! the horror!" – Marlow believes Kurtz has attained a "moral victory," a moment of truth and self-judgement. Is Kurtz's

26

declaration indeed a pronouncement on his life and the moral darkness, or is Marlow's interpretation of these words a saving illusion for this narrator and his audience? The issue is never fully resolved.

Early in the book, Marlow foreshadows Kurtz's ultimate fate as he describes the arrival nineteen hundred years earlier of a Roman soldier bringing civilization to the wilderness of England:

> Land in a swamp, march through the woods, and in some inland post feel the savagery, the utter savagery, had closed around him, – all that mysterious life of the wilderness that stirs in the forest, in the jungles, in the hearts of wild men. There's no initiation either into such mysteries. He has to live in the midst of the incomprehensible, which is also detestable. And it has a fascination, too, that goes to work upon him. The fascination of the abomination – you know, imagine the growing regrets, the longing to escape, the powerless disgust, the surrender, the hate. ([1902] 1975, 9)

Without too much difficulty, readers of Vietnam narratives might place this description within the context of the Vietnam War. The same feelings of savagery, guilt, a love-hate relationship for the brutality of war, disgust for one's moral callousness, and even helplessness mark the pages of these books as soldiers confront the moral and geographical wilderness of Vietnam that exposes the savage nature of mankind. Chris Starkmann, the troubled Vietnam veteran in Caputo's *Indian Country*, eventually confronts these feelings years after his Vietnam battlefield experience ended. He recalls his perverse pleasure in watching a boyhood friend die in a misdirected napalm strike on a US position in Vietnam:

> And he'd [Starkmann] enjoyed it, for it is always gratifying to find what you've been looking for; he'd enjoyed it deep, deep within himself, so deep he'd not been aware of his pleasure. But his conscience had been aware, and the secret delight in the horror that had taken his friend's life had been the source of the guilt that had racked him with

nightmares and had almost led him to take his own life. ([1987] 1988, 432)

Many Vietnam soldier-authors address the same themes and moral questions found in *Heart of Darkness* including exploitative imperialism, the impact of technology and civilization on nature and so-called primitive societies (Conrad's "rapacious, pitiless folly")[6] and evil's fascination and repulsion ("the fascination of the abomination"). But also central to these books, as well as to *Heart of Darkness*, are characters' inner conflicts between savage and civilized behavior occasioned by the suddenness in which normal individuals slip into primitive brutality. Beidler describes this dilemma as follows: "'Out There' in Vietnam, 'Beyond,' is to run the risk of cutting free from whatever it was that once defined humanity and, even worse, perhaps never being able again to get back to it" (1982, 162).

As in Conrad's book, many of the Vietnam narratives also portray individuals' attempts to retain moral certainties and inner character; to overcome their dark, destructive emotions; to master their fear; and to control the creeping madness and chaos. A striking echo of this Conradian theme appears in the following passage from *A Rumor of War*. It reads like a modern version of a passage in *Heart of Darkness* describing the impact of the African jungle on the European ivory-traders, in particular Kurtz:

> Out there, lacking restraints, sanctioned to kill, confronted by a hostile country and a relentless enemy, we sank into a brutish state. The descent could be checked only by the net of man's inner moral values, the attribute that is called character. There were a few ... who had no net and plunged all the way down, discovering in their bottom-most depths a capacity for malice they probably never suspected was there. (Caputo [1977] 1978, xx)[7]

In his perceptive commentary on *Heart of Darkness*, critic Ian Watt similarly assesses the responses of Conrad's European

28

commercial agents to their fear, savagery, avarice, and lust for power intensified by the jungle, the natives, and the absence of civilization's restraints: "those who respond to savagery and succumb, like Kurtz; those who respond but possess 'a deliberate belief' which enables them to resist; and the fools [hollow men] who do not respond at all because they do not notice" (1979, 226). In striking ways, characters in the Vietnam narratives fall into the same categories. They range from the unreflecting fools, the naïve Alden Pyle in *The Quiet American*, to those individuals, as both observers and participants, who are simultaneously attracted and repelled by the horrors of war. The latter group, like Conrad's Marlow, rely on their work, an attention to surface reality, a deliberate belief in the validity of their mission, or even self-deceptions (lies?) to control their actions and psyches and to hold off atavistic regression. The most challenging Vietnam books, as well as other modern war literature, become introspective plunges exploring the depths of these characters and, as the Brussels doctor in *Heart of Darkness* tells Marlow while measuring his head, describing their changes that "take place inside."

Consequently, narrators and characters in these Vietnam narratives embark on heavy heart-of-darkness journeys as they proceed from the world of straightforward facts and John Wayne myths; through the literal and metaphysical darkness of the jungle; to some measure of truth, self-awareness, and judgement – Fussell's three stages. Ultimately, these soldiers or veterans must confront the self. Some are Marlow figures, learning from others and bringing back the tales; others are Kurtzes, enigmatic figures corrupted by the freedom and brutality of their existence. A few are combinations of both characters. All, however, stripped of their protective John Wayne illusions about masculinity, war, and individual conduct, suddenly find themselves facing isolation, alienation, primal instincts, fears, and moral questions suggested by the following exchange occurring in *The 13th Valley*:

"L-T. That Cherry. He gone nuts. He crazy, L-T. You can see it in his eyes. L-T, Cherry becomin a animal."

Brooks looks at Doc and sighs, tired. "That potential exists in every man," Brooks says. He shakes his head.

"The line between man and beast is very thin. He'll come out of it." (Del Vecchio 1982, 571)

But, unlike unreflecting fools, many move beyond this confrontation to insights about their responses to spiritual isolation, destructive impulses, and the disillusionment caused by the horrors of war. Ron Kovic, for instance, finds himself tormented by (what he believes to be) his accidental shooting of a fellow-soldier and his involvement in the deaths of several innocent civilians. Unable to cope with these thoughts and the war, he seeks an easy way out of the horror and moral dilemmas, a million-dollar wound that will send him home, but not severely wounded. Michael Herr, on the other hand, finds that despite the brutality of combat, which as a journalist he can fly to and leave at will, he does not want to escape. War fascinates him. Herr certainly does not become a clone of the unreflecting journalist in *The Green Berets* (film) who readily accepts the military's propaganda. Like numerous other soldiers, however, he is in Conrad's terms "fascinated by the abomination" as the visceral high of combat becomes a significant part of his Vietnam experience. Similarly, in one of O'Brien's imaginative war stories in *The Things They Carried*, a young woman who travels surreptitiously to Vietnam to visit her boyfriend at an American base-camp discovers she, too, is hooked on the allure of combat: "For Mary Anne Bell, it seemed Vietnam had the effect of a powerful drug: that mix of unnamed terror and unnamed pleasure that comes as the needle slips in and you know you're risking something" (1990, 123). Finally, Caputo in *A Rumor of War* arrives at another important insight while evaluating his responsibility in the murder of Vietnamese civilians – an episode appearing in several Vietnam narratives. Citing the confused nature of the war and a body-count military strategy as a contributing cause for his actions, Caputo probes the origins of his inner conflict between savage actions and civilized behavior. Despite the extenuating circumstances, he admits that he momentarily succumbed to the dark, destructive human emotions: "Perhaps the war had awakened something evil in us, some dark, malicious power that allowed us to kill without feeling" ([1977] 1978, 309). Caputo's words could easily come from *Heart of Darkness*.

What appears, then, in much of the American literature about Vietnam is the underlying motif of a John Wayne figure confronting a modern heart of darkness within the context of Fussell's three stages of innocence, experience, and consideration. Several characters and narrators in these books begin as naïve John Waynes ready to act out their best movie fantasies about war and heroism. Even after taking the physical and metaphysical journey from a world of straightforward facts and "B" movies into the moral, emotional, and psychological confusion of the Vietnam jungle, a few of the participants (unreflecting fools) remain unchanged by their experiences. Many, however, grapple with this darkness and in the process are fascinated, repulsed, and inevitably changed by the experience – a story as old as war itself. The best of these tales become confessionals as authors and characters articulate lessons learned about human nature and war and judge their experiences: Dosier's insight in *Close Quarters*, "The war works on you until you become part of it, and then you start working on it instead of it working on you, and you get deep-down mean . . . not movie-style John Wayne mean, you get mean for real" (Heinemann [1977] 1986, 278); Caputo's "I was finished with governments and their abstract causes . . ." ([1977] 1978, 315); Kovic's "All I could feel was the worthlessness of dying right here in this place at this moment for nothing" ([1976] 1977, 222); and the widespread agreement in these books with Kurtz's "The horror! the horror!" as a judgement of individual actions and the war experience – "[We] knew that this was a moment of evil, that we would never live the same" (Heinemann [1986] 1987, 184).

Voices from the Past: Soldiers Seeking Control

In an updated version of George Santayana's observation that "people who forget the lessons of history are condemned to relive them," Philip Caputo in *A Rumor of War* comments on his own failure to learn about war from the history lessons provided by literature and other soldiers:

I had read all the serious books to come out of the World Wars, and Wilfred Owen's poetry about the Western

31

Front. And yet I had learned nothing. . . . So I guess every generation is doomed to fight its war, to endure the same old experiences, suffer the loss of the same old illusions, and learn the same old lessons on its own. ([1977] 1978, 76–7)

Caputo's observation appropriately introduces a fourth thematic context: widely portrayed in modern war literature are soldiers' recurring feelings of insignificance and helplessness on the battlefield. Together, the contexts discussed so far establish a helpful thematic and formal paradigm for examining many Vietnam war stories: an idealistic and confident John Wayne figure undertaking a journey, through Paul Fussell's three stages of change, that ultimately ends in a metaphysical heart-of-darkness experience. But for this next context, voices from the past, we view Vietnam narratives within the broad category of modern war stories ranging over time and place. Specifically, we will consider the similar ways in which soldiers in modern wars perceive their loss of innocence, particularly an absence of purpose and control, and cope with this loss. Such comparisons will again help us appreciate the content and quality of Vietnam war stories, as well as establish bonds among characters appearing in modern war stories.

Certainly, soldier-authors writing prior to Vietnam have described Owen's "the pity of war." But they have also voiced other timeless themes of literary war stories emerging from Troy to the battlefields of Vietnam: fear, courage, cowardice, heroism, camaraderie, survival, brutality, helplessness, alienation, and nostalgia for combat. A few authors have graphically portrayed the physical and mental scars veterans carry with them long after the wars are over, an aftermath stage in a soldier's quest for inner peace. For example, Dalton Trumbo in his American novel *Johnny Got His Gun* (1939) describes the plight of a World War I multiple amputee, Joe Bonham, reduced to a helpless "piece of meat." Yet as Fussell suggests, and Peter G. Jones emphatically states (1976, 6), the thematic cornerstone of most modern war literature is the initiation and education of young soldiers occurring within the crucible of war. A reality of wars is that, for the most part, they are fought by young people for the reasons articulated by the older generations, whom Owen describes as "the masters of men who plan the wars." As previously noted, these youthful combatants usually bring to the experience an idealism, a desire to prove their character and courage, romantic illusions about war, and a patriotic spirit based on abstract words such as "honor," "liberty," "democracy," "freedom," and "decency" spouted by the older generations, literature, and the media.[8]

Much of serious modern war literature, then, including books about Vietnam, probes the soldiers' loss of their youthful naïveté as they acquire a battlefield education. Also important in such books are the ways soldiers respond to these lessons about death, courage, survival, savagery, and responsibility. For example, Frederic Henry's education in Hemingway's *A Farewell to Arms* causes him to view abstract words such as "glory, honor, courage, or hallow" as "obscene" next to the names of actual villages, roads, and rivers where real people died in war. His knowledge eventually leads to a personal separate peace; he decides to leave the absurd war and flee to Switzerland. With the words "I've been fighting . . . to save my country. Now I'm going to fight a little to save myself" (Heller [1961] 1979, 455), Captain Yossarian in *Catch-22* acts on similar insights about war. Educated about the power and absurdity of the military machine and the society that has created it, he also flees the battlefield; his destination is Sweden. And finally, in a different war and in a different setting (Quang Ngai, Vietnam), Paul Berlin, after a six-month initiation into the Vietnam experience in *Going After Cacciato*, rejects his own opportunity for a separate peace. Instead, he chooses to remain with his unit because of his obligations to people (friends, family, and fellow-soldiers) and his fear of "being thought of as a coward."

Underlying these informed decisions by Henry, Yossarian, and Berlin are their struggles to control their fate and fears within the chaotic arena of the battlefield. Within modern war literature, a soldier's pursuit of order and control in his life and in his environment becomes one of the most common responses to this war initiation and loss of innocence. And in the aftermath stage it becomes a prominent coping mechanism in the veteran's adjustment to life away from the battlefield. This obsession with control, as philosopher Peter L. Berger believes, is rooted in human nature (1977, xv). It is also a behavior closely tied to a soldier's prewar life in a modern world often described as bereft of traditions, normative values, and religious or secular mediating structures. In a war environment, any latent feelings of helplessness, confusion, and insignificance brought from society to the battlefield quickly surface. Thus, young soldiers, bearing illusions about war and perhaps holding on to a system of loosely formed values to guide their conduct in combat, may discover their values and assurances crumbling, along with their illusions. They find themselves in a chaotic environment where often they have little or no control over their actions and fate – mere cogs in the military machine. At other times, removed from rules of conduct, decision-making institutions of society, or the veneer of civilization, their moral choices multiply and their confrontations with human savagery and death become commonplace. As these soldiers lose their innocence and their standards for conduct, their struggles with the resulting conflicts, fears, insights, and confusion become important measures of character in modern war literature.

In these war stories, one recurring incident leading to a battlefield epiphany is a death-recognition scene. Here, innocent soldiers suddenly perceive their inability to control their fate as revealed in their own mortality, the fragility of life in general, or the bond through death shared with the enemy. Such an experience may occur early in the soldier's tour and result in an immediate loss of innocence. For example, the naïve and panicked Henry Fleming in Crane's *The Red Badge of Courage* flees his first Civil War battle only to stumble across a dead Union soldier hidden among trees and underbrush:[9]

The youth gave a shriek as he confronted the thing. He was for moments turned to stone before it. . . . The dead man and the living man exchanged a long look. . . . At last he burst the bonds which had fastened him to the spot and fled, unheeding the underbrush. He was pursued by a sight of the black ants swarming greedily upon the gray face and venturing horribly near to the eyes. ([1895] 1976, 59)

Henry's romance of war, nurtured by boyhood dreams of

adventure, heroism, and Homeric struggles, abruptly disappears, replaced by fears of cowardice and helplessness, and images of death.

Such a significant death-recognition experience can also occur much later in soldiers' tours of duty, even after they are veterans of war's carnage. Red Valsen's reaction to this encounter, described in Mailer's *The Naked and the Dead*, is typical as the corporal suddenly realizes his own life's fragility, as well as the ties, through death, binding enemies together:

But the corpse [Japanese] lay there without a head, and Red ached dully as he realized the impossibility of ever seeing the man's face. . . . Very deep inside himself he was thinking that this was a man who had once wanted things, and that the thought of his own death was always a little unbelievable to him. The man had a childhood . . . and there had been dreams and memories. Red was realizing with surprise and shock, as if he were looking at a corpse for the first time, that a man was really a very fragile thing. ([1948] 1981, 216)

A similar sympathetic identification with the enemy occurs in Dos Passos' World War I novel *Three Soldiers* as Chrisfield's hatred for the enemy suddenly ebbs when he stumbles across the body of a German soldier who committed suicide by shooting himself in the face ([1921] 1949, 149).

Perhaps one of the most famous death-recognition scenes in modern war literature portrays Yossarian's ineffectual efforts in *Catch-22* to aid Snowden, the wounded tail-gunner whom Yossarian believes is not seriously wounded. Fussell calls this episode an adaptation of a "favorite ironic scene that the Great War contributes to the Second" (1989, 33–4).[10] It is a perfect example of Fussell's notion of hope abridged and symbolizes the irony of all wars, the conflict between expectation and reality. For Yossarian, the incident reveals man's insignificance and helplessness; it is also an event he recalls in bits and pieces throughout the novel and confronts in its entirety only near the conclusion of the narrative, just before he decides to flee the war. Feeling in control of Snowden's situation, he optimistically works to bandage the tail-gunner's thigh-wound, only to discover that a large piece of flak has eviscerated the airman and his entrails have spilled on to the floor. Suddenly, Yossarian feels helpless and insignificant:

> He [Yossarian] felt goose pimples clacking all over him as he gazed down despondently at the grim secret Snowden had spilled all over the messy floor. It was easy to read the message in his entrails. Man was matter, that was Snowden's secret. Drop him out a window and he'll fall. Set fire to him and he'll burn. Bury him and he'll rot like other kinds of garbage. The spirit gone, man is garbage. (Heller [1961] 1979, 450)

Similar symbolic confrontations with death commonly appear in Vietnam narratives as soldiers quickly discover that they are not fearless John Waynes controlling their destiny. For example, Caputo's illusions about the heroic nature of death and "noble sacrifices of soldiers offering up their bodies for a cause or to save a comrade's life" ([1977] 1978, 153) end early in his tour as he learns the fate of a well-liked NCO unceremoniously killed by a sniper while filling canteens in a muddy jungle river. Or a death scene in Heinemann's *Close Quarters* reminds readers of a similar episode in Remarque's *All Quiet on the Western Front* where Paul Baumer must spend twenty-four hours in a trench alone with a dying German whom he has stabbed. Baumer alternately feels disgust, fear, hatred, guilt, compassion, and identification as he listens to the gurgling sounds of the slowly dying soldier and perceives his own mortality and insignificance. In the Vietnam version Dosier spends the night staring at the "gook" he has gruesomely strangled during a night ambush. Gazing at the body frozen in a posture to ward off his attacker, Dosier seems both shocked and fascinated by the ease with which he killed the man and by the insignificant end to this human life. His thoughts parallel Yossarian's description of Snowden's secret: "I [Dosier] look away and back. I cannot get comfortable. . . . Strangling him, was like wringing out a wet rag, folding and squeezing, refolding it thicker, squeezing it more. It was like crushing a melon in half and that junk, seeds and all, oozing out between my fingers" (Heinemann [1977] 1986, 74–5).

Soldier-authors from all wars use these traumatic death scenes in their stories to emphasize the combatant's basic feelings of mortality, insignificance, and lack of control. But such feelings are also engendered by situations in which soldiers perceive themselves as expendable cogs in a giant war machine moving inexorably forward or, as a soldier in *The Naked and the Dead* describes his plight, "helpless in the shattering gyre of the war" (Mailer [1948] 1981, 630). Obviously the ironic nature of war heightens these feelings of disillusionment and disorder. Soldiers enter battle believing that they control their own destiny and that their individual actions, all carefully coordinated by military strategists, will contribute directly to eventual success. This naïve sense of purpose also contributes to their illusion that, similar to the plot in a war movie, the real war has a readily discernible order, purpose, and end.

But across modern war literature events undercut these notions. Soldiers discover the obscene scale of carnage and brutality of the battlefield, as well as the Russian-roulette nature of war, which increases as modern technology heightens the war's impersonality. Also contributing to an individual's disillusionment and confusion is the insensitive, chaotic bureaucracy of the war machine illustrated by the unreasonable actions of the Italian Battle Police in *A Farewell to Arms*, described throughout Heller's *Catch-22*, and later portrayed in *A Rumor of War* with Caputo's absurdist description of the importance of body-counts during his stint as "The Officer in Charge of the Dead." As a corollary, even noble purposes at the individual level are often reduced to efforts for survival, or at the national level they are diminished to economic gain as suggested by Sergeant Welsh's cynical refrain in *The Thin Red Line* "Everybody dies; and what's it all about? In the end, what's everything about? What remains? Property" (James Jones 1962, 119).

The results of these conditions lead to images of entrapment and victimization throughout the war books. Paul Baumer in *All Quiet on the Western Front* describes the front as "a cage in which we must await fearfully whatever may happen. . . . Over us, Chance hovers" (Remarque [1929] 1987, 101). Frederic Henry, as a result of his disillusioning experiences with the war and his lover Catherine's death in childbirth, describes life as a game which "you never had time to learn. They threw you in and told you the rules and the first time they caught you off base they killed you" (Hemingway [1929] 1957, 327). In a passage from *Fields of Fire*, an American soldier articulates a similar view about the war's chaos: "I get the feeling this [Vietnam War] is kind of like Russian roulette. . . . Just as senseless. And the players aren't excused until the gun goes off in their face, so you get new players but the old ones can't leave until they lose" (Webb, 1978, 201–2).

Perhaps the most sustained use of this theme of entrapment appears in Dos Passos' second of four books about World War I, *Three Soldiers*. He describes the effects of the bureaucratic war machine on the lives of three American combat soldiers (Fusselli, Chrisfield, and Andrews) "in a treadmill" and "lost in the vast machine" ([1921] 1949, 63). Each of his metaphorical chapter titles suggests a result of this conditioning process, which, as critic Jeffrey Walsh notes, is designed to destroy individual identity (1982, 77). The first chapter, "Making the Mould," describes basic training, and the last chapter, "Under the Wheels," relates the ignoble outcomes for the three soldiers – court-martial and desertion. In the chapter labeled "Machines," Dos Passos presents a paradigmatic image for the combat soldier's sense of helplessness and victimization. He describes a unit of American soldiers marching machine-like toward the front:

> The column perceptibly slackened its speed, but kept on, and as the houses dwindled and became farther apart along the road the men's hope of stopping vanished. . . . Men's feet seemed as lead, as if all the weight of the pack hung on them. . . . Each man's eyes were on the heels of the man ahead of him that rose and fell, rose and fell endlessly. ([1921] 1949, 135)

A similar image appears in *The Thin Red Line* with the description of C-for-Charlie Company's grueling march of seven and a half miles through the Guadalcanal jungle:

> The marchers needed every spark of concentration they possessed simply to keep going. Any thoughts beyond that remained their own. After an hour's marching, even

such private thoughts were displaced. The infantry forgot where it was going in the urgent immediate problem of getting there, of keeping going without dropping out. (James Jones 1962, 110)

And in a different war, Vietnam, a similar scene appears in *Going After Cacciato* as Paul Berlin marches machine-like at the rear of his platoon:

He marched up the road with no exercise of will, no desire, and no determination, no pride, his muscles contracting and relaxing, legs swinging forward, lungs drawing and expelling, moving, climbing, but without thought and without will and without the force of purpose. (O'Brien [1978] 1979, 203)

Even after physically and emotionally draining battles, when the marching has ceased, soldiers' feelings of insignificance and helplessness are still acute:

The patrol was over and yet they had so little to antici-pate. . . . They were still on the treadmill; the misery, the ennui, the dislocated horror. . . . Things would happen and time would pass, but there was no hope, no antici-pation. (Mailer [1948] 1981, 702)

Taken together these four passages spanning three wars illus-trate this thematic continuity within modern war literature. The recurring images of victimization emphasize the combat soldiers' confusion and treadmill-like existence as they appear incapable of acting independently or of perceiving an end or purpose for their movements.

As soldiers lose their illusions of war and face their own mortality and the oppressive feelings of fear and insignificance, how do soldiers cope? How do they survive? Two seemingly contradictory responses appear throughout modern war stories: some soldiers give themselves over to the war, a denial of will; others attempt mentally to escape the war by establishing some order and control in their daily existence and thoughts. The first approach is, perhaps, the most common and disconcerting. It manifests itself in the calm, detached way that Frederic Henry shoots a deserting Italian sergeant. It also underlies Müller's insensitive request to Kemmerich in *All Quiet on the Western Front* that the latter give up his fine pair of airman's boots after his leg has been amputated, since only facts are important and "good boots are scarce." Finally, carried to an absurd extreme, it sparks much of the black humor in *Catch-22* or the soldiers' callous explanations for civilian atrocities frequently appearing in so many of the Vietnam narratives.

Psychologists call this complete surrender to war desensitization or psychic numbing;[11] Conrad labels the condition a "descent into darkness"; Owen in his poem "Insensibility" calls it a dullness: "Dullness best solves/The tease and doubt of shelling." Remarque also describes it as a dullness and compares it to "the indifference of wild creatures" ([1929] 1987, 274); and the narrative voice in *The Things They Carried* observes that, by slighting death through seemingly insensitive actions and language, soldiers "had ways of making the dead seem not quite so dead" (O'Brien 1990, 267). Whatever the label, the process involves becoming oblivious to the horrors of combat, to the death of friends, or to the guilt of killing other human beings. The results, temporary or long-lasting, depend on the intensity of the experience and the strength of individual character. Some soldiers easily assume a callousness about human life, a preoccupation with their survival at all costs, or even a further descent into brutality. A Vietnam veteran quoted in Lifton's *Home from the War* describes the effects and cause of this combat numbness:

"We began slowly with each death and every casualty until there were so many deaths and so many wounded, we started to treat death and loss of limbs with callousness, and it happens because the human mind can't hold that much suffering and survive." ([1973] 1985, 109)

Within modern war literature, repeated references to this condition appear. Owen in "Apologia Pro Poemate Meo" writes

Merry it was to laugh there –
Where death becomes absurd and life absurder.

> For power was on us as we slashed bones bare
> Not to feel sickness or remorse of murder.

Sergeant Welsh in *The Thin Red Line* seems exempt from this battle numbness, but recognizes its presence in others:

> Of all the company including officers, Welsh was perhaps the only one as far as he knew who had never felt the combat numbness . . . He understood that it was the saving factor, and sensed the animal brutality that it brought with it. (James Jones 1962, 411)

Mailer associates this numbness with a frequent incident in war stories – a foray among the enemy dead for war souvenirs: "He [Martinez] was filled suddenly with a lust for the gold teeth . . . he looked down again at the gaping mouth of the cadaver. No good to him, he told himself. Tensely he was trying to estimate how much the teeth were worth. Thirty dollars, maybe, he told himself" ([1948] 1981, 214).

Perhaps, because of the psychological impact of brutal and impersonal guerrilla warfare, this theme of combat numbness is even more prominent in the Vietnam narratives. In fact Gustav Hasford centers the plot and characterizations in his first novel, *The Short-Timers*, on soldiers' callousness conditioned by the brutal Marine Corps basic training – "Our rifle is only a tool; it is a hard heart that kills" ([1979] 1983, 13) – and reinforced by the savagery of the battles. Emerging from this "nurturing" environment, one of his characters, Private Pyle, mechanically murders his drill instructor and commits suicide; another, Rafterman, eagerly eats the flesh of a fellow-soldier killed by a mortar round; and Joker, the narrator, describes the deaths, mutilations, and his own mercy killing of a best friend through a mask of black humor and indifference enabling him to survive the psychic trauma.

In addition to soldiers' numbness to the death of fellow Vietnam combatants, the callousness also, at times, surfaces in their attitudes toward civilian deaths. Herr quotes the famous story involving a reporter's question to a helicopter door-gunner about how he could shoot women and children. He gives a Helleresque response – "'It's easy, you just don't lead 'em so much'" (1977, 35). Hodges, a character in Webb's *Fields of Fire*, also describes this condition influencing one soldier's attitude toward civilians: "and the kids would like to kill us I don't blame them I'd like to kill them too not the kids but who gives a shit anymore it's all the same too hard to draw lines seen too many dead kids I don't feel bad for them anymore" (1978, 136).

This numbing effect of war, described in the Vietnam narratives and other modern war books as a way of coping by abdicating individual responsibility, often leads to a level of brutality, callousness, and atavism among combat soldiers that shocks them as well as observers. Several characters temporarily or permanently become Kurtzes, succumbing to primitive emotions of power, survival, and the savagery described earlier in the thoughts of Sergeant Welsh and reinforced by the animal imagery found throughout the books. Paul Baumer in *All Quiet on The Western Front* observes that "At the sound of the first droning of the shells we rush back, in one part of our being, a thousand years. By the animal instinct that is awakened in us we are led and protected" (Remarque [1929] 1987, 56). General Cummings in *The Naked and the Dead* joyously associates the sounds of artillery shells with the opportunities war offers for indulging primitive passions including sexual urges:

> . . . and yet there was a naked quivering heart to it [war] which involved you deeply when you were thrust into it. All the deep dark urges of man, the sacrifices on the hilltop, and the churning lusts of the night and sleep, weren't all of them contained in the shattering screaming burst of shell, the manmade thunder and light? (Mailer [1948] 1981, 566)

And as Phil Dosier in *Close Quarters* prepares to leave Vietnam at the end of his tour, he reflects on how the effects of this combat numbness lead to shocking brutality: "and all I wanted to do was kill and kill and burn and rape and pillage until there was nothing left" (Heinemann [1977] 1986, 279). Phrases from Conrad's *Heart of Darkness* – "fascination of the abomination," "the awakening of forgotten and brutal instincts," and even "The horror! the horror!" – echo throughout these passages as soldiers on their own psychological journeys penetrate "deeper and deeper into the heart of darkness" found on the battlefield and within themselves.

This giving oneself completely to war, a mental and emotional escape from the horrible truths of the battlefield, is more a conditioned response of the soldier's psyche than a choice. It's not willed; it just happens as the war acts on the soldiers and they become controlled by the war rather than remaining in control of it. Yet another method of surviving psychological war also involves escape, but a willed escape. Through tricks of the mind, soldiers try to overcome their feeling of a machine-like existence or their fears of facing the inner truths of their horrible experiences. In *Heart of Darkness*, Marlow's single-minded attention to "mere incidents of the surface" (finding rivets to repair his boat or navigating the river) enables him to avoid temporarily the unpleasant reality of the Congo and imperialism. This response and Sassoon's observation in his World War I poem "Dreamers" (1917) about daydreams as an escape suggest ways soldiers attempt to control their physical and mental environments: "Soldiers are dreamers; when the guns begin/They think of firelit homes, clean beds and wives."

According to Marlow, attention to surface details of life (work, basic needs, familiar routines) keeps people from probing the truths of existence and self and prevents them from asking difficult questions: "the reality – the reality, I tell you – fades. The inner truth is hidden – luckily" (Conrad [1902] 1975, 49). In modern war literature, this attention to surface details as a means of controlling inner conflicts assumes various forms. For example, in *All Quiet on the Western Front*, Paul Baumer becomes preoccupied with eating and defecating – the daily routines of life. Lengthy passages lyrically describe an "idyll of eating and sleeping" in a reinforced cellar and later a carefree two-hour visit to the latrine. Similar passages appear in the other war narratives as soldiers before or after a battle play cards, ritualistically prepare for combat, or focus on the trivial details of their existence. General Cummings in *The Naked and the Dead* attends to the numbers, abstract strategies, and surface details of war in an effort to control this war machine. Members of C-for-Charlie in *The Thin Red Line* concentrate on collecting and bartering battlefield souvenirs or hoarding Aqua Velva aftershave for its alcohol content. Egan in *The 13th Valley* relishes putting together an elaborate gourmet meal with the help of sterno and several varieties of C-rations. Or Joker and his platoon in *The Short-Timers* concentrate on the simple act of marching, escaping into rather than rebelling against their treadmill existence:

> Putting our minds back into our feet, we concentrated all our energy into taking that next step, that one more step. . . . We try very hard not to think about anything important, try very hard to think there's no slack and that it's a long walk home. (Hasford [1979] 1983, 180)

The reason why soldiers engage in these routines, rituals, and surface details of war is, of course, an attempt to keep from thinking about the realities of their existence – the hidden truths and their innate fears. Such routines, or coping mechanisms, establish order and comfort within the chaos of the battlefield, and undertaking these familiar activities temporarily relieves soldiers from guilt, anxiety, and feelings of powerlessness. They temporarily feel in control of their existence. As Lloyd B.Lewis notes, engaging in routine and trivial activity cuts down on choices and tension: "In the same manner that order protects the individual from being engulfed by a terrifying chaos, triviality shields the individual from the agony of constant alertness" (1985, 90).

But sometimes such outwardly directed tricks of the mind are inadequate to flee the horror, fears, and mental anguish. At these moments some participants become daydreamers, escaping into their memories or their imagination. They construct a new reality, one over which they have control and one that in its order and comfort directly counters their chaotic, uncomfortable war environment. Some imagine an end to the war: in Owen's poem "Soldier's Dream" the persona dreams that "kind Jesus fouled the big-gun gears;/And caused a permanent stoppage in all bolts." Some, such as Paul Baumer, daydream about pastoral scenes and tranquil events from their youth: "they [the memories] are always completely calm, that is predominant in them; and even if they are not really calm, they become so" (Remarque [1929] 1987, 120). Others, such as Goldstein in *The Naked and the Dead*, bury themselves in thoughts of the future: "It was the only pleasure he had . . . At night in his tent he would lie

44

awake and plan his future, or think of his son, or try to imagine where his wife would be at that moment" (Mailer [1948] 1981, 205). But it is left to Paul Berlin while on night guard duty in *Going After Cacciato* to construct the most elaborate and complex daydream, one that takes him from Vietnam to Paris. It is a six-hour odyssey through the past, present, and future (via memory and imagination) to escape the war, to conquer his fear, to think about future possibilities, and to establish some order and meaning for his previous six months in Vietnam:

> Paul Berlin . . . stood high in the tower by the sea, the night soft all around him, and wondered, not for the first time, about the immense powers of his own imagination. A truly awesome notion. Not a dream, an idea. An idea to develop, to tinker with and build and sustain, to draw out as an artist draws out his visions. (O'Brien [1978] 1979, 43).

All of these mental gymnastics are ways to survive: to keep soldiers from confronting the horrible truths of war, to stave off madness, or to allow them to act effectively on the battlefield. Some soldiers, especially in Vietnam war stories, turn to drugs and alcohol to escape the darkness. A few embrace ideology and patriotism – overriding beliefs in the value of the war effort – to establish stability in their lives. Even fewer seek relief in the established order and solace of religion. Most, however, rely on their own inventions or the comfort of fellow-combatants to ward off the darkness and to establish, if only temporarily, some measure of power over their fragile lives:

> . . . a man perceives with alarm how slight is the support, how thin the boundary that divides him from the darkness. We are little flames poorly sheltered by frail walls against the storm of dissolution and madness, in which we flicker and sometimes almost go out.
> (Remarque [1929] 1987, 275)

This view from a German soldier in World War I describing the soldiers' fragile inner state reiterates the bonds among warriors throughout modern war literature seeking order, control, comfort, and courage in their chaotic existence, both on the battlefield and later at home.

A Different War: A Different War Story?

The four contexts examined so far in this chapter illustrate the similar moral conflicts, changes among the participants, psychic journeys, struggles to survive, and narrative strategies pervading modern war stories. Underlying these connections is a basic truth for soldier-authors that, no matter where, when, and how a war is fought, "war is war" and that, as Civil War general William Tecumseh Sherman noted, "War is all hell." Doc Peret, the philosopher-medic in *Going After Cacciato*, articulates this link:

> War kills and maims and rips up the land and makes orphans and widows. These are the things of war. Any war. . . . I'm saying that the feel of war is the same in Nam or Okinawa – the emotions are the same, the same fundamental stuff is seen and remembered. (O'Brien [1978] 1979, 237)

Readers of modern war literature would be hard pressed to dismiss Doc's logic, but they would have equal difficulty ignoring the commonly held notion that each war also has its own character – images, political ideology, battlefield strategy, geography, participants, and technology influencing soldiers', civilians', and artists' reactions to the war. This section examines a final context for reading the literature about Vietnam: several special characteristics, real or perceived, of the Vietnam War affect how American foot soldiers responded to this war and how soldier-authors created themes, images, and psychological conflicts within their war stories.[12]

As evidence of various views about the connections among wars, many American historians view World War I, compared to World War II, Korea, and Vietnam, as an anomaly. They suggest that, because Americans viewed this war as one of self-defense, American soldiers, by and large, carried with them a realistic, pragmatic outlook in marked contrast to the idealism and subsequent disillusionment of Americans entering and exiting World War I and Vietnam. At the same time some military historians argue that strong political and military parallels exist between American involvement in Korea and in Vietnam.[13] As Max Hastings observes in his book *The Korean War*, Korea can be viewed as "a military rehearsal for . . . Vietnam" (1988, 10). Other historians, however, note that the Vietnam War differed from other wars in the way it was initiated, fought, and resolved. They also describe the war as a complex melting-pot of revolution, colonialism, civil conflict, communist aggression, and guerrilla warfare.

As suggested by Doc Peret's musings on the subject, this controversy over parallels and contrasts among the various wars makes its way into the Vietnam narratives. In David Halberstam's *One Very Hot Day*, Captain Beaupre, the American advisor in Vietnam, who is also a veteran of World War II and Korea, compares the three wars. For him World War II was "simple," walking in a straight line and never distrusting people; in Korea his distrust grew as Americans began to rely more and more on Korean agents for intelligence; but compared to Vietnam "Korea was simple." According to Beaupre, in Vietnam not only did the soldiers walk in circles, but "here you began with distrust, you assumed it about everything. . . . Even the Americans seemed different to him now, and he trusted them less; in order to survive in this new world and this new Army, they had changed" ([1967] 1984, 133).

This fictional character's assessment of the special character of the Vietnam War mirrors assessments by sociologists, historians, political scientists, journalists, and common soldiers. A *Time* journalist has this to say about the war: "History would have to go on a maniacally inventive jag to top Viet Nam for wild, lethal ironies and stage effects" (1 June 1981, 45). Michael Herr labels Vietnam a "black looneytune." Historian Walter Capps observes that "the Vietnam War did not mean what wars had meant before. Previous frameworks of interpretation did not count. Earlier criteria did not register. Former understanding did not fit" (1978, 20). As further evidence of differences, a sociological study of Vietnam veterans lists several distinct features of this war leading to veterans' special adjustment problems: (1) a soldier's individual entrance and exit from the war rather than in a military unit; (2) the widespread opposition at home to the war, especially after 1968; (3) Vietnam as a "contained conflict" without distinct battle-lines; (4) the emphasis on body-counts as an indication of battlefield success; (5) a limited tour of duty for American soldiers; (6) a brief post-combat transition period for the returning soldier from the battlefield to the United States; and (7) an unusually high incidence of delayed psychiatric casualties after the war (Figley and Leventman 1980, xxiii–xxxi). Finally, another distinct contributing factor to American soldiers' confusion and veterans' later adjustment problems involves the divisive strategic, political, and ideological conflicts, particularly from 1968 on, raging at home and in Vietnam. Neil Sheehan's superb history-biography, *A Bright Shining Lie: John Paul Vann and America in Vietnam* (1988), cites several prominent examples of this turmoil: the corruption and political division within the Saigon government, the inability of both Americans and the South Vietnamese Army (ARVN) to "win the hearts and minds" (WHAMMO) of the Vietnamese peasants, the myopia of high-ranking American military officers, and the strong anti-war sentiment present in the USA as well as in Vietnam. Together these and other special characteristics of the Vietnam War directly or indirectly influence how Vietnam war stories are written and read.

Images. Each war has distinct images, conveyed by literature, oral war stories, and the popular media, that are filed away in a nation's collective consciousness. With World War I, Americans associate the machine-gun, trench warfare, artillery bombardments, gas attacks, and patriotism promoted in songs such as "Over There." Linked to World War II are images of extensive naval battles, submarines, waves of B-29 bombers, tanks, Patton with his six-guns, the mushroom cloud from the atomic bomb, island-hopping in the South Pacific, the American flag raised at Iwo Jima, chocolate bars, concentration-camps, the firebombing of Dresden, the Glenn Miller Band, factory worker "Rosie the Riveter," and parades on VE- and VJ-Days. For Korea, which may now have the dubious distinction of being America's most forgotten war, movies and the television series *M*A*S*H* provide images: jets bombing bridges at Toko Ri, Army nurses and doctors working in front-line surgical hospitals, Marines enduring the bitter cold at Chosin Reservoir, American soldiers undergoing brainwashing at the hands of the Chinese and North Koreans, and both sides negotiating at Panmunjom near the 38th Parallel.

Vietnam, of course, has its own images entering America's collective identity and coloring perceptions of the war. The metaphors "quagmire," "swamp," and "light at the end of the tunnel" are associated with this war. In addition, since Vietnam was the first television war covered nightly by the network news, many of the images come from this medium: General Loan, head of South Vietnam's National Police, placing a pistol to the head of a Vietcong suspect and pulling the trigger; a young Vietnamese girl, arms outstretched, her clothes burned off, screaming as she flees a napalm strike; Cobra helicopters prepping a hot landing zone while Huey helicopters prepare to land their combat assault force from the 1st Air Cavalry; American soldiers using Zippo lighters to burn thatched huts in a Vietnamese village; canvas body-bags, containing dead American soldiers, stacked in a jungle clearing and ready to be placed on a medivac helicopter; back in the States angry protestors and equally enraged Chicago police confronting each other outside the 1968 Democratic Convention; and the poignant scenes of American POWs reunited with their families at an American airbase. These are just a few of the scenes from this "cool" medium's presentation of this "hot" war that stirred the emotions of supporters and opponents of the war and still arouse passions today.[14]

But it is, perhaps, left to the charged language, perceptual overload, and frenetic jump-cut narrative style of Herr's *Dispatches* to give us the most revealing glimpse of the language, sights, and sounds of Vietnam dominating the war stories. Herr's unorthodox style seems appropriate for the unconventional images of this particular war and for the unconventional 1960s in which it originated: peace signs; peace beads; Black Power salutes; the sights and sounds of the ever-present helicopters (Hueys, Cobras, Loaches, Chinooks); music of the Animals, the Doors, Jimi Hendrix, Creedence Clearwater Revival, Janis Joplin, and the Rolling Stones; floppy jungle hats and jungle fatigues; the bars and massage parlors of Saigon's Tu Do Street; and graffiti on the back of flak jackets – "Born to Kill." Herr also gives us images of a weeping African-American NCO at Khe Sanh hearing about the assassination of Martin Luther King; a Vietnamese father standing mute while holding his dead child in his arms; a Marine wearing a necklace made from the ears of dead Vietcong; the flying "Ranch Hands" spraying Agent Orange to defoliate the jungle; a Marine medical team entering a Vietnamese village as part of the Hamlet Pacification Program; a point man stumbling over a trip-wire strung across a jungle path and setting off a booby-trap; and finally Herr and several other soldiers getting stoned on high-grade dope. These and traditional images of battle make their way into the Vietnam narratives and contribute to the familiar as well as special feel of this war.

The Unusual Nature of the War. Regardless of the dates chosen to mark the length of the Vietnam War (beginning with the first deaths of American advisors in Bien Hoa, Vietnam, in July 1959 or the arrival of two Marine battalions at Da Nang in March 1965 and ending with the peace agreements signed in January 1973 ["peace with honor"] or the fall of Saigon to the North Vietnamese on 30 April 1975), this was America's longest war. Unlike the previous three American wars of the twentieth century, with their frequent large-scale battles and clearly defined front lines, Vietnam was a small-unit war lacking a definite front and rear. Except for the rare big battle with a North Vietnamese regiment or the street-to-street fighting in the battle for Hué during Tet of 1968, the ground war in Vietnam revolved around small-scale firefights, ambushes, search-and-destroy missions, reconnaissance patrols, and air (helicopter) assault combat missions. For American military strategists, Vietnam was to be a short war of attrition; the immensely superior US military technology and firepower would ultimately wear down and wipe out the enemy.

But in one more example of war's irony the tiger (the Vietcong and North Vietnamese), as it had done with the French, exhausted the elephant (Americans).[15] America's high-tech military machine often outstripped its military strategy. The "splendid little war," a label first given the Spanish–American War of 1898, turned into a political and military quagmire. From a military standpoint, it was a war in which Americans won most of the battles but still lost the war. Front lines were nonexistent;

enemy rocket attacks could occur anywhere; and battlefield movements seemed more like a game of musical chairs as American soldiers continually captured, exited, and recaptured villages and Vietcong strongholds. The common soldier in most wars has little understanding of overall military objectives and strategy. For the American soldiers in Vietnam, however, their frustration at an apparent lack of purpose, order, commitment, and progress in a limited war was particularly acute, especially as the war dragged on and support on the home front waned. American soldiers wondered out loud, "Why won't the Government let us win this war?" Lloyd B. Lewis labels Vietnam a "formless war," one that participants viewed as "shapeless, disjointed, fragmented" and one that American soldiers were unprepared to fight (1985, 72). As the narrator of *Going After Cacciato* observes about the confusion of Paul Berlin and other members of Third Squad:

> They did not know even the simple things: a sense of victory, or satisfaction, or necessary sacrifice. They did not know the feeling of taking a place and keeping it, securing a village and then raising the flag and calling it a victory. No sense of order or momentum. No front, no rear, no trenches laid out in neat parallels. No Patton rushing for the Rhine, no beachheads to storm and win and hold for the duration. They did not have targets. They did not have a cause. (O'Brien [1978] 1979, 320)

Captain Beaupre in *One Very Hot Day* similarly assesses this type of combat: "here [Vietnam] you walk in a goddamn circle, and then you go home, and then you go out the next day and wade through a circle, and then you go home and the next day you go out and reverse the circle you did the day before, erasing it" (Halberstam [1967] 1984, 119).

Also contributing to the soldier's frustration was the brutal and impersonal nature of guerrilla warfare, which required constant alertness and created a high level of battle stress. The enemy's principal strategy was to cause havoc without being seen through small-scale night ambushes, snipers, heavy use of mines and deadly booby-traps, and extensive mortar-fire on American positions. The soldiers' resulting sense of danger and helplessness took its psychological toll on the Americans: "It was murder. We could not fight back against the Viet Cong mines or take cover from them or anticipate when they would go off. Walking down trails, waiting for those things to explode, we had begun to feel more like victims than soldiers" (Caputo [1977] 1978, 273).

This war was not only fought against the enemy soldier; it was also waged against the elements – heat, rain, and cold; against the land – jungle, elephant grass, rice paddies, rainforests, mosquitoes and leeches, dust, and mud; and even against the civilian population. American soldiers, who for the most part did not understand the Vietnamese language or culture, often found themselves fighting an unseen enemy easily assimilated into the towns, villages, and hamlets. As a result they had difficulty instantaneously deciding whether Vietnamese civilians, including women and children, were friends, foes, innocent bystanders, indifferent observers, or active participants in the war. Rules of engagement were ambiguous. Was a farmer by day a Vietcong at night? Was a quiet village a support-base for a Vietcong unit? Was any running Vietnamese a fair target? The results of this confusion were often disastrous for both groups: innocent civilians killed by callous or confused American soldiers, and sympathetic Americans killed by innocent-looking civilians. The guilt, moral dilemmas, brutality, and darkness of the human spirit emerging from these confrontations haunt many of the soldier-authors writing about Vietnam. Passages from William Ehrhart's poem "Guerrilla War" express a prevailing view of this situation: "It's practically impossible/to tell civilians/from the Vietcong. . . . Even their women fight;/ and young boys,/and girls. . . ./after a while, /you quit trying" (1985, 93–4).

Also contributing to the special character of ground combat and soldiers' brutal acts against civilians was the American military's method for determining battlefield success in a war of attrition – body-counts. Since traditional methods for determining military victory, territory gained or lost, had little meaning within this contained conflict, military planners and the US media turned to body-counts (number of killed and wounded on both sides) to gauge progress in the war and to give shape to this formless conflict. Each evening on the network television news, Walter Cronkite and other anchors would dutifully report the results of that day's activity, the numbers of dead and wounded. These figures, released by the US Defense Department, were conveniently adjusted at every level of the chain of command, beginning in the field and ending at the highest levels of command.[16] The result was a "scoreboard" mentality toward the war reaching the absurd levels described in Caputo's chapter "The Officer in Charge of the Dead." As regimental casualty-reporting officer, Caputo maintained a large acetate-covered board with up-to-date figures of various units" kill ratios:

> And the measures of a unit's performance in Vietnam were not the distances it had advanced or the number of victories it had won, but the number of enemy soldiers it had killed (the body count) and the proportion between that number and the number of its own dead (the kill ratio). ([1977] 1978, 160)

Such an emphasis on numbers in this war of attrition led to inflated claims and, at times, American soldiers' callous disregard for civilian lives. Human beings were quickly reduced to numbers on a scoreboard. Moral dilemmas abounded as distinctions among confirmed enemy, suspected enemy, and innocent civilians sometimes blurred in a unit's quest to produce impressive kill ratios. The guide in such situations often seemed to be "if dead and Vietnamese, then the person must be VC," or "any running Vietnamese, is a potential target." This strategy also adversely affected the conscience and resolve of American combat soldiers as they questioned the value of numbers in determining progress of the war and as they grappled with the moral conflicts attendant to such a strategy. According to Baritz, the absence of clearly defined military purposes and precise external constraints distinguished Vietnam from other wars and led to a degree of "moral independence" for the foot soldier and his officers not found in previous American wars. Within this formless bureaucratic war, "The line beyond which an action would become a transgression was a matter of individual conscience, a Protestant formula" ([1985] 1986, 286).

53

Tour of Duty. Given the war's amorphous structure and other unsettling features, including the frequent adverse political and military turmoil under which American soldiers fought, Americans serving in Vietnam faced a difficult tour of duty, particularly from 1968 onward. Unquestionably the vast majority of these approximately 3 million men and women responded by performing ably, courageously, and quietly. But, as is true in any war among soldiers on both sides, some Americans in Vietnam abused their power and committed unspeakable acts; murdering innocent civilians at My Lai is one glaring example. As described in the underground newspaper *Overseas Weekly*, further complicating Americans' tour of duty were racial tensions, especially in rear areas; drug use, again predominantly in the rear; some anti-war activities among the soldiers; and occasional open hostilities between officers and enlisted personnel erupting in violence.[17] Adding to tensions and confusion on the battlefield were the absence of overriding ideological justification in an undeclared war; inequities of a military draft allowing deferments and loopholes for many middle- and upper-class white young men ("a rich man's war; a poor man's fight"); and on the home front a growing anti-war movement as the war continued. Along with these burdens, American soldiers (average age of 19 compared to their Second World War counterparts' average age of 26) faced problems caused by two special features of their tours of duty – short rotation schedules and individual replacements.

In a policy first introduced in Korea, but greatly expanded in Vietnam, American soldiers served limited tours (twelve months for the Army and thirteen months for the Marines).[18] Included in this limited tour was a one-week rest-and-rehabilitation (R & R) leave taken out of country at one of ten R & R locations ranging from Hong Kong to Honolulu. And, in a new policy aimed at "career building," American combat officers served six months or less in combat and then received reassignment to staff positions in the rear.[19] Although these rotation policies were instituted to improve morale, especially among draftees, the results were self-defeating from a military and individual standpoint. Since their personal war would end after twelve or thirteen months, regardless of the outcome, a majority of soldiers viewed the struggle from an individual rather than

54

unit perspective. Surviving, not winning, became an overriding concern, especially as the war dragged on.

This individualism and constant turnover of men with considerable combat experience often led to a discontinuity of effort and expertise and a lack of cohesiveness in the units. Also, after 1968, as the war escalated and the number of draftees serving in Vietnam increased, the limited-tour policy, as well as President Nixon's planned reductions of some tours by an additional one to two months (drops), sent mixed signals to these troops about the value of their sacrifices. Such policies also heightened the survivor mentality and short-timer syndrome among those soldiers who had only a short time left in their tour. Certainly, the primary goal of the common soldier in any war is survival. But, as American combat soldiers became more and more disillusioned with their experiences in Vietnam and frequently questioned the purposes and progress of the conflict, morale diminished. Efforts to get soldiers to make necessary sacrifices and an all-out commitment to the war became increasingly difficult. As William Ehrhart notes, surviving and avoiding danger became the main preoccupation: " 'Still, it never occurred to me to lay down my rifle and quit. Instead, you develop a survival mentality. You stop thinking about what you're doing, and you count days'" (quoted in Karnow 1983, 472–3).

In addition to the limited tour, another significant feature of Vietnam combat duty was a soldier's individual entrance and exit from a military unit. Instead of replacing whole units, the American military replaced individuals. In theory, such a strategy would keep a constant core of experienced soldiers in combat units. In practice, this replacement strategy proved counterproductive: heightening the new soldier's feelings of isolation and problems of adjustment, increasing experienced soldiers' feelings of loss as friends rotated back to the States, and intensifying the rotating soldiers' guilt as they left their friends in combat. Such a policy also, in some instances, diminished a unit's effectiveness and cohesiveness and reinforced soldiers' feelings of insignificance – replaceable parts in the war machine. Baritz notes that these feelings of separateness and insignificance "induced a sense of fragility, probably more intense and widespread than in other wars" ([1985] 1986, 283). Several Vietnam narratives, including *The 13th Valley*, focus on these adjustment problems among a unit's FNGs ("Fucking New Guys").

The Return Home. Traditional war stories often tell of some warriors' difficulties in returning home from the battlefield as they carry the physical and psychological scars of combat and struggle to adjust quickly to strange civilian life. These veterans grapple with survivor guilt, feelings of alienation, a nostalgia for the war, unresolved questions about the meaning and validity of the conflict, and nightmares about the horrors of war. These are just some of the characteristics of the aftermath stage of a soldier's journey "home." In this sense many Vietnam veterans are no different from their counterparts in other wars, yet for some Vietnam veterans the war's distinctive features continue to make their aftermath stage particularly traumatic. For these troubled individuals, psychologists have labeled their postwar emotional and psychological reactions as Post-Vietnam Syndrome (PVS) or Post-Traumatic Stress Disorder (PTSD). One often-cited contributing factor to the severity of these adjustment problems was soldiers' individual exit from the battlefield and rapid return to the USA. For example, a combat soldier might leave his unit in the field; pass through a processing center at Long Binh or Cam Ranh Bay, Vietnam; arrive at the Army Terminal in Oakland, California, for discharge from the military; and reach his hometown – all within twenty-four to forty-eight hours. Abruptly leaving friends in Vietnam and proceeding individually through this procedure intensified a departing soldier's feelings of guilt and isolation; moreover, having such a short time to adjust from a battlefield mentality to civilian life later caused additional emotional turmoil for some veterans, including nurses.

Thus, unlike their counterparts in previous wars (even Korea) who made leisurely trips home from the battlefield on troopships, Vietnam veterans did not have sufficient time to share their doubts, fears, guilt, and common battlefield experiences with other veterans.[20] They were quickly thrust into the realities of civilian life in the USA, which during the late 1960s and early 1970s seemed just as disordered and, at times, hostile as the battlefield. Chris Starkmann in *Indian Country* experiences these feelings of dislocation:

Only four days before, he had been in the heat and mud of brigade headquarters, surrounded by the threatening hills near the Cambodian border. Now he was in a car with his family . . . and instead of jungle, he was looking at factories, motels, apartment buildings, houses, and automobiles. Everything should have been comfortably familiar, but it wasn't. All of it looked stranger than those hills on the far side of the earth. He grew uneasy. (Caputo [1987] 1988, 98)

Also exacerbating the Vietnam veteran's problems of adjusting to life in the "real world" were the attitudes of the American public toward these soldiers. Victorious American soldiers had returned from World War I and World War II to victory parades, thanks, and respect. These wars, especially World War II, had a positive image, and the soldiers who fought in them were embraced as honorable men. Korean veterans, who some would say had fought to a draw, returned to a largely indifferent country, one that Max Hastings characterizes as having "no interest whatsoever" in their experiences (1988, 330). Especially from 1968 on as opposition to the war increased at home, Vietnam veterans also returned to an indifferent populace, but more often they encountered a highly charged atmosphere of hostility, fear, or suspicion. Contributing to these feelings were war protests across the country and throughout segments of American society. Also, because television news brought this war into American homes on a nightly basis, many Americans found the reports, as well as the war, disturbing: death, destruction, atrocities, and little apparent progress. Furthermore, the entertainment media promoted a stereotype of Vietnam vets as sadistic, deranged, potheads and "killing machines."

Even with an end to America's combat role in Vietnam, many civilians continued to have difficulty separating their feelings about the war from their feelings about the veterans. Thus, civilian reactions ranged from "Let's forget the whole thing," to "You guys lost the war," to "You are nothing more than murderers who participated in an immoral war." A widely accepted notion was that American involvement in Vietnam and the conduct of American soldiers had given war a bad name. Facing these conflicting reactions, as well as the social turmoil of the late 1960s and early 1970s, returning veterans found themselves just as confused and frustrated as they were in Vietnam, perhaps more so. As Thomas Myers notes, "The country could not correlate the historical data of Vietnam with traditional mythic patterns [victory] and celebrate the hero's return as the final typological act in a continuing national drama. It chose to cancel the performance with what Caputo calls collective amnesia or to cast the veteran in a new role [scapegoat]" (1988, 189). Even some families were unprepared or unwilling to aid the adjustments of returning sons and daughters. For example, in *Indian Country* a bitter anti-war activist, whose son has just returned from fighting in Vietnam, comments that "my son left a long time ago. . . . He never came back" (Caputo [1987] 1988, 105). And traditional veterans' support groups (the Veterans Administration, VFW, and American Legion) were ineffectual, or Vietnam veterans considered them part of the problem rather than a solution. Veterans' responses to this alienation included painful silence about their experiences, inner rage about their treatment at home, violence, drug and alcohol abuse, marital conflict, physical isolation, and ironically a nostalgia for the battlefield. Caputo describes this last reaction as a longing for a familiar place: "Though we were civilians again, the civilian world seemed alien. We did not belong to it as much as we did to that other world, where we had fought and our friends had died" ([1977] 1978, xvi).

These, then, are some of the significant features of the Vietnam War directly or indirectly influencing Vietnam literary war stories. Other characteristics include advanced medical procedures leading to a low death rate among seriously injured soldiers, a disproportionate number of combat soldiers drawn from racial minorities and poor economic backgrounds, and the first war in which American combat forces were truly integrated.[21] Overall, the magnitude and number of these characteristics contribute to a widely held notion among soldier-authors that Vietnam was, at times, a different war and occasionally required different war stories. Now, turning our attention to examining specific narratives about this war, the differences discussed in this section, along with the similarities to other wars described in the previous four sections, facilitate understanding and evaluating the Vietnam narratives. These important themes, images, characters, psychological conflicts, narrative strategies, and distinctive features play prominent roles in the Vietnam soldier-authors' re-creations of the Vietnam experience from innocence through aftermath.

2

Innocence

***

"Everyone loses that illusion [immortality] eventually, but in civilian life it is lost in installments over the years. We lost it all at once and, in the span of months, passed from boyhood through manhood to a premature middle age" (Caputo [1977] 1978, xv). With this observation from *A Rumor of War* about the combat soldier's coming of age, we move into the subject for this chapter, two significant memoirs describing the loss of innocence in the Vietnam War. Myers labels this central theme "the personal transformation of the soldier from FNG ('fucking new guy') or 'cherry' to 'short-timer'" (1988, 30). Such a theme in many of the Vietnam narratives connects these works to other modern war initiation stories, to classical traditions of the war story (*The Iliad*), as well as to such traditional coming-of-age literature (*Bildungsroman*) as Dickens's *David Copperfield* or Thomas Wolfe's *Look Homeward Angel*. All of these works portray an individual's education and maturation as he or she acquires insight about self, knowledge about the world, and a philosophy for living. Underlying this chronological, emotional, and psychological progression is the central character's move-ment from innocence through experience to consideration and understanding.

Since combat is traditionally the domain of the young, the connection between a *Bildungsroman* and a war story is not surprising. As suggested by Fussell's tripartite thematic and structural paradigm – "innocence savaged and destroyed" – a recurring theme in much of modern war literature, fiction and nonfiction, is in fact soldiers' education on the battlefield, as they lose their innocence and cope with the fundamental irony that "every war is worse than expected." In two important works of Vietnam literary nonfiction, Philip Caputo's *A Rumor of War* and Michael Herr's *Dispatches*, the authors use this archetypal pattern to shape the content and structure of their war stories. Both books contain the authors' lessons learned about war and the events and people they encountered in Vietnam. But the books differ markedly in their style and the authors' reactions to the Vietnam experience.

As a literary and historical context for examining these two Vietnam books, Erich Maria Remarque's *All Quiet on the Western Front* demonstrates that the connections between war stories transcend time, place, and language. Published in 1929, this German novel about German soldiers in World War I is one of the most famous pieces of modern war initiation literature, the "Bible of the common soldier." Remarque, who enlisted in the German army in 1916 and was wounded several times, turned his tour of duty into a semi-autobiographical novel about the human experiences of war – horror, destruction, struggle, fear, camaraderie, and death. The simplicity and directness of the narrative, as well as the author's avoidance of lengthy moralizing, mask Remarque's passionate anti-war stance. Equally important, the absence of dates and place-names contributes to the universal appeal of the book and transports readers beyond documentary realism into the novelist's realm of theme, character, and interpretation. For this chapter, Remarque's treatment of lost innocence becomes an important touchstone for comparing combat soldiers' experiences in World War I and Vietnam. Furthermore, Caputo's use of several epigraphs throughout his book from the poems of Owen and Sassoon, World War I poets, invites such comparisons of the two wars and the literature written about them.

Against the symbolic backdrop of changing seasons, Remarque uses the three-part theme of change to relate three years of Paul Baumer's literal and spiritual education into the realities of war. This education ends abruptly with his death in the trenches one month before the Armistice ending World War I on 11 November 1918. The novel is Paul's war autobiography and an elegy for his generation. Instead of beginning the novel with the customary innocence-training section, Remarque uses brief flashbacks to cover this material and instead focuses on Paul's experiences on the front line or his moments of reflection away from the front, including a trip to his home. As a 19-year-old German, Paul enlists in the army, along with four school classmates, at the urging of their patriotic teacher who promotes duty to one's country as the greatest virtue. Paul, much like Andrews, the American artist-soldier in Dos Passos' *Three Soldiers*, is a sensitive young man who writes plays and poetry, reads classical literature, and collects butterflies. At his enlistment he is eager to be a soldier and is crammed full of "vague ideas which gave to life, and to the war also an ideal and almost romantic character" (Remarque [1929] 1987, 21). Such an indoctrination comes from schoolteachers and the older generation of Germans. But after ten weeks of harsh basic training, which forces the young recruits to renounce their personality and trains them for heroism "as though we were circus ponies," Paul changes. Most important, he views life, war, and people from a new perspective.

In this psychological study, how and what Paul sees, feels, and thinks are the traditional elements of *Bildungsroman* war literature. Under the horrible conditions of World War I trench warfare, constant artillery barrages, mass charges, hand-to-hand combat, gas attacks, and obscene casualty-figures, Paul's maturation occurs quickly. On one hand, he still considers himself "little more than a boy," yet his combat experiences have aged him so quickly – a natural phenomenon in the crucible of war. "We are none of us more than twenty years old. But young? Youth? That is long ago. We are old folk" (p. 18). Marking this change are his own heart-of-darkness journey and his strong feelings of alienation from the civilian world. From the innocent youth, he typically progresses to the hardened combat soldier, one compared to an animal reacting by instinct and concerned principally with survival and the daily routines of existence:

> life is simply one continual watch against the menace of death; – it has transformed us into unthinking animals in order to give us the weapon of instinct – it has reinforced us with dullness, so that we do not go to pieces before the horror. . . . It has lent us the indifference of wild creatures. . . . (pp. 273–4)

At times, out of control, he is caught up in the savagery of battle, acting out of animalistic rage and survival instincts:

> But we are swept forward again, powerless, madly savage and raging; we will kill, for they are still our mortal enemies, their rifles and bombs are aimed against us, and if we don't destroy them, they will destroy us. (p. 115)

During time away from battles (sentry duty, conversations with fellow-soldiers, or a leave to visit his home), Baumer reflects on what he has become and how he is alienated from almost everything and everyone. His only sense of community comes from being with the other soldiers who have shared this physical and psychological journey from innocence to awareness, a brotherhood of the battlefield: "I belong to them and they to me; we all share the same fear and the same life, we are nearer than lovers, in a simpler, a harder way ..." (p. 212). Trapped in the "cage" of war, Paul and the other young soldiers feel helpless and cut off from their innocent past and an unformed future: "The war has ruined us for everything" (p. 87). Seeing death and experiencing the horrors of war ("A hospital alone shows what war is" (p. 263), they have grown to distrust the older generation's patriotism and so-called wisdom and learned to rely on their own newly gained insights: "we had suddenly learned to see. And we saw that there was nothing of their world left. We were all at once terribly alone; and alone we must see it through" (p. 113). Typical of World War I literature, Paul blames this older generation, including his teachers, for not fulfilling their roles as "guides to the world of maturity" and for not providing young people with a true education about war and its consequences.

Separated from the older generation – Wilfred Owen's "masters of war" – Paul also feels estranged from his family and the people in his hometown. Such feelings become especially acute when he returns home from the front on a brief leave. His behavior foreshadows the actions, feelings, and thoughts described in postwar literature dealing with returning Vietnam veterans. Paul senses that these innocent civilians see the war from a different perspective; they cannot understand the truth about war unless they have experienced it firsthand. Thus, feeling as if he is in a strange country, he wishes to be alone, away from the civilians' stares and naïve questions about the war's progress. But he is also upset that these people have "trivial" desires and worries far removed from the war. Innocent to the realities of war, even his mother and father wish to hear war stories. But Paul hesitates to tell them the truth. He fears that the stories will be too upsetting for them, and he also worries that once he narrates these stories the events will be too horrible for him to consider and to control within his mind:

> I realize he [Paul's father] does not know that a man cannot talk of such things; I would do it willingly, but it is too dangerous for me to put these things into words. I am afraid they might become gigantic and I be no longer able to master them. What would become of us if everything that happens out there were quite clear to us? (p. 165)

After recognizing his loss of innocence and confronting the metaphysical darkness of his war experiences, Paul must develop a way to cope with his thoughts, feelings, and experiences – a philosophy for living with war. Like the typical combat soldier, he tries to control his environment as well as his thoughts, by developing a protective combat numbness. He becomes preoccupied with the surface realities of his existence – food, shelter, mail, rest, and the daily routines of war – at the expense of the horrible truths and painful feelings. His commitments become quite simple – his and his friends' survival. During moments of controlled reflection, however, he ponders his spiritual isolation, weariness, loss of hope, bleak future after the war, and the extent of his change: "I believe we are lost" (p. 123). Yet, armed with this knowledge, he, like Paul Berlin in *Going After Cacciato*, chooses not a separate peace, leaving the war, but a realistic perspective and a stoic acceptance of his situation:

> But for all that we were no mutineers, no deserters, no cowards. . . . We loved our country as much as they [civilians]; we went courageously into every action; but also we distinguished the false from the true, we had suddenly learned to see. (p. 13)

64

Remarque certainly presents nothing glamorous or comforting about the war described in this novel, and he does not temper the brutal realism of the battlefield with the momentary attractions of combat. Paul's death is described briefly and unceremoniously: "He fell in October 1918, on a day that was so quiet and still . . ." (p. 296). Remarque's war story is one that current readers continue to find relevant, moving, and truthful. The book's themes, imagery, language, realism, psychological detail, and structure make their way into the best of the Vietnam narratives.

When Caputo began writing *A Rumor of War* in 1976, he intended to write a war novel, but soon realized that he was using factual material and merely changing the names of characters and places. He discovered, as Hemingway once noted, that "it's difficult to write imaginatively when you know too much about something." Thus, instead of an imaginary re-creation, he produced a memoir with literary intentions and used the shaping power of imagination and literary devices to select, arrange, and dramatize the factual material. Current critics might label the book a successful "nonfiction novel";[1] Fussell would label it a typical war memoir: "the memoir is a kind of fiction, differing from the 'first novel' (conventionally an account of crucial youthful experience told in the first person) only by continuous implicit attestations of veracity or appeals to documented historical fact" ([1975] 1981, 310). Caputo strives to develop and interpret his central character, himself, to the same degree that Remarque creates the fictional Paul Baumer, but the journeys inside Lieutenant Caputo are neither as frequent nor as deep as those forays into Baumer's psyche. Also, compared to Remarque's strong anti-war tone, *A Rumor of War* is more anti-Vietnam War than anti-war.

Although separated from the fictional Paul Baumer by almost eight thousand miles and a half-century, the real-life Philip Caputo finds himself in the Vietnam War undergoing a similar loss of innocence and, as a combination Marlow (observer) and Kurtz (participant) figure, undergoing a similar heart-of-darkness journey: "it [Vietnam] was one of the last of the dark regions on earth and only the very brave or the very dull – the two often went together – could look at it without feeling fear" ([1977] 1978, 105). The structure of the narrative, more than in any of the other Vietnam works, strictly follows Fussell's patterns of innocence, experience, and reflection, and the echoes of language and theme from *Heart of Darkness* and the John Wayne Syndrome are equally prominent.

But the subject of *A Rumor of War*, published in 1977, is more than a literary treatment of spiritual and psychological change. Caputo the author has mixed purposes – autobiography and documentary realism about the Vietnam War. In his "Prologue," Caputo summarizes his intentions:

> This book does not pretend to be history. . . . In a general sense, it is simply a story about war, about the things men do in war and the things war does to them. More strictly, it is a soldier's account of our longest conflict, the only one we have ever lost, as well as the record of a long and sometimes painful personal experience. ([1977] 1978, xiii)

As a result, throughout the book, Caputo maintains two roles. The first is that of the reporter-narrator. From a personal perspective years after his experiences, Caputo gives a limited journalistic account of particular events, places, and people associated with this conflict. He also narrates innocence lost – soldiers and a country – in the arena of war. In the second role, Caputo the character is the subject of this literary treatment of a soldier's inner life.

Three features of Caputo's background influence his narrative: college English major (BA from Loyola University, Chicago); Marine Corps officer (enlisted in the Marines' ROTC unit in 1960, commissioned in 1964); newspaper reporter for the *Chicago Tribune* (1972 Pulitzer Prize for investigative reporting and Middle East correspondent from 1972 to 1977). First, the degree in English perhaps explains the literary intentions for this first book. Scattered throughout the work are numerous literary and biblical epigraphs (especially lines from Wilfred Owen's and Siegfried Sassoon's World War I poetry), literary references (Kipling, Owen, *Augie March*, Dylan Thomas), and echoes of Conrad's *Heart of Darkness*. In short, readers find both a well-read narrator describing the war and a literate character

involved in it. Next, the Marine experiences, of course, provide
the raw material and factual accuracy of the book – sights,
sounds, and emotions of war. But they also have a dramatic
role in this memoir. The mental and physical conditioning,
esprit de corps, and romantic ritual of Marine officer training,
along with Caputo's glorious arrival with the first combat unit
in Vietnam, intensify the romantic expectations of Caputo the
character to such a high degree that they can be notably undercut
by the experienced narrator's ironic vision. The intensity of the
combat also leads to another irony for the veteran narrator – a
nostalgia for war:

> I could protest as loudly as the most convinced activist
> [anti-war], but I could not deny the grip the war had
> on me, nor the fact that it had been an experience as
> fascinating as it was repulsive, as exhilarating as it was
> sad, as tender as it was cruel. (p. xvi)

This theme of Conrad's "fascination of the abomination," notice-
ably absent in *All Quiet on the Western Front*, makes its way into
many of the Vietnam narratives.

Finally, Caputo's career as a reporter shapes both the content
and narrative style of the book. At times, the narrator moves
from storyteller to a reporter intent upon documentary transcription of combat rather than a literary treatment of plot,
character, and conflict. Like a reporter, he describes representative sights, sounds, and details of Vietnam for people
who have never been there. In fact, in introducing one section
of journalistic narrative, Caputo warns readers of its lack of
continuity:

> Because of the sporadic, confused nature of the fighting,
> it is impossible to give an orderly account of what we
> did. . . . The incidents I do remember, I remember vividly;
> but I can come up with no connecting thread to tie events
> neatly together. (p. 90)

Also, after leaving the Marine Corps, Caputo had extensive
experience with war and political turmoil as a Middle East
correspondent, and this allows him to place Vietnam within

contexts. The result is frequently a narrative voice tinged with skepticism, cynicism, and historical perspective. For example, in comparing the stench of dead bodies in Vietnam to dead bodies he later encountered on the Golan Heights, in the Sinai Desert, in Cyprus, and in Lebanon, he notes, "All those dead people, Americans, North and South Vietnamese, Arabs and Israelis, Turks and Greeks, Moslems and Christians, men, women, and children, officer and enlisted, smelled equally bad" (p. 161). Or, after recounting the death in Vietnam of a classmate from Officer Candidate School, Caputo combines an elegy for the soldier with a cynical observation about America's later treatment of its Vietnam veterans:

> You died for the man you tried to save, and you died *pro patria*. . . . You were faithful. Your country is not. As I write this, eleven years after your death, the country for which you died wishes to forget the war in which you died. Its very name is a curse. (p. 213)

Yet, despite the factual detail and limited social – political commentary, Caputo principally concerns himself with the timeless theme of innocence savaged and destroyed on the battlefield. The most succinct statement of this theme appears in the "Epilogue." Narrator-correspondent Phil Caputo observes from a circling helicopter the hasty and chaotic American evacuation of Saigon on 29 April 1975, the day prior to the fall of the city to the North Vietnamese:

> My mind shot back a decade, to that day we marched into Vietnam, swaggering, confident, and full of idealism. We had believed we were there for a high moral purpose. But somehow our idealism was lost, our morals corrupted, and the purpose forgotten. (p. 328)

The "we" of the quote refers to Lieutenant Caputo and the members of the 9th Expeditionary Brigade arriving in Vietnam in March 1965. But, on another significant level, the "we" refers to Americans in general as the first combat units entered the war.

A Rumor of War, then, is a story of an individual's loss

of innocence as well as a country's loss of innocence and coming of age in a war that politically was America's first defeat and left the country scarred. As Caputo describes his own innocent yearning for adventure, the inspirational aura of Kennedy's Camelot, the strong belief in an international role as protector from communism and defender of democracy, and the intoxicating romance of military balls, he is also presenting a tableau of American innocence prior to the Vietnam War. Such innocence initially cracked with President Kennedy's assassination but shattered in the political and military turmoil of Vietnam. Karnow, in describing the Vietnam Veterans Memorial in Washington, comments on this end of national innocence:

> They [names of dead] bear witness to the end of America's absolute confidence in its moral exclusivity, its military invincibility, its manifest destiny. They are the price, paid in blood and sorrow, for America's awakening to maturity, to the recognition of its limitations. With the young men who died in Vietnam died the dream of an "American century." (1983, 9)

And English scientist Freeman Dyson comments that when he came to America in the late 1940s American students "lacked the tragic sense of life" deeply ingrained in every European as a result of World War I. But thirty years later things were different.

> The Vietnam War produced in American life the same fundamental change of mood that the First World War produced in Europe. The young Americans of today are closer in spirit to the Europeans than to the Americans of thirty years ago. The age of innocence is now over for all of us. (1979, 53)

Caputo's personal journey to maturity begins in the forest preserves of suburban Chicago. The young boy faces a typical modern dilemma for youths wishing to prove their courage, toughness, and maturity – how to be heroic in an unheroic age. Roaming the woods near his home, he occasionally stumbles across flint arrowheads, relics of distant adventures: "Looking at them, I would dream of that savage, heroic time and wish I had lived then, before America became a land of salesmen and shopping centers" ([1977] 1978, 5). The same longing for adventure appears almost a hundred years earlier in Henry Fleming's initial musings about the Civil War: "He had, of course dreamed of battles all his life. . . . There was a portion of the world's history which he had regarded as the time of wars, but it, he thought, had been long gone over the horizon and had disappeared forever" (Crane [1895] 1986, 11). These youthful yearnings for danger and challenges, which cut across time, wars, and countries, continue for Caputo as he enters college still unsure of how to fulfill these ambitions.

In 1960, typical of many of the young men of his generation, Caputo at age 19 finds direction for his quest from the significant mythmakers at the beginning of American involvement in Vietnam – President John F. Kennedy, Hollywood, and John Wayne. A teacher introduced Paul Baumer to patriotism and the glory of dying for one's country in World War I, but for Caputo a president's idealism and values spark his interest in war: "War is always attractive to young men who know nothing about it, but we had been seduced into uniform by Kennedy's challenge to 'ask what you can do for your country' and by the missionary idealism he had awakened in us" ([1977] 1978, xiv). Caputo also finds grist for his romantic illusions and heroic fantasies in the score of war movies he has seen, especially those starring John Wayne: "Already I saw myself charging up some distant beachhead, like John Wayne in *Sands of Iwo Jima*, and then coming home a suntanned warrior with medals on my chest" (p. 6).

Acting on these romantic myths, he joins the Marine Platoon Leaders Class and begins training for war on a part-time basis during his summers away from college classes. While on these summer retreats into a world of adventure, the romance of war shifts from the movie theater to the training fields of Quantico, Virginia. Acing like "overgrown kids playing soldier," Caputo and his classmates find that the games of boyhood merely have been upgraded to exercises for war, complete with marching songs, mock battles, survival tests, the ceremonial side of military life including grand parades and military balls, and the fantasies about winning the Bronze and Silver Stars – badges of honor and signs of proven manhood. For Caputo, this war waged in the abstract becomes the ultimate outdoor sport and Hollywood movie where thoughts of failure and death have no place. The greatest fear is the fear of being found wanting. Certainly this section of narrative parallels Fussell's first stage of the "farcical preparation for battle" and mirrors to some degree Paul Baumer's training experiences under Corporal Himmelstoss. Five years after his enlistment, with a college degree, his commission as a second lieutenant, additional training in Okinawa, and command of a rifle platoon, Philip Caputo as part of the Marines' 9th Expeditionary Brigade – a name right out of colonial wars – lands in Vietnam in March 1965 to take part in this "splendid little war." One might expect a 23-year-old officer who has read Owen's and Sassoon's World War I poetry to have a realistic idea of what lay ahead. But Caputo still holds on to the daydreams of John Wayne heroics, a feeling of immortality, and romantic expectations of high adventure. With this arrival in Vietnam, Caputo the narrator begins to merge the innocent character with the naïve country he represents. Both seem to share the same jingoistic spirit, a view of war as "an outdoor sport," and happy-warrior mentality about why and how the war will be waged. They perceive it as no more than a brush-fire war to be quickly extinguished by the Marines' superior forces and technology:

> I guess we believed in our own publicity – Asian guerrillas did not stand a chance against US Marines. . . . There was nothing we could not do because we were Americans, and for the same reason, whatever we did was right. (p. 66)

At this point, Americans in general and Caputo in particular are innocent of the soon-to-develop ironies of this war. In fact, using the familiar movie metaphor, Caputo compares the first days in Vietnam to one more Hollywood movie: "We are starring in our very own war movie, and the howitzer nearby provides some noisy background music" (p. 100).

Up to this point in the narrative, Caputo's innocence, although described in more detail than is typical, parallels that of other central characters in modern war literature, including Paul

71

Baumer. In fact, with few exceptions, this account of innocence and the quest to be a hero parallels Ron Kovic's description (published one year earlier) complete with references to the Kennedy influence and the John Wayne syndrome. But with the increase in enemy contact, the deaths of friends, and the exposure to the brutality of combat, Caputo's narrative moves from the familiar romantic clichés about war to the harsh realities, which also become clichés in this initiation literature. Caputo unwillingly enters the second stage of his education and begins to acquire the familiar combat numbness:

> We learned what war was about. . . . We began to change, to lose the boyish awkwardness we had brought to Vietnam. We became more professional, leaner and tougher, and a callus began to grow around our hearts, a kind of emotional flak jacket that blunted the blows and stings of pity. (p. 90)

The Hollywood adventure film soon becomes a horror film as Caputo and the other soldiers, like Paul Baumer and the German soldiers, gradually sink into a brutish state. They begin to hate the Vietnamese villagers who willingly or unwillingly allow the Vietcong to use their villages for base-camps. They also sense a loss of control over their lives and emotions as events occur randomly and their units occasionally run amok in villages. Their initial optimism, innocence, and missionary zeal disappear as the soldiers face the constant harassment of an unseen enemy, mutilating booby-traps, hostile civilians, and another enemy in the form of the unrelenting land – "It was the land that resisted us, the land, the jungle, and the sun" (p. 82). Typical of grunts in modern war, Caputo and his men also encounter the horrible destruction caused by the impact of modern war technology on the fragile human body. In a passage paralleling Yossarian's description of Snowden's wound, Caputo observes that "The horror lay with the recognition that the body, which is supposed to be the earthly home of an immortal soul . . . is in fact only a fragile case stuffed full of disgusting matter" (p. 121). Frustration, hatred, irrationality, and unrestrained savagery mark their gradual descent into a spiritual darkness. Outwardly the signs of this change appear in the haggard, aged faces and the expressionless eyes with their fixed stare – the "thousand-yard stare" shared by experienced soldiers in all wars. In another passage with a Conradian echo, Caputo comments about the modern-day Kurtzes whom the soldiers are becoming in this alien and chaotic environment:

> Everything rotted and corroded quickly over there: bodies, boot leather, canvas, metal, morals. Scorched by the sun, wracked by the wind and rain of the monsoon, fighting in alien swamps and jungles, our humanity rubbed off of us as the protective bluing rubbed off the barrels of our rifles. . . . It was no orderly campaign, as in Europe, but a war for survival waged in a wilderness without rules or laws. (p. 217)

After only three months commanding a rifle platoon in this geographical and ethical wilderness, Caputo rotates to a non-combat position as assistant adjutant at Regimental Headquarters, where he becomes the casualty-reporting officer. At this point the narrative turns more from "we" to "I" and assumes an almost absurdist tone straight out of *Catch-22*. As he becomes the official scorer in this war of numbers, Caputo's education about the realities of war continues in the abstract. But he also begins to move into Fussell's third stage of "time and quiet for consideration, meditation, and reconstruction" as he ponders the meaning of these casualty figures. His job, which he labels "The Officer in Charge of the Dead," entails identifying bodies of American soldiers, gathering casualty reports, visually verifying enemy body-counts, and maintaining the regimental "scoreboard" with numerical comparisons of the kill ratios (Americans killed versus enemy body-count). The mounting numbers include the deaths of soldiers from his former platoon and the death of Lieutenant Levy, the OCS classmate killed while trying to recover the body of a dead Marine. Given the time to ponder these deaths, Caputo loses his remaining romantic illusions about "good ways to die in war," "noble sacrifices," and a war fought with order, rules of engagement, and battlefield ethics. Names and faces of the dead replace these self-delusions: "Asleep and dreaming, I saw dead men living; awake I saw living men dead" (p. 190). After three months of this job, Caputo describes his changes in typical war-story fashion: "I was twenty-four when the summer began; by the time it ended, I was much older than I am now. Chronologically, my age had advanced three months, emotionally about three decades" (p. 182).

At this point Caputo the character makes a decision that may puzzle readers in light of the insight he has acquired in his position as casualty officer. If this book were a novel, the central character, acting reasonably on his newly acquired knowledge of war, might react such as Frederic Henry or Captain Yossarian and declare a separate peace, thus bringing the story to a dramatic and satisfying closure. Instead, stripped of his illusions about war in general and his convictions about the Vietnam War in particular, Caputo, nevertheless, voluntarily returns to combat. He cites boredom and revenge as principal causes, raising the possibility of a John Wayne "guts-and-glory" finish to the book. But he also mentions the soldier's familiar love–hate relationship with combat, a tension that readers may find inexplicable yet one that frequently appears in modern war literature:

> The rights or wrongs of the war aside, there was a magnetism about combat. You seemed to live more intensely under fire. Every sense was sharper, the mind worked clearer and faster. Perhaps it was the tension of opposites that made it so, an attraction balanced by revulsion, hope that warred with dread. (p. 218)

This section describing his return to combat also allows Caputo the narrator to shape the final pages of memoir to dramatize Caputo the character's final descent into the heart of darkness. Ironically, Caputo is given command of Levy's platoon, and he finds himself back in the midst of ambushes, booby-traps, death, and undisciplined soldiers taking out their anger and increasing frustration on Vietnamese villages. The climactic episode occurs as Caputo, feeling as if he were "split in two" and "watching myself in a movie," increasingly loses control of his emotions and thoughts under the mounting pressures of combat, soaring casualties, and the company commander's appeals to his platoon commanders to increase their kill ratios.

Part of Caputo becomes a Kurtz figure in an isolated outpost doing what "he damn well pleases." The other part acts as a Marlow figure reflecting on the events. Caputo decides to act on his violent fantasies, to retaliate against the Vietcong by secretly ordering a mission to enter a village and bring back two VC suspects for questioning. Caputo's orders to the squad who will carry out the plan are to "Snatch 'em up and bring 'em back here, but if they give you any problems, kill 'em" (p. 300). There is a silent acknowledgement among all involved that the suspects will not be brought back alive, and that is exactly what happens. "Perhaps the war had awakened something evil in us, some dark, malicious power that allowed us to kill without feeling" (p. 309). Serious complications arise when Caputo and the Marine bureaucracy learn that one of the dead suspects is in fact an innocent civilian. Like Kurtz, Caputo pronounces his own judgement on the horrible episode: "We had killed the wrong man. That boy's innocent blood was on my hands. . . . My God, what have we done?" (p. 304).

What emerges, then, is a standard episode in many of the Vietnam narrative – an atrocity incident involving civilians or enemy prisoners. From the rape and murder of two VC nurses in Winston Groom's novel *Better Times than These* (1978) to a scene in *The Short-Timers* (Hasford, 1979) where an American tank runs over a Vietnamese girl sitting on a water buffalo, such episodes are commonplace in both the fiction and nonfiction. Their widespread presence in these works is certainly a result of the brutal character of guerrilla war in Vietnam, including the difficulty of distinguishing combatants from innocent civilians. But their existence also allows authors to present dramatic incidents, raise moral issues, and explore characters' responses to the situations. The results of such probing advance the recurring heart-of-darkness theme and reveal the authors' skills in mapping the psychological landscapes of key characters. In short, one clue to the quality of a war book is the author's success in handling such a scene. Fussell suggests another reason for the presence of this episode, especially in nonfiction war literature – a purging of the narrator's guilt:

Subsequent guilt over acts of cowardice or cruelty is another agent of vivid memory: in recalling scenes and moments marking one's own fancied disgrace, one sets the scene with lucid clarity to give it a verisimilitude sufficient for an efficacious self-torment. ([1975] 1981, 327)

Such an explanation seems particularly appropriate for Paul Baumer's exhaustive description of his night in the shell hole alone with the dying French soldier he has stabbed. Fussell's observation also goes a long way in explaining the detailed confession that Caputo's narrative becomes as he re-creates the kidnapping, murder, and subsequent military trial.

Once more, this time for five months, Caputo finds himself removed from combat. He serves as an assistant operations officer while awaiting his court-martial, along with four members of the patrol, on charges of premeditated murder and subsequent lying under oath. The Marlow half of the divided character contemplates his Kurtzian descent into loss of control, savagery, and the absurdity of the entire war. Who or what is responsible? What can be learned from this episode? These and other moral questions directly or indirectly surface. Critic James C. Wilson claims that Caputo ignores the issue of his personal responsibility for the murders: "By blaming the Vietnamese and their debauched moral landscape, Caputo conveniently denies his own responsibility for the brutality he admits participating in" (1982, 62). What Caputo does is to tiptoe delicately through the issue, not entirely avoiding self-condemnation. Denying that the deaths were murder, he instead argues that they result from his own combat weariness and are inevitable products of war, a war in which the sole aim is to develop high body-counts and favourable kill ratios: "the war in general and US military policies in particular were ultimately to blame for the deaths of Le Du and Le Dung" (Caputo [1977] 1978, 313). Also, in evaluating the significance of these deaths and the subsequent trial, Caputo borrows for the last time from Conrad as he, like Marlow, suggests that the potential to become a Kurtz figure resides within everyone:

If the charges were proved . . . no one was guaranteed immunity against the moral bacteria spawned by the war. If such cruelty existed in ordinary men like us, then it logically existed in the others, and they would have to face the truth that they, too, harbored a capacity for evil. But no one wanted to make that recognition. No one wanted to confront his devil. (p. 313)

In an unintentional parallel to Marlow's lie to the Intended at the end of the story, "that great and saving illusion" (Conrad [1902] 1975, 108), Caputo and the other men are acquitted. Officially, they are not judged moral casualties of the war, but Caputo, like Marlow, pronounces the darkness triumphant: "I already regarded myself as a casualty of the war, a moral casualty, and like all serious casualties, I felt detached from everything" ([1977] 1978, 314).

By the end of his tour in Vietnam, Caputo's innocence has been savaged and destroyed, replaced by a wisdom gained through experience and a cynicism acquired through disillusionment and frustration: "None of us was a hero. . . . We had done nothing more than endure. We had survived, and that was our only victory" (p. 320). Caputo no longer reveres the John Wayne–Hollywood view of war, but instead fully understands Fussell's irony of war. Sounding very much like Paul Baumer attacking the older generation of Germans, he responds to the lessons learned by establishing his own separate peace: "I was finished with governments and their abstract causes, and I would never again allow myself to fall under the charms and spells of political witch doctors like John F. Kennedy" (p. 315).

As Caputo leaves Vietnam in 1966, his "hope abridged" anticipates by a few years the parallel change that the United States will undergo in discovering the ironies, absurdities, and tragedies of the splendid little war. Nine years later, in April 1975, Caputo the correspondent covers the fall of Saigon and the subsequent evacuation of US personnel and South Vietnamese. While on this assignment, he encounters a Marine from his old unit, the 9th Expeditionary Brigade, whose assessment of the war symbolizes America's innocence replaced by cynicism: "The marine looked at the faint blue line marking the Vietnamese coast and said, 'Well, that's one country we don't have to give billions of dollars to anymore'" (p. 328). In the ending to Caputo's story, America, also, has made its separate peace.

Turning from *A Rumor of War* to Michael Herr's *Dispatches* (1977), nominated for the 1978 National Book Award for non-fiction, is to move from the conventional war narrative to the unconventional in style as well as content. The shift is from the traditional war memoir to New Journalism; from memory to a combination of observation and imagination; from Fussell's tri-partite form to fragments, vignettes, scenes, character sketches, and cryptic images culled from Herr's observation of the war; and from a narrator who is a full-time soldier turned part-time reporter to a narrator who is a full-time reporter turned occa-sional soldier. Yet underlying both pieces of nonfiction is the narrator's loss of innocence; Herr's, unlike Caputo's, however, is not savaged and destroyed, but it is irretrievably altered: "I went to cover the war and the war covered me . . . (1977, 20). And like *A Rumor of War*, this book does become a confessional. Herr chronicles his own heart-of-darkness trip that despite the absurdities and horrors of Vietnam leads to his acknowledgement of the "fascination of the abomination." As Paul Gray notes in a review of *Dispatches*, "Herr dared to travel to that irrational place and to come back with the worst imaginable news: war thrives because enough men still love it" (1977, 120).

In late 1967, arriving in Vietnam as a freelance writer for *Esquire* magazine, Herr took his place in the sizable Vietnam press corps populated at various times by such notable American journalists as Ward Just (*Washington Post*), David Halberstam (*New York Times*), Peter Arnett (AP), Neil Sheehan (UPI), and Gloria Emerson (*New York Times*). Also present were many international correspondents and photojournalists, as well as numerous hacks, curiosity-seekers, war freaks, and military mouthpieces – all, once accredited, given incredible freedom to roam the battle zones in covering the war.[2] At age 26 and with previous assignments for *Esquire* and *Rolling Stone* completed, Herr wasn't, one suspects, naïve about the ethos of Vietnam: the politics; the Catch-22 mentality of the military bureaucracy; and the drugs, music, language, and protest of the late-1960s culture transported by the soldiers to Vietnam. He came prepared to give his readers a perspective of the war they would not receive from traditional journalism:

Conventional journalism could no more reveal this war than conventional firepower could win it, all it could do was take the most profound event of the American decade and turn it into a communications pudding. . . . (1977, 218)

Herr wanted to cut through military and media propaganda, to move beyond the facts and statistics, to leave the relative safety of Saigon, and to journey into the field where he would write about the soldiers and tell the secret history of the Vietnam War. His subjects would be death, friendships, lies, cover-ups, the exhilaration of combat, and war stories. He wanted to capture the language, music, culture, feelings, and emotions of the war. Most of all he wanted to give the grunt's view of combat. Without the pressure of daily deadlines or a set number of commissioned pieces, Herr freely traveled the country, primarily via helicopter, and succeeded in capturing the aura of Vietnam in articles eventually published in *New American Review #7*, *Esquire*, and *Rolling Stone*.

These short pieces of journalism, which Herr labels "illumination rounds," are an important part of this book. They become pieces of photojournalism without the pictures, narrative versions of *Life* magazine covering Vietnam. Consequently, in this role as journalist, Herr becomes a Marlow figure who has survived a journey into the Vietnam jungles to bring back for all who will listen traditional war stories told in an unusual way. His tales deal with courage, fear, death, and the self. They range from the extensive account of the seventy-six-day siege of the Marines at Khe Sanh (1968) and the bloody battle for the imperial city of Hué during the 1968 Tet Offensive to the shortest war story of them all: "Patrol went up the mountain. One man came back. He died before he could tell us what happened" (p. 6). Also included are short pieces on the history of American involvement in Vietnam; the geography of the country; the Vietnamese people and their language; the US military bureaucracy; Herr's personal essays on sleep, religion, and combat superstitions; and even an ode to the helicopter.

But Herr does not present this information in conventional newspaper and magazine journalism. Instead, he gives readers his unique images and a particular shape to the war – a perceptual overload of sights, feelings, and sounds (rock lyrics, military jargon, grunt jive, and doper's spaced-out language). The style and language are, at times, lyric, cryptic, tortuous, frenetic, funky, and ornate. In fact James C. Wilson has described the writing and content as most representative of the "dope and dementia" approach to portraying the war (1982, 45). A chronological narrative is not Herr's concern as he often rapidly jumps back and forth in time, subject, and place.[3] These abrupt shifts emerge from Herr's special view of the war:

Some of us moved around the war like crazy people until we couldn't see which way the run was taking us anymore, only the war all over its surface with occasional, unexpected penetration. As long as we could have choppers like taxis it took real exhaustion or depression near shock or a dozen pipes of opium to keep us even apparently quiet; we'd still be running around inside our skins like something was after us, ha ha, La Vida Loca. (1977, 8–9)

Herr's manner of presenting these war stories, the fragmented form mirroring the fragmented content, often becomes as important as the stories themselves and suggests a crucial question for writers attempting to re-create the Vietnam experience. How does one write about the special inner and outer landscape of the Vietnam War? That is, does the writer translate the experiences into facts; conventional language; and narrative patterns, imagery, and themes commonly found in war reporting? Obviously, Herr rejects the style and content of conventional journalism, opting instead for his own patterns, structure, and language to present truths about Vietnam.

What unifies these far-ranging illumination rounds is Herr's focus on people as he strips away the surface detail and examines their feelings about combat. He uncovers truths found in other war literature. For example, Paul Baumer's feelings of alienation as he returns home on leave are echoed by a Marine who has returned to Vietnam for his third tour, " 'I just can't hack it back in the World' " (p. 5). Also, Herr describes one soldier's heart-of-darkness fantasy and sexual release achieved while firing his M-16 on full automatic at a string of VC bodies hanging on perimeter wire. Or Herr, revealing the disturbing combat callousness occurring among soldiers who have spent lengthy periods in the field, notes a soldier's attitude toward civilians in a combat zone: " 'I mean, if we can't shoot these people, what the fuck are we doing here?' " (p.29). And in one of his longest sections Herr describes the friendships forged by the war as he gives a character sketch of an unlikely "salt and pepper" duo of Khe Sanh Marines Mayhew and Day Tripper. But, most of all, in these fragments he chronicles the typical changes soldiers undergo in combat – the loss of innocence and the aging that unites young soldiers from all wars and is revealed in their eyes and faces:

> He had one of those faces, I saw that face at least a thousand times at a hundred bases and camps, all the youth sucked out of the eyes, the color drawn from the skin, cold white lips, you knew he couldn't wait for any of it to come back. Life had made him old, he'd lived it out old. (p. 16)

If all a reader finds to praise in this book is Herr's New Journalistic reportage about the sights, sounds, and people of Vietnam, is this feature enough to validate Ward Just's assessment that *Dispatches* is "the best single work of art about the war" (1979, 64)? Probably not! But ultimately this book – and, indeed, it is a carefully crafted book rather than a collection of articles – becomes, like *All Quiet on the Western Front* and *A Rumor of War*, a first-person account of innocence lost – in this case Herr's. In fact the depth and artistry of the author's treatment of his own heart-of-darkness journey fit Fussell's definition of a literary war memoir and take readers on a more detailed psychological journey than does Caputo's book. The jumbled and fragmentary illumination rounds capture the ethos of the Vietnam experience. But transforming this work from a collection of articles into a unified and coherent book is the pervasive narrative voice of Michael Herr, the war survivor who years after his return from Vietnam re-creates his experiences as a war correspondent and attempts to arrive at truth and understanding (Fussell's third stage). As Hellmann notes about the structure of the book, "These fragments are subsumed within the larger structure of Herr's meditating consciousness as he probes for the essential meaning of his Vietnam experience" (1980, 142). This re-creation and reflection occur years after

Herr's return from Vietnam, since he had a serious bout of deep depression beginning in 1970 and was unable to finish the book for six more years.[4]

Despite the unconventional style and content, Herr relates a conventional progression from innocence, through experience, to reflection as he changes from witness to participant while in Vietnam. As he noted in an interview, he went to Vietnam because "I wanted to write a book. But also like a lot of Marines, I went because I had never been and wanted to go" (Morgan 1984, 52). His changes are, nevertheless, a correspondent's and not a Marine's. Drawing upon his own education through war movies, Herr presents this unusual initiation story as a surrealistic prose film with its frequent jump cuts served up by the ever-present helicopter or drug-induced reveries rather than the movie camera. For this version of *Dateline: Vietnam*, Herr becomes writer, director, and principal actor with a supporting cast of other correspondents:

> In any other war, they would have made movies about us too. . . . But Vietnam is awkward, everybody knows how awkward, and if people don't even want to hear about it, you know they're not going to pay money to sit there in the dark and have it brought up. . . . So we have all been compelled to make our own movies, as many movies as there are correspondents, and this one is mine. (1977, 188)

In this "home movie," Herr arrives in Vietnam for his *voluntary* eleven-month tour sporting political sophistication along with an innocence about combat and about the journalist's ability to remain detached: "If anything could have penetrated that first innocence, I might have taken the next plane out" (p. 22). In an interesting way, he is like the cynical and knowledgeable Fowler, the narrator and British reporter in Graham Greene's Vietnam novel, *The Quiet American* (1955). Fowler understands the political and military machinations of French Vietnam in the early 1950s as the American presence is starting to increase, and he is quick to perceive the harm of the American innocence, idealism, and adventurous spirit of Alden Pyle (a shadowy CIA figure). Still, Fowler also naïvely believes that he can remain detached from the surrounding turmoil and maintain the reporter's objective and uninvolved stance: "... I would not be involved. My fellow journalists called themselves correspondents; I preferred the title of reporter. I wrote what I saw. I took no action – even an opinion is a kind of action" (Greene [1955] 1980, 28). He eventually succumbs to his adverse feelings about Pyle's actions and becomes "*engagé*." Herr, too, initially believes that he will act as a recorder of other people's war stories and remain emotionally and physically detached from the war: "I was there to watch" (1977, 20), but like Fowler he also becomes *engagé*.[5]

As might be expected of a highly motivated and aggressive reporter, Herr travels to Vietnam out of a sense of curiosity and journalistic ambition. But like Caputo he also journeys to Vietnam out of a romantic sense of combat adventure:

> But somewhere all the mythic tracks intersected, from the lowest John Wayne wetdream to the most aggravated soldier-poet fantasy, and where they did I believe that everyone knew everything about everyone else, every one of us there a true volunteer. (p. 20)

Once in Saigon, Herr's equivalent to in-country basic training is a quick trip to the Saigon black market where he purchases a new set of combat fatigues and then returns to his Saigon hotel room where he dresses in front of the mirror, "making faces and moves I'd never make again. And loving it" (p. 22). And, like Marlow preparing for his trip to the Congo by studying maps, so Herr stares at the old French map of Vietnam hanging on the wall of his Saigon apartment. The reporter-soldier fantasy is beginning. Like Caputo and many other American soldiers, he soon departs on his first combat operation filled with Hollywood's images and language of war:

> I didn't know what was going on, I was so nervous I started to laugh. I told him [platoon sergeant] nothing was going to happen to me and he gave my shoulder a tender, menacing pat and said, "This ain't the fucking movies over here, you know." I laughed again and said that I knew; but he knew that I didn't. (p. 22)

Once on the mission, the first few deaths and firefights don't have any meaning since they seem an extension of film images, special effects, and familiar violence from the electronic media: "We'd all seen too many movies, stayed too long in Television City, years of media glut had made certain connections difficult" (p. 209).

Is Herr an aggressive reporter covering the war from an unconventional perspective, or is he a quasi-soldier living his adventure fantasies and playing at war? This is a key question. The answer is blurred by Herr's shifting relationship to his subjects as he loses his innocence and constantly changes his role: "I stood as close to them [soldiers] as I could without actually being one of them, and then I stood as far back as I could without leaving the planet" (p. 67). Instead of just covering the war, he quickly immerses himself in the Vietnam experience as the omnipresent helicopter transports him in and out of the Vietnam hills, jungles, and firebases and back to a Saigon hotel room for the sleep and the grass that cannot erase the images, fears, and faces of the dead. Destroyed in the early stages of his heart-of-darkness trip are his reporter's detachment and his combat-movie illusions:

and when the Cav sent an outfit to relieve the Marines on 471, it killed off one of the last surviving romances about war left over from the movies: there was no shouting, no hard kidding, no gleeful obscenities . . . The departing and arriving files passed one another without a single word being spoken. (p. 158)

As has been true for the soldiers in his war story, he, also, has quickly aged: "I realized later that however childish I might remain, actual youth had been pressed out of me in just the three days that it took me to cross the sixty miles between Can Tho and Saigon" (p. 72). Replacing the illusions is the conventional dose of harsh realism and disillusionment of Fussell's second stage – the horrible images of war and an awareness of how awful Vietnam could be.

But, as Herr's physical and psychological journey into the Vietnam War proceeds deeper and deeper, the Marlow and Kurtz roles – reporter and participant – become intertwined.

Herr develops a deep fascination for combat as he moves increasingly closer to identifying with the soldiers. In fact, in some of these sections of memoir, pronouns shift from "I" and "they" to "we": "*We* were all rubbing Army-issue nightfighter cosmetic under our eyes to cut the glare . . ." (p. 11); "*We* were running some wounded on to the back of a half-ton truck . . ." (p. 79); "*We* sat on the hill and watched while the napalm was dropped against the bunkers, and then *we* set up a recoilless rifle and fired at the vents" (p. 160: *my italics*). Although he does not carry a weapon, Herr, at one point, accepts an M-16 rifle and becomes part of a reaction force protecting a base-camp. On another occasion during a particularly frantic moment at a Special Forces Camp at the time of the Tet Offensive beginning 30 January 1968, he ends up with a .30-caliber automatic firing cover for a returning reaction team in a scene right out of the movies: "they [VC] had Cholon, Tan Son Nhut was burning, we were in the Alamo, no place else, and I wasn't a reporter, I was a shooter" (p. 68). And the next day he finds himself in the hospital compound where "I worked all the next day, not a reporter or a shooter but a medic, unskilled and scared" (p. 68).

With these new roles, Herr establishes a unique place for himself in the war, a reporter and quasi-soldier. At the same time, however, as he moves from innocence to experience, he encounters typical battlefield experiences and feelings described in Remarque's and Caputo's books: "I was in many ways brother to these poor, tired grunts, I knew what they know now, I'd done it and it was really something" (p. 206). For example, as part of his battlefield initiation, Herr undergoes the familiar combat aging ("twenty-seven pushing fifty"), the short-timer's syndrome ("I was short"), and the emotional shock of seeing a close friend die. He also experiences the characteristic death-recognition episode when he jumps into an evacuation helicopter filled with dead bodies wrapped in ponchos but with their faces uncovered. Like the grunts, he also becomes much more aware of luck and superstition while walking on a patrol and staying close to a soldier who appears to live a charmed existence in combat. The closest that Herr comes to suffering the terror of being wounded in battle occurs in a scene reminiscent of Henry Fleming's ironic acquisition of his "red badge of courage" and similar to Paul Berlin's embarrassing moment of fear in *Going*

After Cacciato. Unintentionally kicked in the nose as the soldiers hit the ground during an ambush, Herr mistakes his bloody nose for a head wound: "I made a sound that I can remember now, a shrill blubbering pitched to carry more terror than I'd ever known existed. . . . My hands went flying everywhere all over my head, I had to find it and touch it" (p. 32). Finally, Herr, like Caputo and other soldiers, also discovers the exhilaration of combat and the visceral thrill of being in heavy action. He uses sexual imagery to describe his emotional surge during battle and the later satisfying exhaustion: "It was a feeling you'd had when you were much, much younger and undressing a girl for the first time"(p. 136).

At the heart of Herr's journey into Vietnam and confrontation with the self, the darkest secrets emerge. Herr, like combatants before him, uses war to find his courage and to play the ultimate game – gambling with one's life: "All right, yes, it had been a groove being a war correspondent, hanging out with the grunts and getting close to the war, touching it, losing yourself in it and trying yourself against it" (p. 206). Furthermore, he discovers that accompanying his fear of death and disgust for the absurdity and brutality of the Vietnam War is his growing infatuation with the violence, destruction, and beauty of war – "the fascination of the abomination." Herr reduces his mixed feelings to a simple image. On the one hand, an incoming mortar round at night can be frightening and cause a lot of destruction, but the sight and sound can also be beautiful, "beautiful and deeply dreadful" (p. 132). Throughout the book, whether he is writing about others or about himself, Herr is trying to reconcile this dark secret, his and others' love–hate relationship for war:

> Maybe you couldn't love the war and hate it inside the same instant, but sometimes those feelings alternated so rapidly that they spun together in a strobic wheel rolling all the way up until you were literally High On War, like it said on all the helmet covers. Coming off a jag like that could really make a mess out of you. (p. 63)

Yet these aren't the only feelings Herr must reconcile; he must also deal with the guilt he has as a quasi-soldier and so-called "war profiteer" – a journalist making his living off misery and death. Most of the soldiers readily accept his presence, treating him like a guest, making him comfortable, looking out for his welfare, and admiring his courage. But a few are suspicious of the press, believing that they are traitors presenting a false picture to the readers back home. Even more are simply contemptuous of anyone who would volunteer to go to Vietnam: "They only hated me, hated me the way you'd hate any hopeless fool who would put himself through this thing when he had choices, any fool who had no more need of his life than to play with it in this way" (p. 208).

Ultimately, however, the soldiers and Herr understand that his tour of duty is artificial. He can go on patrols, visit the isolated firebases, talk with the grunts, try to put himself in their place, and become a shooter, but he is still an outsider. He cannot, nor does he want to, ignore that he is a correspondent, not a soldier. He does not face the daily pressure of coping with the Russian-roulette quality of a soldier's precarious existence. Furthermore, Herr has an unusual degree of control over his environment and contacts with the war. Hitching a ride on a helicopter, he can leave the combat zones at will – establishing an order in his life, escaping to the safety of his Saigon hotel, but bearing the guilt of a departing survivor. In the end Herr reconciles the ambiguity of his situation. He realizes that he has an important responsibility for the soldiers he leaves behind to write in an unconventional way about the real war story – "men hunting men, a hideous war and all kinds of victims" (p. 214):

> And always, they would ask you with an emotion whose intensity would shock you to please tell it, because they really did have the feeling that it wasn't being told for them, that they were going through all of this and that somehow no-one back in the World knew about it. (p. 206)

Finally, after eleven months in Vietnam, Herr's meta-movie switches scenes to the States where the survivor finds himself out of the jungles of Vietnam but not out of the darkness. Once more, he unconsciously assumes another role, that of the Vietnam veteran doing the "Survival Shuffle." In a society that neither understands his experiences nor wants to, this war survivor, not the reporter, proceeds through Fussell's third stage of consideration, as he reflects on the personal changes Vietnam has wrought, and into a post-war aftermath stage, as he struggles to adjust to civilian life. Nightmares of dead Marines haunt him, but combat nostalgia accompanies them: "You missed the scene, missed the grunts and the excitement . . ." (p. 245). Herr arrives at his own separate peace, reconciling his real hatred for the Vietnam War with his deep fascination for war. The latter dominates. Granted, he has not changed to the same degree as the reporter in the film *The Green Berets*, who becomes a shooter and completely embraces the political and military propaganda of the Vietnam War. Nor has Herr reached the extreme conditions of his photojournalist friends Sean Flynn and Tim Page still in Vietnam. Psychologically and emotionally, Flynn has journeyed so deep into the war that he doesn't bother to take pictures after a while, and even after being seriously wounded, Page still wholeheartedly embraces the adventure and allure of war: "Take the glamour out of war! I mean, how the hell can you do that?" (p. 248). But Herr, too, is unable to dismiss or repudiate his experiences as he holds on to his war souvenirs, nostalgia, and the comfort of a small community of survivors in the States:

The friendships lasted, some even deepened, but our gatherings were always stalked by longing and emptiness, more than a touch of Legion Post Night. Smoking dope, listening to the Mothers and Jimi Hendrix, remembering compulsively, telling war stories. (p. 245)

Unlike Caputo, Herr in his movie script does not destroy the John Wayne myth of war, even after careful consideration. And he even suggests an ironic twist to Fussell's notion of the irony of war; for Herr, the irony is that the war seems to have turned out better than expected. Thus, when compared with *All Quiet on the Western Front* and *A Rumor of War*, Herr's unusual but realistic treatment of his loss of innocence and his resulting change may be difficult for readers to accept. Some may even agree with a British reviewer's comment that *Dispatches* contains the sick ramblings of a "war freak" (Fenton 1978, 464). But Herr must be admired for his willingness to participate in the war so he can tell the real story. The outcome is not without precedent, just the setting. Herr came to Vietnam to reveal the horrors of the darkness, which he does, but in the process becomes fascinated by that darkness:

> A few extreme cases felt that the experience there [Vietnam] had been a glorious one, while most of us felt that it had been merely wonderful. I think that Vietnam was what we had instead of happy childhoods. (1977, 244)

Moreover, the experience has continued to fascinate him long after completing *Dispatches*. Despite his stated intention never to write another book about war or never to cover another war, he did write for *Apocalypse Now* the interior monologue of Captain Willard, the film's Marlow figure. Later, he joined with Stanley Kubrick and Gustav Hasford to write the screenplay for the recent film *Full Metal Jacket*.[6] Unlike Kurtz, Paul Baumer, or Caputo, Herr does not appear ready to utter "The horror! the horror!" Or, perhaps, he, like Marlow, is compelled to tell the story over and over.

3

Experience

In discussing modern war fiction, Alfred Kazin in *Bright Book of Life* mentions authors' difficulties in presenting realistic accounts of war: "No individual experience, as reported in literature, can do justice to it [war], and the most atrocious common experiences will always seem unreal as we read about them" (p. 81). And Marlow in *Heart of Darkness* laments the problems his listeners have in understanding his own story of violence and atavistic regression:

> "You can't understand. How could you? – with solid pavement under your feet, surrounded by kind neighbors ready to cheer you or to fall on you, stepping delicately between the butcher and the policeman . . . how can you imagine what particular region of the first ages a man's untrammelled feet may take him into. . . ." (Conrad [1902] 1975, 70)

Both of these are literary versions of soldiers' common retorts to civilians' inquiries about what it was like to be in heavy combat. As a Vietnam veteran from *In Country* tells his niece. "Unless you've been humping the boonies, you don't know" (Mason [1985] 1981, 136). This issue of the inadequacy of language to convey accurately and meaningfully the sights, sounds, and feel of war for the uninitiated is central to this chapter. Our particular interest is in three Vietnam combat novels, all "first novels," containing realistic and imaginary treatments of combat: Larry Heinemann's *Close Quarters* (1977), James Webb's *Fields of Fire* (1978), and John Del Vecchio's *The 13th Valley*

(1982). Pertinent to these works is the title of this chapter representing the second stage of Fussell's description of a soldier's evolution in war. Authors of the books discussed in the previous chapter trace a soldier's battlefield education through all three stages, from innocence through experience to consideration. But a significant body of war literature, although briefly touching on innocence and reflection, emphasizes the second stage, the combat experiences, which according to Fussell are "always characterized by disenchantment and loss of innocence" ([1975] 1981, 130). Also a prominent theme in these books is a soldier's culminating journey into the heart of darkness: the face-to-face confrontation with the horrors and evils associated with combat along with the resulting guilt – both collective and individual.

Soldier-authors from all wars writing fiction and nonfiction primarily about this second stage face difficult decisions in determining the audience, purpose, and content for their war stories. For example, an article in the *Wall Street Journal* (9 March 1979, 3) describes Bantam's paperback series about World War II combat, which is intended to restore an appealing, patriotic image of war tarnished by the unsettling experiences of Vietnam. With such titles as *Helmet for My Pillow* and *U-Boat Killer*, the editors, according to the article, hope to promote for a mass audience the glory, heroism, and sporting spirit of war. The series' general editor says, "'Men were admirable in World War II. They weren't just sitting around blowing smoke and listening to rock bands all day. They were admirable men.'" Such a statement alludes to a widely held notion of the mid-and late 1970s that many American combat soldiers in Vietnam had not performed courageously and that serious books about this war did nothing to refute this image. This statement also raises the issue of the purpose and content of combat literature. Should its principal goal be political statement, a romantic portrait of combat, or a brutally realistic account?

As soldier-authors, Heinemann, Webb, and Del Vecchio face these and other artistic issues in writing about Vietnam. How autobiographical should their combat novels be as the authors resolve the creative tension between memory and imagination? Should the authors commit themselves to a factual re-creation (realism) at the expense of story, artistic arrangement, and meaning? In other words, should detailed battle scenes be the author's primary goal, or should they serve as backdrops for imaginary characters, themes, and conflicts? Myers in examining this issue notes that many American authors do an excellent job of powerfully portraying the "daily horrors and boredoms" of Vietnam, but they often "abdicate the tasks of larger historical vision and cultural connection to the reader or critic sifting through the particular images on the page" (1988, 39) – Conrad's higher truths. Under the banner of political statement, should the content reflect Owen's disillusionment and pity of war, or should the content portray an uplifting, positive view of combat – a "guts and glory" John Wayne perspective? Another question: Is there, as Fussell suggests, a "concept of prohibitive obscenity" acting as a cultural censor on authors and preventing them from revealing the graphic horrors of war?[1] And, finally, through saturated media coverage, have readers become so inured to violence, brutality, and the horrors of war that an author's sincere attempt through language to educate an audience about the realities of war is doomed to fail? In short, what can a book tell readers about war that they haven't already graphically learned through television and film?

These are some of the questions guiding this discussion of Vietnam combat novels beginning with a historical-literary context of two critically acclaimed combat novels emerging from World War II. The first is Norman Mailer's *The Naked and the Dead* (1948), a "first novel" dealing with a fictional island campaign against the Japanese in the Pacific. The second is James Jones's *The Thin Red Line* (1962), a fictional account of the bloody battles on Guadalcanal Island in 1942–3 and the second novel in his war trilogy that includes *From Here to Eternity* (1951), awarded a National Book Award in 1952, and the unfinished *Whistle*, published posthumously in 1978. Together, Mailer's and Jones's works serve as helpful introductions to Vietnam combat fiction because of the relationships between these two soldier-authors' combat experiences and their books' fictional content; their use of a conventional melting-pot narrative structure; their handling of the social, political, and psychological issues of combat; their treatment of evil and guilt; and their differing views on the purpose and content of this type of war story.

Both the Harvard-educated Mailer and the Midwesterner

Jones served with the infantry in the Pacific during World War II. Mailer's two years in the Army, including an eighteen-month tour in the Philippines, provided limited background material for *The Naked and the Dead*, which he started planning while still a student at Harvard.[2] Jones's stormy five years in the Army included time at Schofield Barracks, Hawaii, during the attack on Pearl Harbor, which became important background for *From Here to Eternity*. He also participated in the bloody campaign on Guadalcanal where he was wounded and received the Purple Heart and Bronze Star. Jones's war novels are much more autobiographical than Mailer's, especially *The Thin Red Line*, which contains several incidents from Jones's experiences at Guadalcanal. Interestingly, both authors later wrote about the Vietnam War, and their contrasting treatment of this conflict mirrors fundamental differences in the content of their Second World War novels. Mailer's novel *Why Are We in Vietnam?* (1967) is a social and political allegory using a description of an Alaskan hunting trip to discuss the national character leading to America's ill-advised involvement in Vietnam. It's a cynical anti-war, anti-Vietnam War statement. His *The Armies of the Night* (1968), a winner of the Pulitzer Prize and National Book Award, is a New Journalistic account of his arrest after participating in an anti-war protest at the Pentagon in October 1967. In contrast, Jones's reporting trip to Vietnam in 1973, one of those quick VIP tours for visiting journalists and dignitaries that Herr despised, resulted in a series of essays published in *Viet Journal* (1974). With a dedication to "the United States Army," it's a sympathetic portrait of American military personnel and, on the whole, supportive of American involvement in Vietnam.

Such differences in tone also appear in the two Second World War novels. Using a familiar convention of combat literature and film, both Mailer and Jones craft the narratives in *The Naked and the Dead* and *The Thin Red Line* around an omniscient narrator's study of the soldiers in one platoon, a melting-pot of Americans from different classes, races, religions, and cultures. Conspicuously absent in these segregated units are African Americans, but Jews and Hispanics instead become victims of prejudice. This melting-pot narrative strategy enables the authors to describe battles, reveal character, and convey something of the

American social and political ethos through extensive interaction among the diverse soldiers. Mailer, a political radical less concerned with combat action, focuses on extensive political and social analysis about the military machine's and American society's impact on individuals. Despite conflicting critical assessments of his success with this subject, the book represents an important approach to writing combat fiction. Mailer uses the melting-pot narrative and battle scenes as starting-points for a broad socio-literary study of human nature, the military, and American society that transcends the battlefield and moves the work beyond the narrow label of combat novel and into the realm of a book about ideas and characters.

Jones, on the other hand, in *The Thin Red Line* creates a different combat novel. He employs the narrative structure and combat scenes to re-create realistically war and soldiers' psychological responses to these alien and terrifying experiences. Readers learn much about a soldier's daily existence and the feel of war. Readers also sense that, while Mailer is predominantly transmuting his own war experiences, Jones is more often transcribing his. Perhaps Mailer's observations in *Cannibals and Christians* about *The Thin Red Line* accurately assess the book's strengths and limitations. After comparing the book to *The Red Badge of Courage*, he comments that

> it is so broad and true a portrait of combat that it could be used as a textbook at the Infantry School. . . . So he performs a virtuoso feat of letting us know a little about a hundred men. . . . Jones" aim, after all, is not to create character but the feel of combat, the psychology of men. (Mailer 1966, 112)

Yet, although both Mailer's and Jones's books are successful combat novels in their own ways, their strengths are also their limitations. *The Naked and the Dead* strays often and far from the battlefield; *The Thin Red Line* never leaves it.

Taking readers on a heart-of-darkness journey inside men who happen to find themselves in combat, Mailer explores the devils they confront. Especially influenced by the themes and narrative structure of Dos Passos, he intersperses the main narrative with ten sections, each labelled "The Time Machine."

In these he examines the class backgrounds of ten members of the Intelligence and Reconnaissance (I & R) Platoon, as well as their insecurities, sexual hang-ups, prejudices, and guilt formed prior to entering the Army. Thus, in this naturalistic novel, war does not shape their character but merely reveals it. As suggested by a section titled "Argil and Mold" (an echo of Dos Passos' chapter "Making the Mould"), the soldiers' characters have been formed before they enter the military. Thus, Red Valsen, the product of poverty in a Montana mining town and a hobo existence, carries into the military a hatred of authority and fears of commitment that surface as cynicism, rebellion, and isolation in his interaction with the rest of the I & R platoon. Croft, the platoon sergeant, is a power-hungry, evil, anti-Semitic individual who, as the narrator states, is that way "because of the corruption-of-the-society . . . the devil has claimed him for one of his own . . . he is a Texan . . . he has renounced God . . . the only woman he ever loved cheated on him, or he was born that way . . ." (Mailer [1948] 1981, 156). Within this political dichotomy of quasi-liberalism and fascism, Mailer explores the conflicts between the powerful and the powerless; and within the economic context of different classes, races, and religions, he examines the conflicts between the "haves" and the "have-nots," or the outsiders and the insiders. All of this takes place within the oppressive military organization ("The Army functions best when you're frightened of the man above you and contemptuous of your subordinates" (p. 176)) and within a jungle environment taking its physical and psychological toll on the soldiers.

Common war themes appear in this novel: for example, soldiers' brutality, death-recognition scenes, battlefield fear, and the soldier's sense of insignificance and entrapment within the "shattering gyre" of war and the military. Ultimately, however, this is a political novel about power and control with four characters emerging as central figures. General Cummings, who directs the campaign against the Japanese on the fictional island of Anopopei, is motivated by a Kurtzian urge for omnipotence. He views himself as a visionary spouting a fascist philosophy of social and military power: "'the only morality of the future is a power morality, and a man who cannot find his adjustment to it is doomed. There's one thing about power. It can flow only from the top down'" (p. 323). Cummings's equally contemptible counterpart in the field is Sergeant Croft, who also relishes power, but in a less cerebral way – "I HATE EVERYTHING THAT IS NOT IN MYSELF" (p. 164). He, too, wishing to control everything around him, restricts his "vistas of omnipotence" to his platoon and his environment. Like Cummings, Croft also rejects accident and chance as having power over his life, even considering himself exempt from being killed. His power manifests itself in brutal treatment of the enemy, his men, and nature: at one point he crushes a bird in his hands. Eventually, Cummings and Croft collaborate as the general orders Croft's platoon to go on a dangerous jungle reconnaissance mission to Mount Anaka in preparation for a later large-scale assault on the entrenched Japanese. The mission becomes a personal test for Croft, a heart-of-darkness journey with the mountain, looming in the distance, symbolizing this Kurtzian hunger for power, a conquest of nature, and personal insight.

Opposing the powerful Cummings and Croft in this war story devoid of heroes are the powerless Lieutenant Hearn and Red Valsen. Hearn is an upper-class, idealistic quasi-liberal, who initially is an aide to General Cummings and later commands Croft's platoon; Valsen is an outwardly cynical but basically compassionate enlisted man in the I & R platoon. Neither can oppose the power of Cummings or Croft, either at the level of argument or of physical confrontation. Together, Hearn's death (indirectly related to Cummings's orders of transfer and directly related to Croft's duplicity) and Valsen's humiliating submission to Croft's power and brutality during the reconnaissance mission underscore the bleak pessimism of this novel and Mailer's fears of fascist ideology infecting postwar America. Within this battlefield environment, values – personal and religious – crumble; positive actions result in failure; integrity, concern for others, noble struggles for survival, and heroic actions are absent; and rare moments of personal insight are quickly dismissed. As Jeffrey Walsh observes, a strong argument can be made that "not a single actively good man emerges" in this novel and that the story is devoid of "any significant personal or social affirmation" (1982, 112–13). Determinism, primal instincts, and chance (not individual choice) ultimately dominate this combat environment as they control character and thwart power and illusions of control, even Croft's attempt to conquer Mount Anaka. In the final irony of the book, Cummings's carefully reasoned battlefield strategies do not defeat the Japanese, but the blunderings of an incompetent major lead to victory. In this combat novel, soldiers' glorious moments on the battlefield are absent; the resulting oppressive spiritual darkness pervading the narrative is not so much a consequence of individuals' actions but a product of the political, social, and military systems in which the soldiers have existed.

Compared with Mailer's frequent abstract treatment of war in *The Naked and the Dead*, in *The Thin Red Line* Jones substitutes realism for abject pessimism, psychological analysis for social commentary, and combat language and battlefield strategy for political philosophy. And, although, like Mailer, Jones uses the narrative framework of the melting-pot platoon, he is not concerned with exploring the social conflicts within this group of soldiers. We learn little about the social background of his characters. Instead, as suggested by Mailer's earlier comments, Jones focuses on the battlefield. In the process, he resurrects his own experiences in the South Pacific as a corporal with a rifle company in a regiment of the 25th Infantry Division, during the latter stages of the pivotal Guadalcanal Island campaign of 1942–3 against the Japanese.[3] As readers we learn much about the physical dangers and day-to-day existence of infantry soldiers engaged in island warfare, which in its jungle terrain, oppressive climate, small battles, and ferocity might be compared to the small-unit skirmishes in Vietnam.

Within the novel's realistic setting, Jones also intends, as suggested by one of the epigraphs ("There's only a thin red line between the sane and the mad"), to journey into the psyches of combat soldiers. He traces their shifts on the battlefield from sanity to temporary madness, from order to chaos, from an acceptance of death to a struggle to survive, and from inexperienced soldier to skilled combat veteran. Thus, like *The Red Badge of Courage* and O'Brien's Vietnam books, this war story frequently examines individual courage and fear on the battlefield. But with a roster of eighty-four characters drawn primarily from C-for-Charlie Company, which has landed near the end of the campaign, Jones also briefly explores issues such as guilt, helplessness, homosexuality, sexual tensions associated with combat, and endurance. Furthermore, he examines the psychological make-up of an effective soldier, an important subject in Vietnam combat fiction. As numerous critics have noted, this latter theme (a soldier's evolution) is part of a planned thread weaving together his trilogy on World War II and the art of soldiering.[4] Jones's version of the ideal soldier contrasts markedly with the John Wayne figure. As Jones notes in *WWII*, his illustrated non-fiction book about the war, this psychic process culminates when soldiers accept their own insignificance in the larger scheme of things and thus subordinate personality, repress civilian habits of mind, and accept anonymity in death.

> [The soldier] must make a compact with himself or with Fate that he is lost. Only then can he function as he ought to function, under fire. He knows and accepts beforehand that he's dead, although he may still be walking around for a while. (1975, 54)

Such acceptance results in an attitude similar to Paul Baumer's "We are lost," and leads to a spirit of sacrifice, camaraderie, and joy in insignificant rituals present in C Company but notably absent in Mailer's I & R platoon. It can also lead to combat numbness and brutality.

Several of Jones's characters temporarily achieve this state of acceptance, anonymity, and detachment associated with the evolution. But the character who comes closest permanently to reaching the level of the fully evolved soldier is First Sergeant Welsh whose eccentric behavior, bordering on madness and cynicism, conceals his skill as a soldier and his loyalty and concern for the men of Charlie Company. His detached demeanor is a pretense similar to Joker's mask of black humor and indifference enabling Joker to cope with Vietnam's horrors described in *The Short-Timers*. Ironically, Welsh claims that he has never experienced combat numbness because "life had already made him numb like that years ago" or because "combat itself had never yet gotten quite tough enough to freeze up his particular brand of personality" (James Jones 1962, 411). This psychological portrait of Welsh becomes one of the more intriguing elements in this novel.

Also appearing in this book are stock characters and episodes readers expect in combat book. For example; the innocent and cowardly clerk, Corporal Fife, undergoes a battlefield transformation similar to Henry Fleming's in *The Red Badge of Courage* as he temporarily relishes his combat numbness and bellicosity, but eventually succumbs to his survival instincts by getting a medical release from combat.[5] Private Bell displays the stereotypical preoccupation with fears of his wife's infidelity, which ironically come true, and through a combination of motivation and luck Private Doll gradually evolves into an approximation of Jones's ideal soldier. Also present are the commonplace battlefield scenes and feelings found in Mailer's novel – the mutilation of dead Japanese soldiers; the search for battlefield souvenirs; the guilt after the first kill; a soldier's remorse after his brutal hand-to-hand combat with a Japanese soldier;[6] soldiers' recurring feelings of helplessness; and chauvinistic views of women. But, compared to the sources of Mailer's heart of darkness, the evils in this book emerge from individual actions or the battlefield environment. And, despite battlefield absurdities, soldiers" feelings of insignificance, conflicts between officers and enlisted men, an absence of heroes, and Sergeant Welsh's cynical tone, Jones, unlike Mailer, does sympathetically portray American combat soldiers in C Company. Positive values emerge; characters display an enduring and vital human spirit; and occasional moments of valor, loyalty, and compassion occur on the battlefield. According to Fussell, "The actualities of war are more clearly knowable from some books than from others," and Jones's novel falls into the category of the best Second World War combat works (1989, 290). For other reasons, Mailer's novel also has a place within this group, demonstrating that combat fiction can transcend the battlefield and explore broad political, social, and philosophical issues. Together, these two Second World War novels offer Vietnam soldier-authors contrasting approaches for transforming war experiences into combat fiction.

Fifteen years after the publication of *The Thin Red Line*, Larry Heinemann published his "first novel," *Close Quarters*. Although not receiving widespread critical acclaim and commentary, this book is a significant beginning for discussing

Vietnam combat fiction. Following closely the patterns and purposes of Jones's novel, Heinemann draws upon his tour of duty (1967–8) as a 22-year-old combat infantry sergeant with the Army's 25th Infantry Division in Vietnam (ironically, the same division in which Jones had served). Like Jones, he centers the book on the battlefield, examining the psychology of the combat soldier from the grunt's perspective and emphasizing the sights, sounds, smells, emotions, and actions of combat. On the other hand, Heinemann eschews the narrative frame of the melting-pot platoon found in *The Naked and the Dead*, and he also forsakes Mailer's strong underlying plot and continuity of theme in favor of a more journal-like recording of events. Also absent is the lengthy cast of characters appearing in *The Thin Red Line*. Instead, using a first-person narrator, Philip Dosier, Heinemann focuses on the members of a Battalion Reconnaissance platoon. This Vietnam version of Mailer's earlier I & R platoon comprises thirty-six men and "ten boxy squat-looking armored personnel carriers" (APCs, or tracks). More precisely, he centers this novel on the actions, thoughts, and feelings of "Flip" Dosier and his close friend, Charles Quinn, two soldiers with similar backgrounds: high-school graduates from blue-collar families living in the Midwest. Heinemann, for the most part, uses past tense as Dosier recalls the many episodes of his tour of duty and his later return to the States. But there are moments – eight, to be exact – when Heinemann introduces present tense to heighten the immediacy and lyricism of events as Dosier describes night ambushes, maintenance on the tracks, a drug-induced reverie in a chapel, a daydream about sexual fantasies on R & R, his feelings about his tour, and a visit to his dead friend's parents.

As a combat novel, Heinemann's work, without question, shatters Fussell's concept of a cultural "prohibitive obscenity" censoring the horrors of war. This work moves far beyond Mailer's and Jones's limited attempts through language and detail to reveal overtly war's obscenity. The language is vulgar, racist, and sexist; the graphic scenes are, at times, almost poetic in their litany of death, gruesome details, and horrific human destruction. Like Jones's novel, this book portrays the evolution of a soldier and gives readers a feel for war, but Heinemann's portrait is much more emotional and visceral than Jones's.

Furthermore, like *The Naked and the Dead*, it is a much darker and more cynical book than *The Thin Red Line*; in fact, among Vietnam war stories, it is closer to Hasford's *The Short-Timers* in its extensive catalog of horror, cruelty, and callousness.

The novel is also another Vietnam version of *Heart of Darkness*, complete with Dosier's physical and psychological journey as he evolves into a brutal soldier. This literal and spiritual account begins at the battalion's own "central station"; culminates in a horrible battle on New Year's Day; and gradually recedes from this moment into reflection, pronouncement, and a return to civilization. Dosier becomes both Marlow and Kurtz figures as he chronicles his and Quinn's moral collapse and loss of humanity. Their physical journeys are similar to Marlow's trip deep into the jungle to Kurtz's inner station. But the river is replaced by dusty roads, and the steamer is replaced by the powerful tracks providing mobility and protection – yet, like Marlow's boat, becoming death traps. From the battalion base-camp at Dau Tieng, approximately fifty miles northwest of Saigon near the Cambodian border, Dosier's squad travel to the surrounding firebases in their heavily armed APCs leading resupply convoys or rescuing trapped soldiers. Occasionally they journey on foot to establish night ambushes. Along the way, the evils they confront are the customary ones of war and also those of their own making.

Finally, this is a book of comings and goings as Heinemann captures the transience, rituals, odd relationships, and psychological traumas of the unique Vietnam tour of duty with its one-year rotation policy, out-of-country R & Rs, individual entry and exit from the war, and swift evacuation of dead and wounded from the battlefields. A friend wounded in an ambush is suddenly gone, medivaced out of country within hours; or at the end of a tour, a soldier gathers his gear, signs out of the company, and, despite promises to keep in touch with those who remain, is never heard from again. Capping this theme of coming and going is the soldier's swift return from the battle front to the home front. Anticipating his later novel, *Paco's Story* (1986), and other aftermath novels, Heinemann briefly sketches the emotional and psychological stress of the returning soldier's re-entry into civilian life – "climbing down."

Unlike central characters discussed in the previous chapter,

Dosier does not enter Vietnam as a hardened combat veteran or as an idealistic, gung-ho soldier. But he is naïve. Foreshadowing Paul Berlin's character in *Going After Cacciato*, he is a reluctant and somewhat cynical draftee lacking a strong commitment to the Vietnam War and having little sense of why the war is being fought or what combat is like. Thus, as he first enters the battalion camp, he doesn't yet comprehend the significance behind the disturbing 1,000-meter stare of the American soldiers he encounters: "Each man looked over, looked down at me with the blandest, blankest sort of glance – almost painful to watch – neither welcome nor distance" (Heinemann [1977] 1986, 4). Nor does he understand their apathy toward the war and their contempt for the Vietnamese people and country suggested by one soldier's comments:

"you could roll it [Vietnam] into one tight-ass ball and none of it is worth the powder to blow it away with. There ain't one, not one square inch of muck within five or six thousand miles of here that I would fight anybody for, except what I'm standing on." (p. 19)

Although throughout the book readers learn few details about Dosier's background, he does occasionally describe a typical American Puritan upbringing of religion, John Wayne movies, war stories, obedience to parents, and patriotism that has ill-prepared him for what he encounters in Vietnam and contributes to his general confusion about the war: "What in the world am I doing here?" (p. 53). He also carries with him to Vietnam the trappings of civilization and attendant moral values that Jones notes initially inhibit the ideal soldier's development. Much of the narrative deals with Dosier's loss of these feelings and inhibitions and his descent into a permanent state of moral and combat numbness – not exactly what Jones had in mind. He is, in a sense, evolving into what his friend Quinn already is: "Quinn so mean and evil" (p. 336). "[H]e [Quinn] knew the tracks and the killing and the staying alive" (p. 329). Caputo's earlier observation about this spiritual condition becomes an important epigraph for this novel: "Out there, lacking restraints, sanctioned to kill, confronted by a hostile country and a relentless enemy, we sank into a brutish state. The descent could be checked only by the net of man's inner values . . ." ([1977] 1978 xx).

Perhaps shocking readers most in this book is Dosier's rapid decline into this brutish state and his apparent lack of any inner values to check such a plunge. As a result, inner conflicts involving guilt, personal responsibility, and moral dilemmas found in both Mailer's and Jones's novels receive little attention. Receiving considerable attention, however, is the nature of evil within this modern heart of darkness. In writing about *Close Quarters*, critic Cornelius Cronin categorizes the evils portrayed in modern war literature:

> veterans of World Wars I and II who turned their experiences into literature tended to see "the war," "the State," or "the system" as the evils with which they must come to terms, while Vietnam veterans who have written about their experiences tend to see themselves as evil. (1983, 124)[7]

Such an assessment holds true for *The Naked and the Dead*, but Jones's treatment of evil, which is of minor interest in his novel, seems more in tune with that of Vietnam writers. Unquestionably, Heinemann portrays Dosier and Quinn as embodiments of evil. The causes and ramifications of such a state are rather murky and not directly addressed. Is the evil individual (one soldier) or collective (a whole unit)? Are there extenuating circumstances created by the war environment? Do Dosier and Quinn express remorse for their descent into an animal-like existence?

Dosier's initial responses to war's realities are commonplaces within combat novels. First, in the midst of his first firefight, his gun misfires, he is frozen by his fears of being killed, and he begins to hyperventilate. Soon after he displays typical "new guy" naïveté as he becomes upset that another member of the platoon murders a severely wounded VC prisoner to prevent his groans from exposing an ambush. These moments will be the last of Dosier's debilitating fear and battlefield remorse. His innocence disappears quickly. Unlike its thematic treatment in the books from the previous chapter, a soldier's loss of innocence in *Close Quarters* is not really an issue; it's a given. The turning-point, narrated in present tense and punctuated with Heinemann's characteristic graphic detail, is also a conventional rite-of-passage episode in combat fiction, but with a twist. Like Private Bead in *The Thin Red Line*, Dosier engages in gruesome hand-to-hand combat with an enemy soldier; however, he does not experience Bead's subsequent guilt after killing the Japanese soldier. Consciously deciding not to kill the Vietcong with his bayonet, Dosier chooses instead to strangle him:

> I squeeze his Adam's apple with both thumbs. I lift his head and push it back into the turf with a muted splash. My fingernails work into the back of his neck. The little man grabs both my wrists. He gurgles and works his jaw. . . . [I] Lift. Push. Squeeze. Like working a tool smooth. (Heinemann [1977] 1986, 73)

Later, as the tracks arrive to take the platoon back to camp, Dosier dwells on the incident, clinically comparing the strangling to "wringing out a wet rag" (p. 74). He also decides that, instead of trying to avoid the body of the dead VC, "I want to see this out. I want me and Atevo [dead friend] and this little dude here [VC] to ride in the same car" (p. 75). Unlike Paul Baumer in *All Quiet on the Western Front* or even Yossarian in *Catch-22*, Dosier is not haunted by this direct encounter with death; he seems fascinated by the experience.

Dosier proceeds swiftly into a moral darkness as the restraints of civilization and inner character quickly recede and as combat numbness becomes a permanent part of his condition, both in and out of the combat environment. He soon becomes the competent soldier Jones describes, numb to the horror of war and indifferent to his survival. He quickly falls into the numbing routine of night ambushes; rescue trips in the tracks; search-and-destroy missions in nearby villages; the booze, drugs, and card games at the base-camp; and most of all the body-counts. With this routine comes the loss of decent feelings for all but a few people in his platoon. Compassion is replaced by hatred, vengeance, and power; self-control is replaced by whim. For example, as chaos breaks loose in a suspected VC village, Dosier turns his shotgun on a bull buffalo and pumps round after round into the flinching animal as a terrified mama-san looks on:

> And it all came on a whim. She was a gook. The hooch was gook. The buff was a gook buff. But it always came with that hard-faced, uncaring, eye-aching whim. . . . [T]hose two or three scraps of good and real and soft things left of you are sucked down into a small hard pea. And the rest? Everything else brazes over and thickens and blackens – even the nap dreams (p. 110)

Such comfortable violence also influences Dosier's treatment of Claymore Face, the toothless Vietnamese prostitute who becomes "the platoon punchboard." At one point Dosier's callousness and power turn a common sex act into a despicable and ugly scene of sexual exploitation as this woman is reduced to a performing animal.

Dosier's journey into the heart of darkness culminates in two scenes, the first described in present tense to heighten the dramatic impact and emotional intensity. This episode, a standard Vietnam atrocity scene, occurs as one of the tracks in the platoon is destroyed by a booby-trap detonated from a nearby village. After his squad captures two VC, a young boy and an old man both suspected of being involved in ambush, Dosier stands guard over the boy. As he observes his prisoner, he gradually loses control over his anger, and his desire for vengeance surfaces. Finally, he turns the job over to someone else, stating that "I'm gonna do something fucked up if I gotta stand there one more minute" (p. 218), but deep down he hopes that someone else – Quinn in particular – will shoot the boy. Eventually, Dosier can no longer control himself. He returns and takes back his weapon from Quinn: "I clicked off the safety, looked again, and blew the top of his [the boy's] head off. . . . I hated him when he was alive and I hated his corpse" (pp. 219–20). Thus, the tale has come full circle as the young soldier, who in his first days in combat questioned the killing of a wounded prisoner, now callously commits the same act. Absent is the lengthy period of soul-searching Caputo engages in after his prisoners' deaths. Instead, Dosier immediately covers up the act with a phony story about an escape attempt for which he receives a stern look from his commanding officer: "I could have [sic] cared less what he thought, the dink was dead" (p. 220).

From this action, it's only a short distance to the horror and carnage of the dark center of the novel, an uncharacteristic (for Vietnam) large-scale battle occurring, ironically, during a New Year's Day truce. The night-long battle becomes a grunt's worst nightmare with sounds of rifles, machine-guns, mortar rounds, claymores, and artillery rounds filling the air, and the smell of death and napalm dropped by Phantom jets filling the nostrils. Confusion reigns as waves of enemy soldiers assault American positions and the coffin-like tracks. But the battle is also exhilarating for Dosier as he completes his evolution into Jones's ideal soldier. Excitement supplants panic; thoughts of his own safety become irrelevant; mechanical actions replace conscious decisions; and the physical joy of heavy combat action ends in a form of sexual release: "It almost amounted to a spark arcing between the thumbs. My body was all used up; all screams and gasps and migraine ache" (p. 233). At first light next morning, Dosier indifferently views the remaining flotsam and jetsam of a land battle and the obscenity of war – a collage of death including the charred remains of a friend in the hulk of a burned-out track and the all-important enemy bodies. These bodies, over 400, are carefully counted by the body-count details, quickly stripped by the souvenir-hunters, and gruesomely photographed by the media vultures flown in for the occasion.

Who or what is ultimately responsible for Dosier's and Quinn's descent into this brutish state becomes a critical issue in this novel, as well as in other modern war literature. Does the burden of responsibility rest with individuals (the evil within), or is the war environment to blame (the evil without)? Just as Caputo skirts this issue of individual responsibility, so does Heinemann. But evidence in this novel points more to an environmental cause. Dosier finds himself in a war that, from a moral and military perspective, appears much more complex than that portrayed in Mailer's and Jones's combat novels. Certainly present in the Second World War novels are conflicts between officers and enlisted men, some racial and religious tensions, and soldiers frustrated with the war. But in *Close Quarters* such feelings are intensified. Racial conflicts between blacks and whites erupt into open hostility and violence at the base-camp. American soldiers' contempt for the Vietnamese ("I never met a squint eye that I would call anything but Gook": p. 19), heightened by the military's emphasis on body-counts, sparks atrocities against civilians and elicits an officer's praise when several ARVN soldiers are mistakenly killed in an ambush. Also characterizing this milieu are confusion, war weariness, and ennui – "Who fucken cares?" – that quickly pervade the soldiers' attitudes toward the war. When these feelings mix with an overriding survivor mentality, the transient nature of the war, the short-timer syndrome, and temporary escapes through R & Rs, dope, and booze, the situation is particularly chaotic and numbing. Not even Dosier's contacts with civilization – the letters from his family and from his girlfriend Jenny or the thoughts about his brother blinded in Vietnam – can prevent him from being drained of compassion, concern, and humanity.

At one point, Heinemann merges this pessimistic portrait of a soldier's numbing existence with Dosier's feelings of helplessness. Using surrealistic images, the author suggests that a grunt's chance-filled, precarious existence is similar to standing in the middle of a "red-and-black bull's-eye" of death or to participating in a footrace with death. In a drug-and-booze-induced reverie, ironically taking place in a base chapel, Dosier's thoughts about dead friends and premonitions about Quinn's death, narrated in present tense, merge with scenes from a race among young children. The event is presided over by an unfeeling higher power who arbitrarily decides the fate of the participants racing around the thirty-two polished points of a compass-rose parquet. Onlookers, who are military brass and "housecats" (soldiers with cushy jobs in the rear), watch as bodies and body parts pile up. Soon Dosier also participates in the race and is smothered by bodies piling on top of him:

> Higher and thicker the dead pile until I begin to climb up and out among the corpses, using the leg bones and arm bones, gaping mouths and mushy bellies, and heads of straight black hair for handholds and footholds, like a person would climb the inside of a pile of neatly stacked tires. (p. 161)[8]

Soon these images of bodies and thoughts about death in the abstract give way to a shattering vision of Quinn's death and Dosier's unsuccessful attempts to revive him. The dream ends with Dosier's arms locked around the corpse and Dosier whispering in Quinn's ear, "Don't die, don't die, don't" (p. 164). But it's only a dream; Quinn's death won't occur until well after Dosier departs Vietnam.

As Dosier becomes a short-timer, he must prepare psychologically to return to civilization. During these final days, he remains stoned and drunk waiting for his flight home, and he goes through the soldier's ritual of leaving: the strained goodbyes to those remaining behind, the promises to write, and the meaningless plans with Quinn to meet back in the World, "I knew that Quinn and I would not see much of each other anymore – probably never after I went home. A person does not like to look into another man's face and see all those bad days and bad feelings reflected back, as though the other face was a fisheye lens" (p. 270). Most important, during the night before he leaves Vietnam, he ponders his now completed journey into the heart of darkness and struggles to understand and judge the experience (Fussell's third stage). But like Kurtz's ambiguous pronouncement "The horror! the horror!" Dosier's present-tense reflections on the death of the "dream" are also ambiguous, becoming either a harsh judgement of self (his inability to resist the evil) or merely a detached assessment of what he has seen.

In this long interior monologue, Dosier catalogs his losses. He has lost his physical well-being, replaced by calluses, a numbness of senses, and filth; he has lost the simple rhythm of breathing; and he has lost the ability to sleep. Connecting himself to the fraternity of grunts we have already encountered (Paul Baumer, Philip Caputo, Corporal Fife), he reviews the soldier's archetypal loss of innocence – the dream – on the battlefield, beginning with the first death and ending soon after when suddenly "there was no caring, except for the things I could reach out and grasp with a hand" (p. 278). The phrase "I don't care" becomes a refrain as Dosier chronicles his evolving combat numbness and the enveloping brutality: "The war works on you until you become a part of it, and then you start working on it instead of it working on you, and you get deep-down mean" (p. 278). Finally, he arrives at a startling insight as he acknowledges the fascination that the abomination holds for him and the grip that evil has on his soul. Yet even at this point he is still confused as to whether this is an external or internal evil:

How did I come to love it [the war] so? What evil taller than myself did I grapple and wrestle and throw to the ground? Subdued. Did it come with a night moon, or is it something inside, this pain in my chest? Did it enter quickly, leaving this crablike scar on my eye, or does it hover here like a poltergeist, whispering? (p. 279)

After this night of reflection, the next morning, Dosier departs Vietnam, his separate peace not willed but merely a part of military policy in this strange war. He leaves behind all his possessions, hoping that he can also leave behind the memories of Vietnam. But as he realizes – "I can never go home" – he is doomed, like Marlow, to carry the war stories with him and to tell them repeatedly. As he re-enters civilization, he returns not as a hero but merely as a survivor gradually shaking off the combat numbness and futilely attempting to tell the real story to Jenny, whom he quickly marries. Later, on learning of Quinn's death in a truck accident in Vietnam, Dosier narrates the final present-tense sequence as he travels to southern Indiana to visit his friend's parents and to tell one more war story. This time while looking at the family's mementos from their son's tour, along with the medals and letters of condolence from the military, Dosier matter-of-factly narrates the war slides from Vietnam sent home by Quinn. Paralleling the meeting with Kurtz's Intended after Marlow's return from the Congo, Dosier also preserves a lie – this time the parents' inextinguishable image of an innocent son who has remained unchanged by the war and who has died in a heroic way. The words in the commanding officer's letter about Quinn somehow ring hollow: "He was a credit to the uniform of the United States Army, a sterling example of American manhood and devotion to duty" (p. 332). But Dosier does nothing to undercut this lie –

or is it a saving illusion for him? – about "Quinn so mean and evil" (p. 335). Dosier survives, left with isolation, self-recognition with his soulmate Quinn, and the death of part of himself: "I stopped and drew my hands out into the cold, making fists and letting go. 'Goddamn you, Quinn'" (p. 336). As was true with Conrad's story, this novel ends with issues unresolved and a character living with memories and an inner darkness.

"I would like to reaffirm my undying pride in having been a part of that anomalous insanity embodied in the word Marine." With this acknowledgement and a dedication to "the 100,000 Marines who became casualties in Vietnam, [a]nd for the others who became casualties upon their return," Vietnam combat veteran and former US Secretary of the Navy (1987–8) James Webb establishes the tone for his own "first novel."[9] *Fields of Fire* passionately defends, not the American government, but American soldiers fighting in Vietnam, and attacks young Americans who conveniently avoided the war. Many Vietnam veterans might wholeheartedly support Webb's views and his combat realism; skeptics might derisively comment that the John Wayne–Hollywood vision of war and patriotism is alive and well in this novel. Nevertheless, like Jones's *The Thin Red Line*, this is a grunt's novel. Truths about human nature and the realities of the Vietnam War dot many pages. The brutal realism and exhaustive detail of the day-to-day life of a combat soldier found in *Close Quarters* also appear in this novel. But, unlike Heinemann, Webb introduces a strong political undertone and often, unsuccessfully, attempts to move away from the fictional memoir to a more developed dramatic plot.

In the three combat novels discussed so far in this chapter, authors provide few reasons to believe that glorious moments of heroism, honor, and self-sacrifice regularly occur on the battlefield, or that a brotherhood of grunts – strong bonds of attachment and mutual concern – is widespread among combat soldiers. Instead, Mailer focuses on the prejudices and personal conflicts separating the soldiers in his I & R platoon; Jones seems more intent on isolating individuals as he re-creates the psychology of combat and battlefield realism for his Charlie Company; and Heinemann examines the combat numbness and external and internal evils producing callous soldiers. In contrast, Webb's combat novel promotes the images of the noble warrior, the glory of combat, and the strong loyalties among soldiers. In fact, it is an antidote to the cynicism and pessimism in *Close Quarters*, restoring some of the luster to the tarnished image of American soldiers. As a result, this novel, nominated for a Pulitzer Prize, becomes an elegy for the courage and sacrifices of Marine combat soldiers in Vietnam and stands as a startling paean for the glory of combat: "Man's noblest moment is the one spent on the fields of fire" (Webb 1978, 22). Attempting to change readers' opinions, Webb directs this book at an audience opposing American involvement in Vietnam and condemning American soldiers who fought there. Certainly at the time he wrote the novel this audience would have been substantial. Webb's underlying message warns these readers not to judge so quickly the war or the American soldiers who fought in it. The combat soldier's refrain – "You can't understand what it was like unless you've been there" – becomes an overriding theme for this book. Thus the narrator's stance is that the moral issues of the real Vietnam War were not as simple as those portrayed by anti-war activists or the media. In Webb's view, hasty judgements about the evils of American soldiers are a disservice to some of the best young people America has produced.

For some readers in the 1970s and the present, such a message is unpopular, dogmatic, and also simplistic, yet Webb does not shrink from including such political statements throughout the book. Thus, the novel, like Mailer's, contains a political message. But, unlike *The Naked and the Dead*, this work is not filled with sweeping political ideology or abstract political philosophy about the nature of power. Instead, the author, through the third-person narrator, is more pragmatic and focused. He directly attacks draft-avoiders, self-interested draft-resisters, college anti-war protestors, the Peace Corps, Americans at home who abandoned American soldiers fighting in Vietnam, and civilians' hostile attitudes toward returning soldiers. His message promotes traditional values of duty, sacrifice, and responsibility to others and to one's country.

Using his omniscient narrator, Webb focuses on a Marine platoon operating in 1969 throughout the An Hoa Basin just west of Da Nang. In the "Prologue" he introduces three main characters – Snake, Goodrich, and Hodges – who, along with the rest of the unit, are guarding a disabled tank sitting in an unprotected rice paddy. This scene symbolizes the failure of American technology in Vietnam. Almost 290 pages later, the narrator returns to this narrative frame of the night defensive around the tank. In between, the narrator portrays the lives of the platoon members and the unit's activities. Heaping violence upon violence, Webb combines the battlefield realism found in *The Thin Red Line* and *Close Quarters* with the fictional devices of the melting-pot platoon, character profiles, multiple plots, and political statement found in *The Naked and the Dead*. But, as frequently occurs with first novels when inexperienced authors move unsteadily from memoir to fiction,[10] the soldier-author may compromise the book's potential strength, its realism. Such is the case with Webb. At times, he ineffectively uses narrative and dramatic structures and strident political commentary delivered by the narrator or a few of the characters. In the process, he diminishes the power of the book's battlefield scenes and grunt psychology.

Without question, however, the strength of *Fields of Fire*, as is true with *The Thin Red Line* and *Close Quarters*, lies in the author's descriptions of combat – language, events, emotions, conflicts, and tragedies inherent in the physical and psychological realities of war. Webb has a remarkable understanding of the combat soldiers' psychological relationships to Vietnam. He also has an ear for the grunts' language and an eye for the precise details conveying the horrors and miseries of war. Because he has observed, listened, felt, and considered well, his descriptions of the soldiers' rituals, relationships, and emotions are on target. Most impressive is the authentic grunt dialogue pervading the book – speech patterns, vulgarities, jargon, fear, threats, hate, and black humor. And, like Jones and Heinemann, Webb accurately describes the day-to-day life of combat soldiers, but ones fitting a more traditional mold than those represented by Dosier's and Quinn's valid but disturbing attitudes and excesses in *Close Quarters*. Such sympathetic portraits of American soldiers, along with Webb's passionate defense of them as "The Best We Have," dominate the book.

A brief glimpse into Webb's own life perhaps helps readers

understand the author's narrative stance, his relationship to the raw material, and the military and political views found in *Fields of Fire*. Like Mailer, Jones, and Heinemann, Webb in his novel draws heavily upon his own war experiences ("the fuel of this fiction was, of course, actual experience": "Acknowledgements"). A graduate of the US Naval Academy, Lieutenant Webb was a platoon and company commander in 1969 with the 1st Battalion, 5th Marine Regiment, operating in the An Hoa Basin (the time and fictional setting for the novel). Unlike Mailer, Jones, and Heinemann, however, Webb is a highly decorated war hero (Navy Cross, Silver Star, and two Purple Hearts) who, after his discharge from the Marines for severe battle injuries sustained in Vietnam, became a lawyer and assumed various positions within the Federal Government.[11] Particularly significant for this novel is the fact that Webb comes from a military family. His father was a colonel in the Air Force, and members of his family had fought in the Revolutionary War and all subsequent American wars. Such a tradition of military service appears to influence this novel in which Webb develops a theme of fathers and sons sharing the bonds of war.

Out of his military experiences and traditions, Webb fashions an unusual melting-pot platoon, not unusual for Vietnam but uncommon when compared to typical platoons portrayed in many Second World War novels and films. As Edward Palm notes, Webb's platoon, for the most part, does not fit the conventional definition: "the myth that Catholic and Jew, intellectual and laborer, the disenfranchised as well as those to manner born, all put aside their differences and pulled together for the common good" (1983, 105). Although there is a racial mix (white, black, Hispanic) and geographical variety (urban and rural, North and South) in Webb's platoon, the soldiers share some key traits. Basically, they are young and come from similar lower-class backgrounds. A few, also, are using the military to escape their poverty or to escape the criminal justice system. If statistics are to be believed, such a portrait represents an accurate profile of the poor, uneducated, young, blue-collar American soldiers who predominantly bore the brunt of the fighting in Vietnam.[12] Webb describes his platoon by quoting an anonymous general's assessment of his troops: "They are the best we have. But they are not McNamara's sons, or Bundy's. I doubt they're yours. And they know they're at the end of the pipeline. That no-one cares. They know" (1978, 1).

Overall, this novel praises the fighting spirit and self-sacrifice of this small unit of blue-collar Marines. Yet within his limited cast of characters and focused narrative, Webb does not whitewash the Vietnam War, the American military hierarchy, or the brutality and callousness of the soldiers. He assembles a supporting cast including a group of career officers and senior non-commissioned officers who, more concerned about getting undeserved medals, ignore their soldiers' welfare. Also present are a few soldiers who, preoccupied with their own survival, have no interest in fighting and are constantly looking for expedient ways to avoid combat. Webb also superficially includes a forgotten voice in the largely ethnocentric American Vietnam narratives – the Vietnamese soldier, represented by Dan, a former Vietcong who has joined the US Marines as a "Kit Carson Scout" and interpreter. By the end of the novel, he is recaptured by the VC and seems unconcerned with this turn of events, realizing that the war is merely a "game" and its participants rather naïve. Webb also briefly focuses on typical negative themes: racial tensions in rear areas; fraggings of unpopular officers and non-commissioned officers; the heavy heart-of-darkness journey with the attendant dehumanization taking place on the battlefield; the absurd rules of engagement in the bush ("Shoot a prisoner from five feet away, it's a kill. Touch him and then shoot him, and you're a murderer": p. 280); and the random, meaningless killing that occurs ("I get the feeling this is kind of like Russian roulette, myself. Just as senseless. And the players aren't excused until the gun goes off in their face": p. 202).

But at the core of this novel is Webb's celebration of combat and its skilled practitioners. Although much more serious and complex than a John Wayne movie, the novel does reaffirm the typical John Wayne values of honor, courage, sacrifice over survival, and the resiliency of the human spirit. Furthermore, a few characters appear to have surfaced from a John Wayne movie. An inner circle of six characters (Snake, Hodges, Phony, Bagger, Cat Man, and Cannonball) find themselves thrown together in a struggle to survive the war, to withstand an incompetent military bureaucracy, and to protect each other.

What bonds them is their ultimate trust in each other, their combat skills, their love–hate relationship with the war's violence and absurdity, and their strong sense of being abandoned by the people at home:

> It ain't what happens here that's important. It's what's happening back *there*. . . . Airplane drivers still drive their airplanes. Businessmen still run their businesses. College kids still go to college. It's like nothing really happened, except to other people. It isn't touching anybody except us. (p. 175)

These grunts also understand what is needed to survive in combat – "dedication and craziness." Because of their race, poverty, or lack of education, they were not part of the mainstream back in the World. But once reaching Vietnam, they assume new identities, as signified by their nicknames, feel pride in their combat skills, and acquire a sense of belonging and meaning in their lives – even if that meaning is only helping themselves and their friends stay alive. Phony comments that "'I never had a home in my life till I came out here.' Nowhere to go back to. Stay forever" (p. 201). And Bagger, after returning from R & R with his wife in Hawaii, comments that his entire time on leave he was

> "thinking about the bush. Like I belong here, and all the other stuff is only important because I *earned* it here, because it's a part of being *here*. Like I been here all my life, and the people in the bush are real, are my people. Like nobody in the world except for us understands this, or gives one flying fuck about it, but that's all right, because it matters to us." (p. 201)

The key members of this battlefield brotherhood are Snake and Lieutenant Hodges, the contemporary warriors who because of their skills and indifference to their own survival perfectly fit Jones's definition of the ideal combat soldier. Their foil is Senator, who with his affluent background, conscience, and critical attitude toward the fighting and his fellow-soldiers is an outsider from the circle. The different backgrounds of these three characters and their interaction with each other on the battlefield spark the novel's principal dramatic conflicts.

As Mailer does with his key characters in *The Naked and the Dead*, Webb also provides brief biographical sketches of eight characters. But Webb is not as successful or consistent as Mailer in linking past with present, biographical background with combat performance. An example of Webb's sketchy characterization is his portrait of Snake. "There was a recruiting station at the wasteland's edge. It fed on creatures from the run-down row-houses. They were vital sustenance" (p. 16). One of these creatures from this concrete urban wasteland is Snake (nicknamed for his tattoo), product of a dysfunctional family and a world of pimps, prostitutes, and drug-pushers. To survive, Snake has become a fighter, literally and figuratively, but he has no status, no sense of belonging to his family or to his world. Snake is a military recruiter's dream come true. Whether believing the recruiting propaganda or having seen too many John Wayne movies, Snake is the stereotypical 18- or 19-year-old looking at the military as an institution to provide order, direction, and fulfilment, a place where his meanness will be prized. After becoming a Marine, his experiences in basic training only confirm his high expectations; he's successful: "And to fight, to grant his natural ferocity its whims, now brought him accolades instead of trouble" (p. 18). Such an optimistic portrait of Marine training's effects is antithetical to Hasford's emphasis on the degrading, dehumanizing, brutalizing treatment of Marine recruits in *The Short-Timers*. But this perspective is consistent with Webb's pride in the Marine Corps.

Corporal Snake's toughness and heroic actions in Vietnam reflect the success he has had in basic training. But little else from his ghetto background, including psychological residue, carries over into Vietnam. Once the narrative moves to Vietnam, Webb, unlike Mailer, largely ignores his characters' backgrounds. In this new environment, Snake is a natural leader, a person the other men respect because of his confidence and control during tense situations, his common-sense approach to battlefield strategy, and his concern for the safety of his fellow-soldiers. Although he is not afraid to question commands when he believes that they unnecessarily endanger his and his friends' lives, he still seems more a part of the establishment than outside it. In fact, Snake feels so much a part of this world of violence and is so good at being a combat soldier that he even extends his tour so he can remain in the bush with his unit. The decision results not from patriotism, a strong belief in the war's value, or even from a fascination with the abomination; it's made because Snake finds that combat fills a void in his life in a way that nothing else will ever be able to – a sentiment echoed in several Vietnam memoirs:

> there was a fullness that no other thing in the remainder of his life would ever equal. . . . If he were to go back now . . . there was nothing, not a thing, that would parallel the sense of urgency and authority and – need. Of being part of something. And of being needed and being *good*. (pp. 275–6)

Eventually, Snake's strong attachment to the other soldiers leads to the conventional atrocity episode, but with a twist. The VC kidnap two members of the squad, execute them, and mutilate the bodies. Soon after, on a sweep of a village, Snake and a few other members of the squad, who have been searching for their friends, detain two villagers, a man and a woman, who they believe are VC. Nearby the squad discovers the graves of the two American soldiers. Snake and the others, ignoring Senator's pleas not to kill the Vietnamese, calmly avenge their friends' deaths by executing the two villagers. Were the pair VC? Were they involved in the Americans' deaths? Is their execution a legitimate act of war or an atrocity? Are Snake's actions justifiable, or are they the aberration of a soldier turned animal? Webb doesn't answer these questions; nor do the participants, except for Senator, agonize over their actions. As later events in the book suggest, the narrator's sympathies, however, do lie with Snake.

The other half of this brotherhood of heroic warriors is Lieutenant Robert E. Lee Hodges, Jr, the platoon commander who "had spent his life preparing for the Marines" (p. 30). As a Marine officer from a mining family in Harlan County, Kentucky, his upbringing is far different from Snake's. But they share their attraction to combat and Webb's portrayal of them as traditional war heroes. Such roles, according to the reader's political views of the war and of the American soldiers, may be either the principal limitation – an attempt at patriotic propaganda – or an admirable feature of the novel – a tribute to the young combat soldier. But from a literary perspective, Hodges's character, like Snake's, is limited. He remains relatively unchanged during the book. Once in combat, he quickly realizes that "it wasn't fun any more" (p. 45), yet this innocence lost is never a significant issue in the novel. Hodges, like Snake, never deviates from his role as the good soldier avoiding a heart-of-darkness journey. Unlike Dosier in *Close Quarters*, insights about self and the nature of war are rare, and moments of agonizing introspection about moral dilemmas are absent. Furthermore, Webb's attempts to develop Hodges's character away from the battlefield are contrived, especially the lieutenant's relationship with a Japanese girl who works on the Marine base at Okinawa.

Although much more realistic, Hodges is nonetheless a John Wayne figure displaying honor, courage, pride, and loyalty. But, unlike Wayne, he does not display larger-than-life dominance over his men, unrealistic heroic actions, unthinking patriotism for his country, or an all-out allegiance to the military. Hodges is in the truest sense of the word a fighter, a throwback to the western gunfighter. "It was the fight that mattered, not the cause. It was the endurance that was important, the will to face certain loss, unknown dangers, unpredictable fates" (p. 28). Vietnam just happens to be the place where the fight is occurring. Hodges's motivation for fighting is family tradition, a bond of war throughout history between fathers and sons. Like his father, who died in World War II before Robert could meet him, Hodges is named after General Lee and has been raised on his grandmother's stories about the "glory in them fields! Fields of fire." He is the last of the Hodgeses who have fought in every American war beginning with the Revolutionary War. (The parallels to Webb's own family traditions are obvious.) Hodges, like so many other soldiers (fictional and real), has also been indoctrinated by the movies:

They [movies] were their own communion. If John Wayne wasn't God then he was at least a prophet. Hodges and a

118

half-dozen friends would walk the five miles into Hillsville on Saturday afternoons and sit in awe through the *Sands of Iwo Jima, The Bridges at Toko-Ri, The Guns of Navarone, Anzio, The Battle of the Bulge*, and dozens of others. It was all there on the screen. Standing up and fighting back. (p. 29)

Yet, arriving in Vietnam eager to enter combat, Hodges does not carry the typical inflated Hollywood expectations of personal heroics. Thus, the conventional stage of innocence lost, experience gained is absent in the novel. He is cryptically warned about what to expect on his tour and what changes he will undergo, much as the Brussels doctor warns Marlow before the latter departs for the Congo. But, once arriving at Snake's company in the An Hoa Valley, Hodges quickly settles into the routine of being a platoon commander with a company that sees heavy action. Unlike many officers portrayed in war literature, especially about Vietnam, Hodges is a positive figure. He gets along well with his men because he cares for them and fights the military hierarchy that disregards their welfare. He is also very skilled in combat and wise enough to rely on the advice of the experienced members of his unit, particularly Snake. Despite their differences in rank, Snake and Hodges quickly develop a close relationship because they are committed to the safety of the other men in the unit and because they are proud of their combat skills. In a rare moment of reflection, Hodges, like Snake, articulates the converging misery and fulfillment (love–hate relationship) combat provides, reaffirms his place in his family's long line of warriors, and unintentionally raises the controversial notion that soldiers are mere robots:

All my life I've waited for this, he mused. Now I've joined you and your losses are a strength to me. . . . I breathe the dust and yet I know that Grandpa breathed the gas that made a hero out of Pershing. . . . And I have learned those things, those esoteric skills and knowledges, that mark, me as one of you. . . . I do these things, experience these things, repeatedly, daily. Their terrors and miseries are so compelling, and yet so regular, that I have ascended to a high emotion that is nonetheless a crusted numbness. I am an automaton, bent on survival, agent and prisoner of my misery. How terribly exciting. (pp. 171–2)

Snake and Hodges share another similarity. Both have opportunities to declare a separate peace and quit fighting. As mentioned earlier, Snake quickly chooses to extend his tour; Hodges's decision is more difficult. During the fifth month of his tour Hodges is wounded, medivaced to Japan, and then sent to Okinawa to convalesce. As he reflects on his situation, his thoughts become part of Webb's constant us-versus-them message to his readers: "Nobody gives a rat's ass whether any of us live or die. They've sold us out back in the World" (p. 245). He also echoes Phony's earlier comments about the brotherhood of the bush: "He missed the people in the bush, more than he had ever missed any group of people in his life. There was a purity in those relationships that could not be matched anywhere else" (p. 245). At this moment Hodges is offered a chance to stay in Okinawa for the rest of his tour and to marry his Japanese mistress: "A simple yes, and the war would be over" (p. 257). But, like Snake, he realizes just how attached he has become to combat. This career soldier answers "no" to this opportunity for a separate peace; the result is a quick return to his unit in An Hoa and an unheroic death while guarding the disabled tank introduced in the "Prologue."

Perhaps the most intriguing of Webb's Marines is Will Goodrich (Senator), who literally and figuratively remains outside the circle of warriors while in Vietnam. His relatively complex character is interesting because of the changes he undergoes. He begins the novel as an innocent idealist, becomes a cynical outsider while in Vietnam (similar to Dosier), evolves into a defender of the American soldier upon his return to the States, and ironically ends the novel as an outsider on American college campuses. Prior to enlisting in the Marines, Goodrich lived a sheltered life in a world of books and abstract ideas. A brilliant but lazy student, Senator quit Harvard to enlist in the Marine band, "a compromise to all competing emotions" about school, the war, and his family. But, true to military logic, he was sent to Vietnam as a combat soldier. Unlike the other soldiers in his platoon, Goodrich comes from a different social background,

Harvard-educated brothers and father; the latter is a lawyer. Senator also comes from an academic and social environment whose members for the most part have avoided the war. In Webb's vitriolic attack on this privileged class, the narrator notes that Mark, Will's Harvard roommate, went to Canada to avoid the draft, and "Everybody else went to grad school" (p. 89):

> It was academic, like studying for an exam. The draft counselors schooled you and helped you determine your own best approach [avoiding the draft], and you worked on it, cultivated it, and usually it worked. After all, Harvard breeds achievers. (p. 89)[13]

Further isolating Senator from the other soldiers are his indifference to the war or to them, his cynicism about the Russian-roulette nature of the conflict, his articulated pessimistic view of life fueled by his reading of the philosopher Schopenhauer, his ineptness as a soldier, his fear, and his conscience. Furthermore, Senator possesses strong principles and is passionate about the sanctity of human life, primarily civilian life. In Caputo's terms, his net of inner values does prevent him from sinking into a brutish state, but it also prevents him from recognizing the humanity of his brutish fellow-soldiers. Nevertheless, he becomes the moral conscience of the platoon: upset that he has mistakenly wounded a Vietnamese civilian, worried about the treatment of VC prisoners, or concerned about the safety of Vietnamese children. In short, he is a reluctant soldier desperately trying to hold on to his humanity and wanting to be liked by the Vietnamese whom he is protecting. Such idealism and disdain for the other soldiers place him at odds with these people, including Snake and Hodges. At the same time, Senator's dilemmas lead to a depth of characterization missing in the other character portraits. The problem with his well-intentioned stance from a combat soldier's perspective is, as Webb suggests, that standards (idealism) have a way of conflicting with reality (survival) in combat. What may appear a clear-cut case of immoral behavior under normal conditions becomes a confusing question of survival in combat. Absolutes get well-meaning people killed, as well as

fellow-soldiers. The inflexible Goodrich often fails to acknowledge certain facts: Vietnamese civilians, including children, try
to kill Americans; some villages are actually VC-controlled;
and even well-intentioned soldiers cannot always control their
feelings of revenge and brutal impulses, especially under the
mental and physical stress of combat.

Webb artfully brings these issues of standards and survival
into conflict. As the person in the platoon committed to maintaining moral standards, Goodrich reluctantly files a complaint
with the Regimental Legal Officer about Snake's involvement
with the murder of the two Vietnamese. He carries through,
despite the officer's attempts to convince Senator that a crime
did not occur. (The result will be a posthumous revoking of
Snake's award of the Silver Star.) A few days later, before any
official action has been taken against Snake, Goodrich is with
the unit as it sits in the rain and darkness protecting the
disabled tank and waiting for an imminent enemy attack. In
a brief moment, his standards are once again tested. Seeing an
American soldier aiming at a distant target that appears to be
a young Vietnamese girl, Goodrich instinctively lunges at the
soldier to prevent him from firing the weapon. But, immediately
after, Goodrich realizes that he has erred. The young girl is part
of a VC ambush team, which kills the American soldier and
blows off Senator's leg. Ironically, in the ensuing battle, Snake
dies saving Senator's life, and Hodges also dies.

Fields of Fire ends with a chapter devoted to the returning veteran, in this case Senator, and to final commentary
about draft-avoiders, war protestors, and naïve perceptions of
war. This chapter is important within the body of Vietnam
combat narratives because Webb anticipates postwar conflicts
dealt with more substantially in the aftermath novels. He also
describes an interesting sociological and political phenomenon
within American society during the late 1960s and early 1970s
– the Vietnam veterans' presence on college campuses. Thus,
months after the climatic battle in Vietnam, Senator arrives
home as a survivor who begins the long, agonizing process of
dealing with his physical disability, working through the nightmares and memories of his war experiences, and re-entering
an unfamiliar society. Obviously, Will's war experiences have
changed him, tempering his idealism, standards, and antipathy

for the members of his unit. Typical of so many returning veterans and echoing the feelings of Bagger, Snake, and Hodges, the cynical Senator even finds himself nostalgic about the experience and the soldiers: "'I have some *bad* memories. But I do have some good ones, I even miss it in a way. I can't explain that. But the hard part is now'" (p. 325).

As part of his adjustment, Will must work through two traumatic experiences, both involving opponents to the war who as straw figures in this novel have their views easily undercut by Webb's patriotism and his prominent advocacy for American soldiers. The first occurs when Will's Harvard roommate surreptitiously returns from Canada to visit Senator. As they briefly discuss political beliefs, Will suddenly becomes angry that Mark, taking the position that Will previously assumed with members of his unit, lectures him about the absurdity of the war and the meaningless physical sacrifice that Will has made. "For the first time, Goodrich felt the itches of unreasoned anger. 'Now what the *hell* do you know about it? What standing do you have to tell me how or why I lost a leg?'" (p. 329). Soon after, Will's father calls the police and has Mark arrested for draft evasion. Will halfheartedly defends Mark ("He hasn't harmed anyone"), but he also accepts the logic and passion behind his father's rebuttal, which becomes Webb's patriotic sermon directed to his readers on individual responsibility and self-interest:

> "He's harming a whole nation. Those people have no sense of country. They don't look beyond themselves. That's as far as their obligation goes. Well, so be it. But if they're willing to accept the benefits of this society – like a Harvard education – they should also accept the burdens." (p. 331)

A second encounter with anti-war sentiments forces Senator publicly to speak about his war experiences and feelings. After resuming his studies at Harvard, he becomes a campus curiosity – a veteran. He also finds himself alienated by student protests and the abstract political rhetoric about the war. One group asks him to join a protest and speak out against the war: "'Yeah, man. You could really lay it on everybody about how bad Nam stinks. Like what did you see that was worth giving a leg for –'"

123

(p. 335). His comments at the rally, which become part of Webb's final message to his readers, outrage the students. He believes the war should end, but the protestors' isolation from the reality of war enrages him – "How many of you are going to get hurt in Vietnam" – as does their "childish game" of waving the Vietcong flag or chanting "HO CHI MINH IS GONNA WIN." Bewildered by his conflicting feelings about the war and his memories of Snake and the final ambush, he cannot repudiate his Vietnam experiences or accept the protestors' evaluation of the war as immoral and the American soldiers as murderers. For Senator, making such a judgement isn't so easy: "What you guys are missing is the confrontation. It loses its simplicity when you have to deal with it" (336). He even begins to question his decision to report Snake to the authorities, as he – like Baumer, Caputo, and Dosier – comprehends war's insidious brutalization of combatants:

> "You drop someone in hell and give him a gun and tell him to kill for some goddamned amorphous reason he can't even articulate. Then suddenly he feels an emotion that makes utter sense and he has a gun in his hand and he's seen dead people for months and the reasons are irrelevant anyway, so *pow*. And it's utterly logical, because the emotion was right. . . . It isn't even atrocious. It's just a sad fact of life." (p. 336)

Senator's insightful evaluation of war's contradictions and evils and Webb's vision of war in *Fields of Fire* are, like Fussell's, ironic; not only is war worse than expected, but also the moral issues are not as simple as the uninitiated expect. A person of principle has a difficult time trusting the infallibility of civilization's and individuals' moral standards in the complex environment of the Vietnam battlefield. Such a message seems reasonable and supports similar insights in Caputo's book. But Webb's novel does polarize readers to a degree that other Vietnam works do not, simply because of his political messages. Yet the politics is not based on strong ideological arguments but more on a populist vision of duty, sacrifice, and responsibility to others and country. Cynics of the war might claim that Webb's book merely resurrects John Wayne characters in the form of

Snake and Hodges and conveniently subverts and converts the one soldier in the book, a quasi-liberal, willing to question the war's validity and American soldiers' sacrifices.[14] Supporters of the war, or of American soldiers, however, might praise the book, claiming that it is one of the few Vietnam novels sympathetically describing the valor, patriotism, and sacrifice of American soldiers fighting in Vietnam. Despite such controversies over the work's overt politics, and in spite of Webb's amateurish use of some dramatic devices and over-reliance on plot, *Fields of Fire* is an important Vietnam narrative. In the tradition of Jones's approach to writing combat fiction, the combat realism in this novel, particularly the soldiers' interaction in the field, is its notable strength. Furthermore, the book reveals the "pity of war"; at the same time, Webb's three main characters express legitimate attitudes toward war and military service – viewpoints supported by a significant segment of Vietnam veterans but often ignored in serious Vietnam literature.

The 13th Valley, John Del Vecchio's Vietnam novel published in 1982 and nominated for an American Book Award, continues the traditions of the combat novel on a grand scale.[15] Like Webb's *Fields of Fire*, it becomes a tribute, although more subtle and less political, to the skills and self-sacrifice of the American soldiers fighting in Vietnam. Also like Webb's novel, this piece of fiction focuses on the brotherhood of combat soldiers, in this case not the common grunt but the "boonierat," who one character in the novel defines as "more than a grunt. Marines are grunts. Soldiers from the Big Red One are grunts. We're boonierats. We live in the boonies, we don't just visit. The jungle is our home" (1982, 378–9). In this novel, an appropriate work to end our study of combat fiction, Del Vecchio weaves together many of the characters, ideas, actions, themes, and narrative conventions discussed in this chapter and found in other war literature. If we take the naturalism, melting-pot narrative structure, and philosophical underpinnings of *The Naked and the Dead*; throw in the theme of lost innocence encountered in the works examined in the second chapter; mix the combat scenes and psychological detail of *The Thin Red Line*; and for good measure introduce the graphic realism and character types found in *Fields of Fire*, along with Dosier's heart-of-darkness odyssey into callousness and savagery appearing in *Close Quarters* – then we have the raw material of *The 13th Valley*.

Despite the derivative nature of much of the form and content, the book is a flawed but impressive "first novel" treating historical events and familiar war themes in an interesting fashion. The large scope of Del Vecchio's work is the source of the novel's strengths as well as its weaknesses. Other than *The Naked and the Dead*, it is the most ambitious and multi-faceted work we have encountered. Although lacking the political sharpness of Mailer's novel, it does have more in-depth character studies than Jones's, Heinemann's, and Webb's books. Also, Del Vecchio, like Mailer, attempts to give his combat novel breadth and depth by exploring the larger philosophical issues of human conflict and by introducing some of the "historical vision and cultural connections" Myers claims are missing in most Vietnam works. In describing the novel, critics use such phrases as "classic war novel," "important," "distinctly American," "big," "lumbering," and "rhetorically uncombed." Hellmann cites its significant setting in a mythic wilderness populated by mythic characters (1986, 128), and Myers discusses in detail the resonant symbols, narrative structure, mythic quest, and other Melvillian echoes turning this combat novel into a modern-day *Moby-Dick* (1988, 57–61). Yet ultimately what Del Vecchio has accomplished is imaginatively to rework the theme of combat brotherhood against the backdrop of Vietnam military history and the raw material of his own combat tour of duty.

Specifically, as sources for his fictional combat unit and characters, he uses his experiences as a decorated Army combat correspondent for the 101st Airborne Division's newspaper, *The Screaming Eagle*, and brief "Significant Activities" reports cited at the end of key chapters. He adapted the latter from official Defense Department documents detailing events related to an actual operation of the 101st Airborne Division in the Khe Ta Laou Valley (located about halfway between Hué and Khe Sanh), beginning 13 August 1970 and ending 30 August 1970.[16] Over three-quarters of the book deals with this thirteen-day operation to find the headquarters of the 7th NVA Front. The mission begins with an airmobile combat assault and ends with the brief capture and destruction of the headquarters located on a knoll in the valley. Adding to the realism, Del Vecchio, like Jones, provides readers with a complete roster of his fictional American unit, Company A, 7th Battalion, 402d Infantry (Airmobile). Within this group of eighty-nine characters, the author focuses on three – Lieutenant Rufus Brooks, Sergeant Daniel Egan, and Specialist Four James Chelini – and an inner circle of supporting characters who together journey into the heavily fortified NVA transportation and resupply center located in the Khe Ta Laou Valley. This American melting-pot unit has the conventional mix of African-Americans, Hispanics, a Jew, an Italian, WASPs, a Vietnamese scout, and the middle-aged sergeant (Pop) on his third Vietnam tour. During frequent "bull sessions," each, introduced with a brief biographical sketch (*à la* Mailer), dispenses his perspective of life in the United States and views about the Vietnam War.

Despite this diversity and some superficial ethnic and racial tensions (an African-American soldier voicing revolutionary ideas of the late 1960s), American popular culture, principally through television, provides these soldiers with a common background. Also unifying this unit are their pride in effective combat skills and an admirable loyalty to each other: "'We soldiers . . . Boonierats. Brothers. Here we are one'" (Del Vecchio 1982, 88). Mirroring the best characteristics of Hodges's platoon in *Fields of Fire*, Company A becomes the ideal combat unit fighting in Vietnam, successfully blending with the environment and assuming the enemy's fighting strategies – hide and hit; hit and run. Along the way members, for the most part, support official American policy for fighting in Vietnam: "'We're here to establish peace'"; "'We've made a commitment to your country . . . and to your people. . . . We've committed ourselves to guarantee you the right to choose your own government'" (p. 304).

Compared to the other war literature discussed so far, *The 13th Valley* stands apart because of its precise and detailed combat realism, even more thorough than Webb's. Certainly, Mailer's comment about the "textbook quality" of *The Thin Red Line* could also aptly apply to this work. Like Jones, Del Vecchio extensively describes combat, military history and organization, weapons, strategy, military jargon (including an extensive glossary), and psychology. Like the prototypical World War II narrative, this novel also deals with a large-scale combat operation against a massive number of North Vietnam Army regulars in a section of country isolated from the civilian population. Thus, the combat scenes and moral dilemmas are more consistent with World War II combat novels set in the South Pacific and markedly contrast with most of the Vietnam works describing constantly shifting small-unit actions and guerrilla warfare waged among the Vietnamese populace. Atrocity scenes involving Vietnamese civilians are missing from this novel.

Conspicuous in *The 13th Valley* are prominent similarities to *The Naked and the Dead*, not just in the cumbersome length but also in the content as the author explores issues as well as characters. Del Vecchio's use of a melting-pot platoon, along with brief biographical sketches describing individuals" prewar lives, is an obvious parallel. Furthermore, similar to Mailer's war story, questions about social conflicts between the "haves" and "have-nots" and 1960s notions of the legitimacy of violence in the political process surface in Del Vecchio's book. Nevertheless, the strong undercurrent of anarchy and the blatant antagonism, prejudice, and cynicism present among Mailer's characters are missing in *The 13th Valley*. Del Vecchio's soldiers display a sense of mission and a physical–spiritual camaraderie that one character grandly labels as "symbiotic intellectual relationships," which involve the soldiers "exchanging and defining against each other their cultural heritage and in that, themselves" (p. 143).

Also present in this novel is a parallel to Mailer's preoccupation with soldiers' symbolic adversarial relationships to their natural environment. The grueling metaphysical and physical quest of Mailer's I & R platoon under Sergeant Croft through jungle terrain to reach Mount Anoka becomes a similar quest by Company A to journey through the Khe Ta Laou Valley to reach the NVA headquarters, marked by a towering teak tree on a knoll in the jungle valley. In discussing the symbols in his novel, Mailer describes the mountain as representing "many things . . . things like death and man's creative urge and man's desire to conquer the elements, fate" (Lennon 1988, 7). Such an interpretation of Mailer's symbol also seems appropriate for Del Vecchio's symbolic tree in *The 13th Valley*. The tree, like Mount Anoka, becomes a recurring physical reference-point for the operation – "In the center of the valley, rising out of the cloud . . .

was a small brush-covered knoll with the immense tree rising hundreds of feet" (Del Vecchio 1982, 224). More important, the tree takes on a haunting aura: "Perhaps the valley itself was a malicious adversary. And there in the middle above the misty ugliness, above it all, alone, stood that immense tree. Brooks sat still, hypnotized by the tree" (p. 450). These lines echo Croft's hypnotic attraction to Mount Anoka: "[It] tormented him, beckoned him, held an answer to something he wanted" (Mailer [1948] 1981, 497). In *The Naked and the Dead*, the mountain also symbolizes the failure of the I & R platoon to achieve its objective, thwarted by its perverse leadership and the hostile terrain. Although Del Vecchio's Company A reaches the knoll and captures the NVA headquarters, success is momentary as the NVA rally and drive the remaining platoon members away. And, although the tree is blown up, it falls off the knoll, landing defiantly upright in a nearby river. Like Webb's disabled tank, it becomes a symbol of Americans' transitory combat successes in Vietnam and their inability with overwhelming technology to conquer the jungle environment: "'I'll be a horse's ass,' FO mutters to himself. 'That son of a bitch looks like it's been growing there forever'" (Del Vecchio 1982, 575).

Another feature of *The Naked and the Dead* adapted in *The 13th Valley* is Mailer's ideological interest in the dual nature of man as seer and beast. Through his characters' interactions and occasional moments of self-reflection, Mailer explores questions of power and vision at the abstract and personal levels. On a more populist level, Del Vecchio introduces his own extensive philosophical thread as several characters, a small circle of the company's Command Post (CP), are led in nightly discussions by Lieutenant Brooks to explore the origins of conflict. Specifically, the lieutenant solicits the views of his men on "An Inquiry Into Personal, Racial And International Conflict," a dissertation that the soldier-philosopher Brooks is composing while on the thirteen-day operation. As suggested by this title, these conversations examine racial and class conflict in the United States, gender conflicts, and above all the origins and dynamics of war, which Brooks initially believes have their roots in the language of power and conflict inherent in Western civilization. For these "rap" sessions, Del Vecchio brings together an atypical melting-pot of Vietnam soldiers to debate these issues, for the inner circle of the CP comprises articulate and introspective enlisted men, many of whom are college graduates (engineering, psychology, history, and English). As Myers notes, "Del Vecchio's soldiers in the field are the most self-conscious and sophisticated in the history of American war fiction" (1988, 67). Therefore, the complex reflections and arguments about home, jobs, women, injustices, and conflict may seem out of place within the jungles of Vietnam and, as Aichinger has claimed for Mailer's "turgid" philosophical digressions, may dilute the book. But such moments move the novel out of the realm of mere combat realism and into the arena of ideas, allowing Del Vecchio to engage in some interesting, albeit at times rambling, considerations of American society, marital discord, and the Vietnam War. Such discussions, or digressions, also allow the author to develop characters' inner lives to a degree missing in most combat fiction. Unfortunately, unlike Mailer, he rarely transforms these individuals' views of power and control into specific actions within the war environment. Thus personal beliefs do not often become clues to characters' battlefield behavior.

Nevertheless, the novel's strength is its detailed battlefield realism and its controlling theme of combat brotherhood. Here, too, are parallels to other World War II and Vietnam combat fiction. For example, typical combat scenes occur as American soldiers, rummaging through enemy soldiers' possessions, identify with the enemy or mutilate the bodies – cutting off ears for souvenirs. A few passages describe innocent soldiers' guilt over their first kills, similar to Bead's experiences in *The Thin Red Line*. Del Vecchio's soldiers also engage in typical battlefield rituals momentarily to escape their environment, or at least to establish some measure of self-control in counteracting their anxieties:

> But anxiety came from being away from wives and friends and family and being totally out of control in a life where control seemed the utmost criteria [sic] for survival. (1982, 100)

Accordingly, the elaborate eating scenes from *All Quiet on The Western Front* surface in this novel as Egan orchestrates "grunt gourmet" meals out of mundane C-rations. Or the boonierats engage in the time-honored ritual of escaping into their memories or daydreaming about the real world, R & R, career plans, and – most often – women. As a result, typical of combat fiction, women play a prominent role – in the abstract. As is true in both *The Naked and the Dead* and Jones's novel, outrageous stereotypes of women abound in *The 13th Valley*. Del Vecchio's chauvinistic soldiers, worried about girlfriends' or wives' infidelity, view women as sex objects, foils, or sources of constant anxiety. Doc, the Harlem-born medic in *The 13th Valley*, becomes so agitated over this subject that he even compares women to the enemy: women are "all the time doin somethin jus so you can't expect why. They's like the dinks" (p. 94).

Like other war stories, *The 13th Valley* also illustrates Jones's epigraph to his novel that "There's only a thin red line between the sane and the mad." For Del Vecchio the phrase becomes "The line between man and beast is very thin" (p. 571). As he, like Jones and the other authors, explores the changes within soldiers undergoing heart-of-darkness journeys, he presents some familiar portraits. For example, his soldiers experience the conventional "hardening of hearts." As a result, the World War II soldiers' refrain "Fuck It" evolves into the "Who Fucken Cares" of *Close Quarters* and becomes in this novel the mantra of the Vietnam boonierats – "'Fuck it. Don't mean nothin. Drive on'" (p. 476). Yet some of these boonierats progress much further in their change. Egan evolves into the perfect embodiment of Jones's ideal soldier ("He must make a compact with himself or with Fate that he is lost": James Jones 1975 54). Thus, late in the novel, on the eve of the final assault. Egan has premonitions about his death and becomes indifferent to his existence, instead focusing his attention and energies on other soldiers' survival and the operation's success.

> Egan had relaxed more and more and everything had changed. He found he could think of himself as non-existent, as dead. . . . He was at peace. . . . He thought of himself in the third person. His fate is sealed, he thought. He can go forth without apprehension. (Del Vecchio 1982, 548–9)

And Cherry regresses the deepest into savagery, as he, like Corporal Fife in *The Thin Red Line* or Dosier in *Close Quarters*, changes from innocent to animal: "'That Cherry. He gone nuts. He crazy, L-T. You can see it in his eyes. L-T, Cherry becoming a animal'" (p. 571).

Cherry's spiritual journey from innocence into the heart of darkness becomes a central narrative thread in *The 13th Valley* and mirrors the paths taken by other characters we have encountered – Paul Baumer, Caputo, Herr, Corporal Fife, and Dosier. He, like Dosier, is an anti-hero who becomes evil. What sets him apart most from these other characters, however, is the degree to which he steps over the line between man and beast. He not only quickly slides away from the moral restraints of civilization and human feelings and into the combat numbness, but he also firmly remains in this condition at the end of the novel. James Vincent Chelini enters the war, like Del Vecchio, a college graduate from Bridgeport, Connecticut, who as a wireman arriving in Vietnam expects a housecat job. Instead, he finds himself assigned to an army infantry unit as a radio-telephone operator (RTO). Chelini's reasons for being in Vietnam seem contradictory, a desultory response to his draft notice but also an eagerness to reestablish family honor after his brother fled to Canada to avoid military service. Typical of the Vietnam rotation policy, he enters alone into an experienced combat unit, and he quickly acquires the derisive nickname given to all new soldiers – "Cherry." His notions about himself, war, and Vietnam are typical of the numerous "new guys" portrayed in other war literature. He's scared, believes he is an integral part of American forces bringing peace and prosperity to another country, and trusts the competency and value of the military organization. Furthermore, during his in-country training with various weapons, he has the typical John Wayne fantasies about heroism: "He came away beaming, imagining himself holding a hill alone, a hero" (p. 13).

As a member of the best company in the 7th Battalion of the 407th, his real training begins when he is assigned as Egan's RTO. As Company A's best boonierat, Egan resolves to mold Cherry into an excellent soldier, educating him about combat procedures, such as setting an ambush; exposing him to the realities of life in Vietnam; and developing within Cherry the boonierat mentality for survival. Egan also teaches his pupil the slogan of combat numbness: "It don't mean a fuckin thing." The lessons are slow and painful for the self-conscious new soldier, but gradually the uninitiated outsider begins to feel involved with the war:

> It was the beginning of understanding, the beginning of Cherry's loss of innocence. Chelini was at war. "You are finally goina see it," he mumbled to himself. "You're finally goina be a part of it." (p. 147)

Typically, the death of one of his few friends in Company A and his first kill hasten his loss of innocence. With these deaths Cherry moves from a mere observer of war to an emotional and physical participant. For days after the shooting, like Private Bead in *The Thin Red Line* or the speaker in *The Things They Carried* haunted by "The Man I Killed," Cherry broods over his killing of the NVA soldier – "'I killed a man in cold blood. I coulda screamed. I coulda fired high'" (p. 255) – and he carries with him the image of the dead NVA soldier.

With these rites of passage behind him, Cherry begins to change quickly, assuming more of his mentor Egan's qualities: becoming more aggressive in combat, controlling his actions, directing other experienced soldiers, and like Fife in the *Thin Red Line* enjoying the emotional high of combat. As a result, veterans consider him an experienced soldier:

> He had changed from play-soldier to trainee, then from state-side soldier to REMF soldier and then to cherry soldier. . . . Those changes were not great. On 17 August he changed greatly, he changed to just plain soldier. (p. 341)

Nevertheless, Cherry's journey from innocence to experience is incomplete. As his skill increases, along with his feeling of power, so does his callousness toward the enemy and even his friends. Combat numbness, taught by Egan as a necessary *means* for emotional survival, quickly becomes for Cherry an *end* in itself. His journey into darkness, like Dosier's, reaches the heart as Cherry loses himself in evil or insanity; the fine line is never clearly delineated. He is out of control! After one combat ambush, Cherry casually walks among the mangled enemy bodies, cutting off the ears for souvenirs. In another scene of hand-to-hand combat with an enemy soldier. Cherry turns into a literal animal, reminiscent of Rafterman in *The Short-Timers* who eats a dead American soldier's flesh (Hasford [1979] 1983, 74):

> Cherry is infuriated. He digs his fingers into the enemy's face. . . . Cherry bites his face, the nose crushes, Cherry bites, mad-dog, bites and rips the soldier's neck simultaneously thrusting his bayonet into the enemy stomach. Blood explodes in Cherry's mouth. (Del Vecchio 1982, 556)

Later, during the climactic battle, aware of Egan's inordinate fear of spiders. Cherry perversely torments his seriously wounded friend by toying with an immense spider slowly crawling toward the helpless Egan. In describing Cherry's physical and emotional changes, Del Vecchio uses images similar to Heinemann's description of Dosier's physical changes and atavistic regression in combat: "Indeed, Cherry was becoming callused hands, shoulders and mind" (p. 498). By the end of the novel, Cherry has, willingly or unwillingly, given himself completely to the darkness. But Dosier's moment of self-evaluation at the end of his journey into evil is missing with Cherry. There is no introspective pronouncement of "The horror! the horror." As signaled by his "intense, crazy" eyes, Cherry has crossed the thin red line into combat madness, with the saving veneer of battlefield numbness becoming a permanent part of his character. Although most of the members of Company A die or are left behind during the final assault on the knoll, Cherry survives, believing himself a "mangod" with the spirit of the dead soldiers living in him. His final response to the deaths is an inappropriate incantation of Egan's cynical refrain: "He laughed. 'Fuck it. Don't mean . . .'" (p. 589). Cherry, unlike Egan, firmly believes this.

If Cherry is the novel's anti-hero, then two of its traditional combat heroes are Daniel Egan, a platoon sergeant, and First Lieutenant Rufus Brooks, the African-American company commander. In their positive attitudes toward the war, their skills as combat soldiers, and their compatible officer–NCO relationship, these two characters are markedly similar to Lieutenant Hodges and Sergeant Snake in *Fields of Fire*. Del Vecchio's characters, however, have more depth and complexity than Webb's. Like their counterparts in *Fields of Fire*, Egan and Brooks are skilled soldiers who, rather than feeling helpless or victimized in the "swirling gyre of war," believe they control their lives, at least in combat, and relish playing the "game" of war. Both, like Snake and Hodges, for various reasons have extended their tours in Vietnam and formed Company A into an elite combat unit. Egan, a college graduate with a degree in engineering, away from combat rebels against the Mickey Mouse military regulations controlling his life. But on the battlefield he, like Snake, has a natural instinct for waging war and is a "soldier's soldier." Beneath his cynicism, apparent invulnerability, and machine-like actions in combat is a sensitive individual performing with the skill and commitment he expects from the men in his platoon. Hellmann labels Egan "the ideal American soldier in the mode of Davy Crockett and John Wayne" (1986, 131). Emphasizing Egan's harmony with his combat environment, Del Vecchio describes him in naturalistic terms: "Egan swayed with the bamboo, bent with the grass. Egan was born for the jungle valley, raised for a jungle valley war. He was the essence of the infantry" (1982, 547).

Brooks, the novel's other hero, is the ideal company commander who, confident on the battlefield, approaches the war intellectually: probing the philosophy of conflict, relishing the strategy of small-unit warfare, engaging in moves and countermoves with the enemy, and recognizing war's absurdity. With his competitive spirit, he also desperately wants his unit to be successful in combat. But Brooks is not a body-count officer measuring success by the number of enemy killed and gambling with the lives of his soldiers. Rather, like Hodges, he respects the men in his company, worries about their welfare, appreciates their sacrifices, and draws upon their experience to establish strategies for the company. He also hesitates to return to the States, fearing that his men will be assigned an incompetent and insensitive company commander. As a result of his skill and attitudes, Brooks enjoys the respect of the enlisted men in Company A, who accept him as a fellow-boonierat.

In addition to being skilled soldiers, Brooks and Egan share another trait – the soldier's familiar escape from the unsettling battlefield into the normally safe haven of memory and imagination:

> a man conditions his mind to be the place where most of his time is spent. Themes develop. An infantryman easily falls to thinking about his themes. Sometimes they are dreams, sometimes desires, sometimes compulsions, sometimes obsessions. (p. 65)

For both of these foot soldiers these mental escapes involve women, and their related thoughts conveyed through letters, memories, and daydreams become one more way for Del Vecchio to develop his characters and explore their lives away from the war. Thus, ironically, although both Egan and Brooks are self-assured on the battlefield, they are vulnerable and helpless in their strained relationships with women. Egan's wanderlust while in college and his unwillingness to share his feelings with other people have prevented him from making a commitment to a girl he first met during a summer vacation from college and continued to see sporadically until his enlistment in the Army. More significant are Brooks's difficulties with his wife, Lila, an artist and model, who neither embraces her husband's commitment to the war nor understands his loyalty to his men and his pride in the brotherhood of the bush. Undermined by the war and the Army, their marriage is doomed. In one significant daydream, Brooks recalls a night on R & R with Lila in Hawaii. The episode becomes a microcosm of the problems facing returning veterans in the aftermath stage as they attempt to re-enter prewar relationships – his spontaneous flashbacks to the battlefield, impotence, silence, moodiness, and a husband's and wife's inability to understand each other's feelings about war:

> They had come from different worlds, had merged, and had been separated by the army. They came together again in Hawaii and again they were from different worlds. They embraced a good-by embrace. They both felt it but neither said it. That would take much longer. (p. 380)

At times, therefore, tormented by these thoughts of their unsatisfying domestic relationships, Brooks and Egan unexpectedly escape into combat as they lose themselves in its machine-like repetition, physical exhilaration, or mental gymnastics of planning strategy. Most of all, they find comfort from their inner demons in the brotherhood of the boonierats. Hence, by the end of the novel, as Company A's literal and symbolic quest is about to end, Del Vecchio brings his characters to a final stage of development – levels of commitment, insight, acceptance, or indifference. Egan acknowledges his insensitivities toward other people and finds perverse comfort in believing that his recurring nightmares of his impending death are going to come true. Brooks decides that after the final assault on the knoll he will leave Vietnam and attempt to resurrect his marriage. He also arrives at a rather simplistic and obvious answer to his complex question about the causes of war, "When there are no more people . . . then there will be no more war. War is part of being human" (p. 575). And Cherry has learned far too well from Egan's instruction. He has become a cool, detached killing machine who has completed his heart-of-darkness journey, crossing over the "thin red line" and believing he is now invincible.

In a heavy-handed symbolic scene on the night before the final assault, the CP – thirteen boonierats – share a last supper prepared by Egan; and all, except Lieutenant Caldwell, who has lost the respect of the company, sip from one beer provided by Brooks:

> They sat in silence . . . They all felt close. Brooks glanced at them all. It was a great company, he thought. Quietly Brooks rose, went to his rucksack and returned with a single can of Budweiser beer. With his B-52 [sic] can opener he made two small holes in the top, took a drink and passed it. (p. 542)

The next day, Company A succeeds in destroying the NVA headquarters and in briefly holding the knoll before NVA soldiers retake the area. During the harried evacuation of the company, Egan, Brooks, and a medic, each attempting to save the others' lives, are seriously wounded and left behind, later

to be listed as Missing In Action. The last few words of the
book emphasize the ultimate irony of the whole experience, a
Vietnam perversion of Fussell's "All war is ironic":

> "Well fuck," Cherry smiled. He was happy they [Egan,
> Brooks, Doc] were not listed among the known dead. In
> me, he thought. He laughed. "Fuck it. Don't mean. . . ."
> Thomasin cut him off. "Don't say it, Soldier." (p. 589)

With this ending to *The 13th Valley*, the fates of Del Vecchio's
three major characters in some ways parallel the destiny of
Webb's soldiers – Snake and Hodges, killed while guarding
the disabled tank, and Senator, changed drastically by his
war experiences. Both novels, sympathetic portraits of the
American combat soldier, emphasize the themes of combat
brotherhood and self-sacrifice, but Del Vecchio presents his
combat realism without Webb's overt political commentary
and within a more sophisticated dramatic structure. Also in
contrast to *Fields of Fire*, this book moves more smoothly from
the battle scenes to moments away from combat. Furthermore,
Del Vecchio's efforts, although occasionally amateurish, to
establish a multi-faceted psychological depth to the characters set him apart from Webb and Jones and place him in
the Mailer tradition of the soldier-author who emphasizes
characterization and ideas. At the same time, Del Vecchio,
like Heinemann and Webb, takes the modern combat novel
to a new level of literary realism in portraying the gruesome realities of war, as well as the disturbing psychological truths about soldiers' instincts to kill and to survive.

4

Consideration

"So you see," said Li Van Hgoc as he brought down the periscope and locked it with a silver key, "things may be viewed from many angles. From down below, or from inside out, you often discover entirely new understandings."

Tim O'Brien, *Going After Cacciato*

The Vietcong major in Tim O'Brien's second novel relates this advice to a squad of American soldiers in Vietnam. He is indirectly encouraging them to engage in Fussell's third stage of a soldier's journey through his war experiences, a period of quiet consideration away from the battlefield. The major's advice also establishes a critical framework for this chapter, viewing a recurring theme in war literature from many angles and in the process arriving at new insights. Obviously, such critical consideration has occurred in the previous chapters as we examined soldiers' loss of innocence and lessons learned on the battlefield. But in this chapter the specific theme is a soldier's contemplation of fear, courage, and cowardice on the battlefield. Specifically, soldier-author Tim O'Brien in two of his Vietnam works, the autobiographical *If I Die in a Combat Zone* (1973) and his fictional *Going After Cacciato* (1978), considers two central questions: whether to flee the battlefield or fight, and once on the battlefield how to control one's fear. Not surprisingly, these two themes, along with O'Brien's self-reflective commentary on the nature of creating war stories, also emerge as central issues in his most recent Vietnam narrative, *The Things They Carried* (1990).[1] Thus, *If I Die* and *Going After Cacciato* serve as helpful critical introductions to this latest critically acclaimed novel.

Difficult moral choices in war and such attendant concepts as fear, cowardice, manhood, courage, heroism, and control are commonplaces within the war genre. Not commonplace, however, are the various ways modern authors explore in war stories the traits associated with these words and deeds: Crane's heroic actions, Dos Passos' stoic acceptance of one's fate, Hemingway's "grace under pressure," and Heller's wisdom combined with courage to make a separate peace. Indeed, a few American soldier-authors writing about Vietnam invoke well-worn John Wayne images to represent the ideal warrior: fearless, self-sacrificing, in control, grandly heroic. But other authors and their characters grapple with the complex meanings of these words within the military, cultural, and moral ambiguities of Vietnam. What causes fear? Is it courageous for soldiers to fight in a war they believe to be wrong, or is it more courageous to flee the battlefield and establish a separate peace? Are heroic acts unthinking ones? Is mere endurance in a war a type of courage? What exactly are society's expectations of a soldier's conduct? What obligations do soldiers have to society, to comrades, and to themselves? What are the characteristics of a hero? Such questions in any war are difficult to answer, but within the Vietnam literature authors' and characters' efforts to consider these issues lead to particularly important insights about the self and fundamental truths about human nature and responsibilities.

Characterizing O'Brien's writing are his creative efforts to examine these questions and words from multiple perspectives. Equally important is the resulting opportunity for readers to study this soldier-author's different connections to his raw material, the relationship between memory and imagination. In his first nonfiction book O'Brien engages in what Fussell terms "documentary transcription" (although names and physical characteristics of the persons depicted have been changed). But in his novel, through the powers of imagination and invention, he transmutes the raw material of his combat experiences into fiction. Thus, *If I Die* is an episodic but carefully crafted memoir of his own heart-of-darkness experiences and difficult choices during basic training and later with an Army combat unit in Vietnam. Within the realistic milieu, the book becomes a straightforward confessional of O'Brien the soldier's efforts to understand courage, fear, wisdom, cowardice, responsibility, and control within his own and other soldiers' lives. In *Going After Cacciato*, O'Brien the artist approaches the same themes from a different perspective – a fictional world with both author and characters using imagination and fact to grapple with the same issues raised in the memoir.

Within this discussion of O'Brien, an appropriate historical–literary context for examining his two books is Stephen Crane's Civil War novel, *The Red Badge of Courage* (1895). Some critics, including Peter Jones, have labeled it the first modern war novel: the archetypical book for "any American who sets out to write of a young man going to war in the twentieth century" (Jones 1976, 6). The reason is that Crane, one of the two non-soldier-authors discussed at length in this book, changed the way American authors wrote about war. He moved away from the traditional romance or diary-like realism found in previous war literature and instead presented an imaginative psychological portrait of a soldier's reactions to the confusion, horror, and random death associated with combat. With Crane's exposure to the military limited to ROTC activities at prep school, research from books written about the Civil War, and conversations with one of his teachers who had been a field officer in the Civil War, Crane gathered his raw material secondhand. Relying on this information and his imagination, Crane crafted a realistic, naturalistic, and at times impressionistic account of one soldier's experiences in battle.[2] His creative motivation for writing this psychological novel is found in his reaction to authors of previous Civil War memoirs and novels: "'I wonder that *some* of these fellows don't tell how they felt in those scraps! They spout eternally of what they *did*, but they are emotionless as rocks'" (Levenson 1975, xxxv). Thus, thoughts and feelings, not actions, dominate Crane's narrative written by one who, at the time, imagined war rather than participated in it. Nevertheless, his work becomes an important touchstone for judging the quality of other modern war novels written by participants. Also making *The Red Badge of Courage* an appropriate context for reading O'Brien's two books are the narrative conventions, the impressionistic scenes, and the content. Specifically, Crane focuses on the psychological themes of fear and control within a war that because of its wholesale mobilization of people and resources, military tactics, and technology is often designated the first modern war.

Crane's initiation story is a relatively simple account of Henry Fleming's first combat experiences as a Union soldier in the battle at Chancellorsville. Henry, who Crane labels the "youth" throughout the novel, has joined the Army fueled by his Homeric notions of battle: "He had read of marches, sieges, conflicts, and he had longed to see it all. His busy mind had drawn for him large pictures extravagant in colour, lurid with breathless deeds" ([1895] 1986, 12). His visions of heroism and a visible badge of courage also excite him: "As he basked in the smiles of the girls and was patted and complimented by the old men, he had felt growing within him the strength to do mighty deeds of arms" (p. 15). Yet once this stage of war innocence passes, and as he gets closer to the actual fighting, Henry questions his courage, seeks reassurances from other soldiers, and wonders whether he will actually fight or flee the battlefield. His doubts come true in the midst of his first battle; believing that his skirmish line will fall, he panics and flees. Ironically, while fleeing he accidentally receives a head wound in a scuffle with another fleeing Union soldier. Later, when he finds his unit, the soldiers believe that Henry's wound is from the battle, "a red badge of courage." Bolstered by his new status as a hero, he performs courageously when he next faces the enemy.

Crane's novel is an in-depth study of different types of fear and the ways Fleming attempts to control them.

> In the darkness he saw visions of a thousand-tongued fear that would babble at his back and cause him to flee, while others were going coolly about their country's business. He admitted that he would not be able to cope with this monster. (p. 28)

Away from the battlefield, as Henry increasingly has time "to wonder about himself and to attempt to probe his sensations" (p. 33), this haunting image of fear appears in various forms: a phantomlike enemy easily evading the shots of the Union soldiers, an embarrassing moment early in Henry's first battle when in a panic he fires his rifle before he has control, or an unexpected confrontation with death as he stumbles upon the corpse of a Union soldier hidden in the thickets. But his greatest fear is that of being considered a coward. Age-old questions of manhood and society's censure surface as Henry worries that his fellow-soldiers will question his courage.

The ways in which this young soldier deals with these real and imagined fears become central to Crane's novel and foreshadow similar issues treated in O'Brien's works. As British World War I poet Siegfried Sassoon observes, and O'Brien reiterates, "Soldiers are dreamers." Fleming is no exception as he employs various tricks of the mind to assuage his fears. First, through his daydreams he escapes from the immediate situation. As he imagines himself acting heroically, he wishes for a visible symbol of bravery much in the same way that both Paul Berlin, O'Brien's central character in *Going After Cacciato*, and Norman Bowker in *The Things They Carried* wish for Silver Stars:

> At times he [Fleming] regarded the wounded soldiers in an envious way. He conceived persons with torn bodies to be particularly happy. He wished that he, too, had a wound, a red badge of courage. (p. 67)

Once he flees the battle, however, Henry's imagination becomes an enemy, tormenting him with scenes of ridicule: "He imagined the whole regiment saying: 'Where's Henry Fleming? He run, didn't 'e? Oh, my!' He recalled various persons who would be quite sure to leave him no peace about it" (p. 84). At other times, however, he also avoids confronting his fear by rationalizing his flight from the battle as the appropriate actions of an "enlightened" soldier who knew the battle was to be lost and had fled because of "his superior perceptions and knowledge" (p. 57). Later he views the wholesale retreat of his unit as a vindication of his conduct, and because his own flight remains undiscovered, he considers his cowardice in a new perspective: "He had performed his mistakes in the dark, so he was still a man" (p. 105), and "he had fled with discretion and dignity" (p. 106) unlike many of the other retreating soldiers from his unit.

In fact, he quickly moves from rationalization to imagination as he creates war stories that he intends later to tell his family: "he felt quite competent to return home and make the hearts of people glow with stories of war" (p. 107).

Obviously, Henry does brood about his moment of fear on the battlefield and subsequent flight, but he does not realistically ponder the reasons for and nature of this action. He does, however, through these tricks of the imagination, begin to control his fear as he constructs a primitive revisionist history of his conduct and explores possibilities for his future conduct. As a result, Henry's self-image changes, as does his outward conduct. His fears no longer paralyze him; fleeing the next battle is no longer a possibility. Therefore, with "an air of courage" he leads his unit into the next battle, fighting like a "war devil" and motivating his comrades to continue the fight. Along with this newfound courage also emerge an understanding about the soldier's insignificance in war, a sense of self-satisfaction in his performance, and insights about battlefield sacrifice and death. Most important, within the crucible of war, he maturely assesses his changes from an innocent youth to an experienced adult:

> with this conviction came a store of assurance. He felt a quiet manhood, nonassertive but a sturdy and strong blood ... He had been to touch the great death, and found that, after all, it was but the great death. He was a man. (p. 158)

In two books about the Vietnam War – one fact, the other fiction – Tim O'Brien, like Crane, examines battlefield courage and manhood. The results of Henry Fleming's tricks of the mind and consideration of war differ, however, from those achieved by Tim O'Brien and Paul Berlin in their own battlefield confrontations with questions of fear and flight. But, because both O'Brien and Berlin experience, confront, and control their fears, helplessness, and indecision in ways similar to Henry's efforts, all three books contain similar dilemmas, psychological themes, and narrative strategies. *If I Die in a Combat Zone: Box Me Up and Ship Me Home* (the title comes from a popular marching song in basic training) is O'Brien's autobiographical treatment of these issues. Relying upon his memory rather than upon imagination, the author describes portions of his tour of duty as a decorated combat soldier in Vietnam. His narrative begins as the 21-year-old Phi Beta Kappa graduate (Macalester College) receives his induction notice in the summer of 1968. Raised in a small town in southern Minnesota, O'Brien, whose parents both served in the military, departs on a journey taking him through basic and advanced training at Fort Lewis, Washington. This experience culminates in a twelve-month tour served mainly as a radio-telephone operator (RTO) with the 46th Infantry near Chu Lai, South Vietnam.

While on this tour of duty, O'Brien, the well-read, well-travelled college graduate, kept a journal that later provided basic information for this book. But *If I Die* is not the conventional chronological combat memoir like Caputo's *A Rumor of War*. Instead, this war story is a series of poignant vignettes describing O'Brien's personal dilemmas as a reluctant draftee, the emotional and psychological crises facing combat soldiers, and portraits of the people of war – a mortally wounded NVA female nurse, an elderly Vietnamese villager abused by American troops, and an American officer who becomes O'Brien's embodiment of courage. This arrangement of stories with interwoven themes and characters anticipates the somewhat similar narrative structure of *The Things They Carried* with its twenty-two intertwined war stories. In *If I Die*, O'Brien also reveals the simple truths of war, ones that Crane dealt with years earlier and ones that O'Brien later examines in his fiction:

Men die. Fear hurts and humiliates. It is hard to be brave. It is hard to know what bravery *is*. Dead human beings are heavy and awkward to carry, things smell different in Vietnam, soldiers are dreamers. ([1973] 1979, 31)

Throughout his literate memoir, O'Brien sprinkles literary references to Owen, Pound, Plato, and Aristotle, and he arranges the scenes, much like Herr in *Dispatches*, for dramatic effect. This latter feature, along with his attention to scene, character, and dialogue, gives the work a fictional aura. Further contributing to the book's depth and sophistication is O'Brien's focus on truths about human nature. Thus, at times, Paul Fussell's assessment of Robert Graves, the British World War

I poet, is appropriate for O'Brien: "As a memoirist, Graves seems most interested not in accurate recall but in recovering moments when he most clearly perceives the knavery of knaves" ([1975] 1981, 219). For readers, one of these more revealing and unsettling episodes of knavery involves the author's experiences in Pinkville (GI slang for Song My, an area harbouring communist soldiers and sympathizers and including the village of My Lai), one year after the infamous "My Lai Massacre." Certainly, O'Brien does not write this brief narrative section to justify earlier atrocities committed on Vietnamese civilians by a platoon of American soldiers under the command of Lieutenant William Calley.[3] But he does suggest how the special features of guerrilla warfare in Vietnam and how the emotional and psychological factors of combat contributed to such abhorrent acts: freed from the restraints of civilization, decent human beings, along with immoral ones, as they had done in previous wars, released their savage emotions. One year earlier, Lieutenant William Calley's troops found themselves frequently harassed by a phantom-like enemy ambushing American soldiers and detonating booby-traps as villagers silently watched. Now O'Brien's unit encounters similar conditions. The result, as described earlier in a more heavy-handed way in *A Rumor of War*, is an all-consuming hatred of enemy soldiers and civilians alike and a desire for revenge emerging within the frustrated American soldiers who helplessly watch their friends die:

> Scraps of our friends were dropped in plastic body bags. Jet fighters were called in. The hamlet was leveled and napalm was used. I heard screams in the burning black rubble. I heard the enemy's AK-47 rifles crack out like impotent popguns against the jets. There were Viet Cong in that hamlet. And there were babies and children and people who just didn't give a damn in there too. But Chip and Tom were on the way to Graves Registration in Chu Lai, and they were dead, and it was hard to be filled with pity. ([1973] 1979, 122)

If in this book's tightly crafted narrative style, dramatic heightening, and psychological insights we glimpse the budding novelist at work, we also find in the content the raw material for *Going After Cacciato* and *The Things They Carried*. As O'Brien comments in an interview for *Modern Fiction Studies*, "There are many passages in *If I Die* that really presage *Cacciato* . . . a lot of events which I use in both books" (Schroeder 1984, 141). For example, from *If I Die*, O'Brien's 1967 conversation about the Vietnam War with a North Vietnamese student in Prague becomes the basis for the imaginary conversation about war with Major Hgoc in *Going After Cacciato*. O'Brien's autobiographical episode about destroying Vietcong tunnels in a Vietnamese hamlet evolves into a central episode in the novel involving the death of Frenchie Tucker and Bernie Lynn. A night of guard duty for O'Brien while in basic training ("A sense of privacy and peace. We talked about whatever came to mind . . . and it was a good time. We felt . . . what? Free. In control. Pardoned": [1973] 1979, 55) foreshadows the central narrative framework in *Going After Cacciato* – Paul Berlin's night of spiritual freedom and imaginative control while on guard duty at Quang Ngai. And in the earlier work a pointedly moralistic scene describing American soldiers' random firing at some Vietnamese boys herding cows in a free-fire zone becomes in the later work a subtle emblematic event involving Americans shooting two water buffaloes.

Also similar images, people, and key words appear frequently in his memoir and in *Going After Cacciato*. Kline, a bewildered and timid trainee wearing two left boots, whom O'Brien encounters in basic training, is, according to the author, the genesis for the character Cacciato (Schroeder 1984, 150). The mechanical act of marching emerges as an important image in both books symbolizing the soldiers' monotonous treadmill existence. Additionally, in both the nonfiction book and this novel, O'Brien, like Crane, is fascinated with the soldier's powers of memory and imagination (tricks of the mind) in the midst of combat to control his fears and establish some order in his life. Both O'Brien and his fictional Paul Berlin recall pleasant scenes, fantasize about possibilities, and plan for life after war: "For a time we just sat there. We watched the dark grow on itself, and we let our imaginations do the rest" ([1973] 1979, 39).

Yet the most important connections between these two works, as well as to *The Red Badge of Courage*, involve O'Brien's interest

147

in the issues of fear, doubt, commitment, and courage – the things soldiers carry into war. Like Crane, O'Brien explores a foot soldier's various fears, his self-conscious attempts to define courage and manhood, and his fundamental doubts about whether to flee the battlefield altogether or stay and fight. In *If I Die*, O'Brien initially explores these issues within his own Vietnam War experiences, which differ significantly from Henry Fleming's in that they become inextricably linked with a war many historians and participants characterize as "a wrong war." Some of O'Brien's fears typically emanate from the hazards of being a combat soldier – the overriding fear of death along with the gnawing feelings of helplessness caused by the numerous land mines and booby-traps dotting the South Vietnam landscape. In one chapter, O'Brien offers a comprehensive catalog of mines – seven, to be exact, including the most feared, "The Bouncing Betty"; and he describes the psychological and physical responses such devices elicit among the soldiers walking through enemy-controlled areas:

> The moment-to-moment, step-by-step decision making preys on your mind. The effect sometimes is paralysis. You are slow to rise from rest breaks. You walk like a wooden man, like a toy soldier out of Victor Herbert's *Babes in Toyland*. Contrary to military and parental training, you walk with your eyes pinned to the dirt, spine arched, and you are shivering, shoulders hunched. (p. 126)

The most important fear, however, O'Brien examines in this book, as well as in *Going After Cacciato* and in a few of the stories in *The Things They Carried*, entails the abstract concepts of commitment, responsibility, and courage – whether to flee or fight. He describes his response to his draft notice and his later involvement in the Vietnam War as a "sort of sleepwalking default. It was no decision, no chain of ideas or reasons, that steered me into the war" (p. 31). A 21-year-old college graduate and confirmed liberal who believes the war is "wrongly conceived and poorly justified" (p. 26), O'Brien is not the best soldier material. In spite of this, he reports for induction and carries with him into basic training doubts about fighting in a war that he does not enthusiastically support. Once at Fort

Lewis, Washington, this internal debate continues as he and a soulmate consider the alternatives to accepting orders for Vietnam. Is O'Brien's opposition to fighting rooted in moral issues – a deep-seated conviction against the Vietnam War; or does his opposition emerge from selfish reasons – a fear of being wounded or dying in the war? If he opposes the war, why has he remained in the Army? Is it, as Pound claims in "Hugh Selwyn Mauberley," because of a fear of "society's censure . . . . Fear of weakness. Fear that to avoid war is to avoid manhood" (p. 45)? In the midst of advanced infantry training, O'Brien, much like the fictional characters Orr and Yossarian in *Catch-22*, ponders his options and temporarily resolves the dilemma. He decides to establish his own separate peace by deserting the Army for the safety of Sweden. He elaborately plans the trip, saves enough money, and compiles the proper documents, but at the last moment, opting not to carry through with his decision, he validates Pound's belief:

> It was over. I simply couldn't bring myself to flee. Family,
> the home town, friends, history, tradition, fear, confusion,
> exile: I could not run. I went into the hallway and bought
> a Coke. When I finished it I felt better, clearer headed, and
> burned the plans. I was a coward. I was sick. (p. 73)

Once in Vietnam, O'Brien still believes the war to be "silly and stupid": "Vietnam was under siege in pursuit of a pretty, tantalizing, promiscuous, particularly American brand of government and style" (p. 145). Nevertheless, such views do not keep him from becoming the good soldier as, in the midst of war, he considers courage and bravery, his own and others'. Drawing upon authors (Hemingway's "grace under pressure"), philosophers (Plato's "wise endurance"), fictional heroes (Frederic Henry's courage mixed with love and justice), and fellow-soldiers (Captain Johansen's "John Wayne" charge against a Vietcong position), O'Brien, like Henry Fleming, tries to define courage and measure his own conduct against this standard. He realizes that unthinking brave actions – for example, an instinctual act to save another soldier's life – are not courageous. Neither are fearless actions courageous. Rather, "proper courage is wise courage. It's acting wisely, acting wisely when fear would have a man act otherwise" (p. 137). Citing Plato, O'Brien notes that "men must *know* what they do is courageous, they must *know* it is right, and that kind of knowledge is wisdom and nothing else" (p. 141).

Within the boundaries of this philosophical definition of courage, O'Brien assesses his own courage. Is his failure to act on his opposition to the war and to establish a separate peace a sure sign of cowardice? Or is his commitment to his country, his family, and the war – another admirable principle – a type of courage and a sign of manhood? Obviously, these inner conflicts are much more complex than the ones Crane raises in *The Red Badge of Courage*; they reflect O'Brien's philosophical bent. They also represent the special social, ethical, and political ambiguities of the Vietnam War. O'Brien conveniently sidesteps his apparent failure to act upon his political convictions, only to raise the issue again in *Going After Cacciato* and later in the autobiographical story "On the Rainy River" in *The Things They Carried*. But, in a passage anticipating events surrounding Paul Berlin's own moment of fear on the battlefield, O'Brien places himself in a middle category of common courage, neither coward nor hero. This category recognizes the average soldier's stoic endurance in the midst of fear and hardship:

> The easy aphorisms hold no hope for the middle man, the man who wants to try but has already died more than once, squirming under the bullets, going through the act of death and coming through embarrassingly alive. The bullets stop. . . . You tentatively peek up, wondering if it is the end. Then you look at the other men, reading your own caved-in belly deep in their eyes. The fright dies the same way novocaine wears off in the dentist's chair. You promise, almost moving your lips, to do better the next time; that by itself is a kind of courage. (p. 147)

And, like the quietly self-assured Henry Fleming after his "trial by fire" in combat, O'Brien also ends his tour in Vietnam armed with truths about his own manhood: "You learned, as old men tell it in front of the courthouse that war is not all bad; it may not make a man of you, but it teaches you that manhood is not something to scoff" (p. 204).

With his second novel, *Going After Cacciato*, which won the 1978 National Book Award for Fiction, O'Brien returns to the same battlefields of *If I Die* and once again explores fear, courage, and manhood. But, following the advice of his fictional Major Li Van Hgoc, he views the Vietnam War from a different angle, specifically through his imagination rather than just through his memory. He turns to imagination's creative playfulness to extend his memories and to travel along different imaginary paths; and he uses fictional craft to develop character, to heighten dramatic effect, to raise moral questions, and to examine consequences of a soldier's actions. Paul Berlin, the central character in this novel, seems, at times, to be both a modern version of Henry Fleming and the *alter ego* of Tim O'Brien the soldier. Like Fleming, Caputo, and so many other soldiers we have encountered, Berlin's greatest fear is that of being found wanting on the battlefield – to have his courage and manhood questioned; like Henry Fleming, he is haunted by the memory of a particularly embarrassing moment of fear on the battlefield; and, like Tim O'Brien the soldier, his desire to flee the war conflicts with his obligations to friends, family, and country to remain a soldier. As O'Brien has noted, however, in comparing his own character in *If I Die* with Berlin, the latter is "more of a dreamer than I was. He takes the war and the possibility of running from war more seriously than I did. . . . He's more frightened . . . more sensitive" (Schroeder 1984, 142). Nevertheless, Berlin's literal and figurative odyssey through his Vietnam tour recapitulates important thematic elements of *The Red Badge of Courage* and *If I Die*, and it serves as a paradigm for Fussell's third stage of a soldier's consideration of his war experiences.

This novel, like so much of modern war literature, also focuses on issues of control: in this instance, the soldier's control of his environment and fear and the author's control of his raw material and creative processes (memory and imagination). Because this book, like *The Things They Carried*, frequently becomes a story about writing a war story, critics" comments about the difficulties in writing modern war literature become an appropriate context for understanding *Going After Cacciato*. These critics often note a novelist's problems in gathering appropriate Vietnam war experiences and shaping them into a tightly focused work similar to novels emerging from previous wars. Vietnam with its fragmentation, complexity, and seeming illogic presents special problems for an author attempting to order the chaos in a meaningful way: "The novelist's disadvantage is that this was a war with no center, no decisive battles; it was all circumference and it is therefore difficult to filter the thing through unified plot and point of view" (Pochoda 1978, 344). Not surprisingly, an author's difficulty in controlling literary elements mirrors the American soldiers' extensively chronicled problem of handling Vietnam experiences by establishing meaning, order, and control in their lives or in understanding the musical-chairs pattern of engaging the enemy. Of course, a combatant's struggle to cope with the Russian-roulette quality of a precarious existence is a recurrent theme in most war literature, but it assumes special significance in Vietnam war stories, especially *Going After Cacciato* where both author and main character seek control.

Within the formal and thematic implications of the soldier's and author's struggle to order their experience and war stories, O'Brien also involves readers in the pursuit of control as they struggle to master the disordered events in this book, find the center, and separate the book's facts from fantasy. In an unconventional approach, he uses a third-person limited point of view and three narrative strands (randomly juxtaposed and roughly equal to past, present, and future) to take the reader deep into the heart and mind of Specialist Four Paul Berlin.[4] For both the reader and the central character, this book becomes one more literal and figurative journey into a heart of darkness. During over six hours of night guard duty, the central character attempts to regulate his external and internal conditions by controlling his fears and destiny. To accomplish this, he becomes a literary rememberer, randomly recalling the facts of his six months in Vietnam, and he assumes the role of an inexperienced author transforming these facts into an uncommon war story about himself. Such an act of remembering and imagining eventually leads to self-knowledge and a measure of control. Berlin, a soldier-author-character, discovers, like Henry Fleming, particular truths about courage, fear, cowardice, willpower, and war. He also discovers, like Tim O'Brien the soldier in *If I Die*, the difficulty for a soldier in establishing a separate peace. Furthermore, this novice storyteller learns general lessons about the creative process. As a result, Berlin's quest for order and control serves as a metaphor for O'Brien's and other soldier-authors' efforts to structure their memories of the Vietnam experience. Thus, at times, the novel becomes a piece of metafiction, a commentary on its own fictive nature. As O'Brien, through his central character, examines basic questions involving the art of narrative and the creative interplay of memory and imagination, this literary theme frequently overshadows his portrayal of the politics and physical realities of the war.[5] The result is one of the few Vietnam combat narratives truly transcending the battlefield.

O'Brien devotes fifteen of the book's forty-six chapters to the facts of Berlin's six months in Vietnam. This soldier is an average 20-year-old grunt attached to the Americal Division near Chu Lai. A "straightforward, honest, decent, sort of guy" from the Midwest, he is confused by a meaningless war and brief dreams of heroism. He is an "Everyman," out of control, lost in the immense physical and metaphysical darkness of Vietnam, and plagued by a constant fear, which the squad's medic attributes to Berlin's "overabundant fear biles." In these chapters, which appear randomly placed, Berlin remembers, without order, the facts: fears, deaths, rituals, and horrors of war.

If the form of the chapters reflects disorder, so does the content. The comparison of fighting in a war to playing Russian roulette, suggested in several books and films about Vietnam,[6] appropriately describes Berlin's plight and the war's futility. As noted earlier, a character in Webb's *Fields of Fire* articulates a soldier's view of this game whose rules have been altered so that play is compulsory and ends only when the player dies: "If you want to know, I get the feeling this [Vietnam War] is kind of like Russian roulette. Just as senseless. And the players aren't excused until the gun goes off in their face" (Webb 1978, 201). Thus, although mathematically the cumulative odds do not increase (one only feels that way), Berlin and the other members of Third Squad feel powerless as they wait for the gun to go off. Such feelings among soldiers that they are expendable are common in modern war literature; but, compared to other wars, the chaotic conditions of the Vietnam guerrilla warfare intensify the sense of vulnerability and insignificance among the ill-prepared soldiers in Berlin's squad. For example, members of Third Squad do not know the Vietnamese language, the people, or friends from enemies. They are also incapable of knowing the validity of this war, "good from evil," or the simple things:

> a sense of victory, or satisfaction, or necessary sacrifice. . . .
> No sense of order or momentum. No front, no rear, no trenches laid out in neat parallels. No Patton rushing for the Rhine, no beachheads to storm and win and hold for the duration. They did not have targets. They did not have a cause. (O'Brien [1978] 1979, 320)

O'Brien's order among these chapters of disordered fact is the portrait of Berlin as an innocent among the lost whose uneventful Midwest childhood has ill-prepared him for war's physical and psychological realities. Although a participant, he lacks commitment to the war; in fact, he has never thought about whether it is right or wrong. Instead, he went to war because of the law, a desire to avoid censure, and a trust in country – automatic responses echoing O'Brien's earlier quoted reaction to the draft in *If I Die*, "But I submitted . . . by a sort of sleepwalking default" ([1973] 1979, 31). Once Paul Berlin is in Vietnam, this pattern of reflex overriding reflection and will continues. The dark side of war does not fascinate him, nor do the horrors of war – Frenchie Tucker and Bernie Lynn killed in a Vietcong tunnel and Billy Boy Watkins literally scared to death when his foot is blown off by a booby-trap. Always marching, machine-like, at the rear of Third Squad, he is helplessly dragged along by the day-to-day events: "Powerless and powerful, like a boulder in an avalanche . . . [he] marched toward the mountains without stop or the ability to stop" ([1978] 1979, 203). Berlin has simply endured without reflection.

The recurring activity in these random chapters of fact is the central character's quest to control his fear and his environment through rituals and daydreams, an activity linking him to soldiers in all wars seeking control. From his first day in country, Berlin wants only to survive and maybe to win a Silver Star, his equivalent of Henry Fleming's Red Badge of

Courage. The first goal is a possibility; the last, merely one more romantic daydream, his only manifestation of the John Wayne Syndrome. To survive, he must master his fears: "True, the war scared him silly, but this was something he hoped to bring under control" (p. 57). Also, he must develop a sense of order, rhythm, and meaning in his life. In three significant ways, O'Brien portrays this soldier's struggle, "how to act wisely in spite of fear," and probes the attendant concern of "whether to flee or fight or seek an accommodation" (p. 101).

First, O'Brien draws upon a common episode in war stories where an outward action symbolizes an inner condition. For example, soldiers" fears in battle are signaled by precise physical signs, such as soldiers defecating in their pants.[7] Thus, Berlin's control of his excretory functions becomes a significant barometer of his success in controlling fear. Soon after arriving in Vietnam, and before experiencing fear on the battlefield, Berlin, calm and in control, defecates in the enlisted men's latrine at the in-processing center. The words describing this ritual parallel Remarque's portrait of a similarly pleasurable activity for Paul Baumer: "And for a long time he sat there. At home, comfortable, even at peace" (p. 61). But during a particularly harrowing experience with a booby-trap Berlin defecates in his pants, and much later, in the novel's climactic scene, when fantasy and reality merge, Berlin loses control of his gun, loses control of his fear, and loses control of his body: he urinates in his pants.

Next, O'Brien uses an elaborate game metaphor to portray this soldier's pursuit of control. Faced with his own helplessness and a confusing war, Berlin seeks refuge in an on-going basketball game played by the Third Squad who, travelling from village to village, carry a "Spalding Wear-Ever basketball" and a wicker grain-basket. The game provides these soldiers with order, control, clarity, and meaning absent in their Russian-roulette existence and missing from this particular war. Thus, Berlin views basketball in the following way:

Winning – you knew the score, you knew what it would take to win, to come from behind, you knew exactly. The odds could be figured. Winning was the purpose, nothing else. A basket to shoot at, a target, and sometimes you

scored and sometimes you didn't, but you had a true thing
to aim at, you always knew. (p. 36)

Finally, for this study in controlling fear, O'Brien selects, as an
epigraph to the novel, an insight about soldiers from World War
I soldier-author Siegfried Sassoon: "Soldiers are dreamers." As
has been true for Henry Fleming, Paul Baumer, and the rest of
the combat brotherhood, daydreams allow escape and partial
solace for Berlin the soldier as he follows his father's advice "to
look for the good things" during his Vietnam tour (p. 85). At
times, he momentarily orders his life through thoughts about
the past (home, parents, and childhood) and through plans for
the future (a trip to Paris and a literal escape from the war).
This dreaming, which becomes the central activity in the book,
assumes added significance; it shapes the form and content of
the other two groups of chapters and influences Berlin's other
roles as author and character.

Perched high in a tower at Quang Ngai during a night of
guard duty, Berlin appropriately finds himself at the midpoint of
his tour of duty, an appropriate moment for a reflective journey
into his heart of darkness:

The real issue was the power of the will to defeat fear. A
matter of figuring a way to do it. Somehow working his
way into that secret chamber of the human heart, where
in tangles, lay the circuitry for all that was possible, the
full range of what a man might be. (p. 102)

Over the next six hours, he not only recalls the facts of
the previous six months, presented in the random chapters
already described, but he also devises his most elaborate
trick to escape the war, to control his fear and destiny, and to
consider possibilities. Through his imagination this confused
soldier leisurely views the war from a new vantage-point and
attempts to transform the chaos into logical, ordered, and
understandable events. To accomplish this feat of consideration,
he becomes an author creating his own fictional war story, an
extended daydream beginning with the question "What if?"
The plot involves Third Squad's mission to bring back dumb,
round-faced Cacciato, who in reality had earlier deserted the

unit and was inexplicably walking to Paris. In a little over six hours, Berlin imagines a six-month, 8,600-mile odyssey as Cacciato leads Third Squad through a host of countries in Asia and Europe. The twenty chapters devoted to this story contain snatches of adventure, realism, surrealism, allegory, black humor, psychology, and philosophy. Since even in this mission Berlin the character is still a soldier and still part of a war, the ordered narrative emerges as Berlin the author's elaborate metaphor for Berlin the soldier's relationship to the actual war. As a result, parallels between the fictional and real worlds abound: activities (a real search-and-destroy mission in a village becomes a fantasy mission on a train to Chittagong); horrors (a beheading in Tehran); and issues of responsibility, courage, and cowardice ("tell me that it [the mission after Cacciato] is an alibi to cover cowardice": p. 276). Once again, Berlin, this time a character in his own creation, seeks to control his fears and to confront the ultimate question of whether to pursue a separate peace.

Surprisingly, despite the free play of his imagination, Berlin the author does not turn his central character into a brave and self-assured John Wayne figure. Instead, like Berlin the soldier, this imaginary Berlin marches at the end of the squad, daydreams, and is frequently afraid. He, too, is incontinent during moments of fear: "falling, he felt the fear fill his stomach. He had to pee. . . . He couldn't control himself" (p. 104). Furthermore, Berlin the character searches for order and rhythm, not in a basketball game but in the cities to which Third Squad travels. In Mandalay and later in Paris, Berlin is happy: "There was order in the streets. There was harmony . . . there was concord and human commerce and the ordinary pleasantries" (p. 143).

Yet the Berlin of the fictive world differs from his double. He is part of a mission having order, sequence, and purpose – to bring back the deserter Cacciato. As a result, Berlin frequently breaks out of his role as follower and actively searches for Cacciato. In Tehran, he drives the escape car; in Mandalay, he becomes angry, disrupting the monks' evening prayers as he struggles to capture Cacciato ("such a hero. . . . Such a brave Spec Four": p. 150); and when the train finally arrives in Paris, he is the "*first* to step down" (p. 344; my italics). Most important, Berlin the character cannot ignore the major decision that Berlin the soldier has steadfastly avoided – "Whether to flee or fight." Cacciato, through his spontaneous or brilliantly planned desertion (the answer is never clear), has provided Berlin with a possible model of courage to leave the war and to attain freedom. Will Berlin act in a similar way and like soldiers before him (Frederic Henry in *A Farewell to Arms* and Yossarian in *Catch-22*) declare a separate peace? As any good author knows, Berlin must fashion a dramatic ending for his story. In Paris he must decide whether to desert Third Squad or to continue the mission.

In his own version of the Paris Peace Talks, Berlin the author presents Berlin the character with the carefully delineated choices. When Third Squad reaches Paris in this imaginary journey, Sarkin Aung Wan, Vietnamese refugee from the war who has accompanied the squad and has often been its spiritual guide, challenges Berlin about his desire to escape the war. She presses him to overcome his fears and to act bravely on his dreams by remaining in Paris and declaring a separate peace:

> "I [Sarkin] am asking for a break from violence. But I am also asking for a positive commitment. . . . Give up this fruitless pursuit of Cacciato. Forget him. Live now the dream you have dreamed. See Paris and enjoy it. Be happy. It is possible. It is within reach of a single decision." (p. 374)

Despite the attractiveness of such a life, Berlin's response, one typical of many soldiers, is to remain with the Third Squad.

Citing reasons strikingly similar to Tim O'Brien's explanation in *If I Die* for not deserting the Army ("Family, the home town, friends, history, tradition, fear, confusion, exile": [1973] 1979, 73), and anticipating Tim's similar response to his draft notice in "On the Rainy River," Berlin justifies his decision by citing obligations and tacit promises "to my family, my friends, my town, my country, my fellow soldiers" ([1978] 1979, 376). He admits that fear of social consequences also controls his action: "I am afraid of running away. I am afraid of exile. . . . I fear the loss of my own reputation. . . . I fear being thought a coward" (p. 377). Even in his imagination, he cannot escape the soldier's fear of society's censure, the fear of being found wanting. To his credit, Berlin acknowledges his temerity, but reasons that he hopes to attain an "honorable and lasting" inner peace by continuing the search for Cacciato. Neither the bonds of community – with the soldiers in the Third Squad and with the people at home – nor the fears of estrangement are to be broken. His words to Sarkin Aung Wan echo those of a German soldier from World War I explaining in Erich Remarque's *The Road Back* why he did not leave his unit in the midst of combat:

> But we have seen the other side [the horrors of war]. Yet we went through with it – we went through with it because there was something deeper that held us together, something that only showed up out there, a responsibility, perhaps, but at any rate something of which you know nothing and about which there can be no speeches. (p. 126)

Berlin, making a decision of the head rather than of the heart, assumes responsibility for his actions and reaffirms his commitment to Third Squad and its mission. At this moment, Berlin the character, unlike the soldier, no longer unthinkingly follows events. His actions are no longer reflexive. He briefly acknowledges his fears, acts upon them, and consciously controls his destiny, if only momentarily. His decision is not based on political considerations but upon social and human realities, including his own frailties (cowardice?) as well as his sense of obligation.

Even if this decision is only one more imaginary act in this odyssey played out in this quasi-author's imagination, it still troubles some readers. Arthur Saltzman condemns Berlin's refusal to leave the war as a "disqualification of imagination as a means of salvation" (1980, 36) from chaos; and other critics, as well as readers of "On the Rainy River," might cite Berlin's decision as more evidence of his failure to act upon his convictions – as a soldier, an author, and a character. For them, he is a coward. But, for readers of *If I Die*, Berlin's decision is, perhaps, not surprising. Not only has O'Brien's real-life decision about desertion anticipated Berlin's, but also this decision in Paris extends O'Brien's examination of various forms of courage throughout both books: "THE ISSUE, OF

COURSE, was courage. How to behave. Whether to flee or fight or seek an accommodation. The issue was not fearlessness" ([1978] 1979, 101).

From O'Brien's perspective in this particular novel, Berlin's rejection of Sarkin Aung Wan's plea to leave the war requires a form of courage. In fact, in discussing O'Brien's "myth of courage," critic Milton J. Bates characterizes Berlin's action to commit himself to Third Squad and to the flawed human community of family, friends, and country as a "kind of courage" combining "masculine endurance with feminine commitment" (1987, 278). Furthermore, reading carefully O'Brien's chapter on "Wise Endurance" in *If I Die*, we find a long philosophical discussion of courage interspersed with examples of brave men from literature, film, and his own Vietnam experiences. Citing Plato, O'Brien defines courage as a "wise courage": "It's acting wisely, acting wisely when fear would have a man act otherwise. It is the endurance of the soul in spite of fear – wisely" ([1973] 1979, 137). Courageous people do not commit unthinking acts of bravery. They confront their fears, consider the consequences of their actions in terms of right and wrong, and *act*. Thus, Paul Berlin in his exchange with Sarkin displays a spiritual courage combining understanding, endurance, and commitment. He realizes that, because of his background, his relationships with people at home and in Third Squad, and the stigma attached to deserters, leaving the war will bring him an uneasy peace – embarrassment as well as a physical and spiritual exile. Even in imagination, authors must be guided by wisdom and be true to their feelings; therefore, after careful consideration, Berlin chooses to fight rather than to flee.

The final group of chapters (ten), each entitled "Observation Post" and set in the present time of the book, also contains Berlin's meditations about courage (again presented in the third person) during this night of remembering and creating. These short chapters serve as the fulcrum for the book: the point at which the "what really happened" chapters extend into the "what might have happened" chapters. The observation-post sections also allow Berlin the quasi-author and O'Brien the real author to pause momentarily in their jumping back and forth in time and place and between fact and fantasy. More important, in these chapters O'Brien continues to focus on Berlin's struggle with fear and control: "This night posted by the sea, he was brave and wide awake and nimbleheaded. His fingers tingled. Excited by the possibilities, but still in control" ([1978] 1979, 84). In these ten chapters, O'Brien also complicates Paul's consideration of these issues. Through the reflections of Berlin, a surrogate, O'Brien examines the author's quest to control his materials and his imagination in creating a war story, a subject taken up again in *The Things They Carried*. Thus, although Berlin is constructing only an elaborate daydream about the journey to Paris, he struggles with the rudiments of artistic creation: musing on such issues as the power and limits of imagination, the strategies of narrative, and the relationship between the author's experiences and the world he creates.[8] O'Brien, portraying the artist as a young soldier, reveals Berlin's thought process as this soldier turned author imagines events never consciously anticipated or moves back and forth between facts of his Vietnam tour and their transformation into fiction. Finally, O'Brien, through Berlin, explores how creation may lead to consideration and self-knowledge.

Thus, sitting in a tower adjacent to the South China Sea, Berlin the author periodically reflects on his problems in shaping the basic elements for the tale – the facts of the soldier's stint in Vietnam. As noted earlier, he, like real soldier-authors, has difficulty giving form to these Vietnam experiences. They lack order, development, and a unified plot:

> Order was the hard part. The facts even when beaded on a chain still did not have real order. Events did not flow. The facts were separate and haphazard and random, even as they happened, episodic, broken, no smooth transitions, no sense of events unfolding from prior events. (p. 248)

Yet, like any skilled author, Berlin trusts his imagination to transform the material into a coherent story: "A truly awesome notion. Not a dream, an idea. An idea to develop, to tinker with and build and sustain, to draw out as an artist draws out his visions" (p. 43). He believes that such an act of invention will give him the sense of order, control, and meaning missing for Berlin the soldier. The activity will be an opportunity neatly to separate past, present, and future; to explore the possibilities;

to find answers about fear and flight; to view the war from a new angle; and to survive.

Berlin begins with the last known fact, Cacciato's actual desertion, and proceeds carefully with his story of what might have happened. He anticipates arriving at a logical conclusion and a happy ending. Inspired by his fear biles, he is "excited by the possibilities" and secure in his control over the story. After a relaxed bowel movement in the sea, he returns to the tower ready to create his imaginary journey: "That was the important part – he was in control. He was calm. Clear thinking helped. Concentrating, figuring out the details" (p. 84). This apprentice author builds and sustains his idea; orders the facts; describes appropriate sights, sounds, and feelings; establishes cause-and-effect relationships among events; provides proper motivations and background for characters; and even anticipates skeptical critics' remarks. His imagination swiftly cuts through obstacles in the narrative – the trivial details such as money, passports, and plausibility – and moves to the important issues – courage, fear, flight, accommodation, and happiness.

Despite Berlin's confidence in controlling his creation, the narrative does not proceed smoothly. He unexpectedly learns lessons about pitfalls novelists face and limits of the imagination. Soon he finds himself unable to concentrate solely on the story, as past and present (chapters of fact and the observation post) momentarily interrupt the tale and eventually merge with it. Other moments occur in the creative process when Berlin also loses control of the narrative as his imagination lapses and events lead to unexpected events. The anticipated story, a smooth arc from war to peace, assumes a direction and tone independent of the author's plan: "How it started as one thing, a happy thing, and how it was becoming something else. No harm intended. But it was out of control. Events taking their own track" (p. 166). Consequently, during the climactic Paris episode, the anticipated happy ending is impossible. Order in the final episodes of the Cacciato story is achieved; however, it is not imposed by this author. Instead, the order emerges internally from the logic of the narrative and externally from the realities of Berlin the soldier's character and his impending decisions. Art and life merge as Berlin's imagination fails to break the constraints of the empirical world. As a result, this author, like many artists, must acknowledge his limitations. Just as the character Paul Berlin acknowledges his obligations to others, so Berlin the author accepts the realities of the fictive world he has created: "Even in imagination we must be true to our obligations, for, even in imagination obligation cannot be outrun. Imagination, like reality, has its limits" (p. 378). In the final scene, the quasi-author loses complete control as fiction merges with reality. After Berlin rejects a separate peace, the novice author cannot imagine an ending for the Cacciato tale, only remember it: Berlin the soldier's fear during the real confrontation with Cacciato at dawn on a hill in Vietnam.

In the book's final chapter, Berlin's past, present, and future narrative strands collide as Berlin the soldier, character, and author loses control. O'Brien, as a result, intrudes and assumes control. He orders the disordered form and content by weaving together the three narrative strands and completing this exploration of the three Berlins' consideration of courage and their quest for control. After Berlin the character, taking control of his destiny, decides not to accept Sarkin's offered peace, happiness, and order of Paris, he joins Third Squad in a dawn ambush outside Cacciato's Paris apartment. Crouched outside the door, he feels his fear coming on, but he also thinks about the elusive Silver Star. "Go" – he enters the apartment – "Then he felt his fear" (p. 388). O'Brien and Berlin, the soldier-author, have been inexorably moving to this scene, for with this line the three Berlins – author, soldier, and character – merge, as does past, present, and future. Berlin's fear of consequences if he deserts merges with his physical fear on the battlefield. In this last chapter, the "Go" uttered in Paris returns O'Brien, Berlin, and the readers to the "Go" uttered on the seventh day of the real journey after Cacciato, which ends the first chapter: "'Go,' whispered Paul Berlin. It did not seem enough. 'Go,' he said, and then he shouted, 'Go'" (p. 42). Throughout the intervening pages, Berlin's imagination and memory have avoided the most important fact of the book, the real event occurring after the "Go" of chapter 1 – Berlin's embarrassing moment of uncontrollable physical fear. Perhaps Berlin's fantasy tale about Cacciato has been merely an escape, a simple alibi to cover cowardice. But unavoidably the character's fear in the imagined Paris ambush suddenly turns into a remembered fear in the actual ambush of

Cacciato: a moment when the soldier lost control of his fear, lost control of his weapon (fired wildly), and lost control of his body (urinated in his pants). With this final fact, Berlin and O'Brien arrive at the end and the beginning, for this event marks the point where reality ended and fantasy began.

The significance of Berlin's six-hour imaginary journey through a physical and metaphysical darkness is that this soldier turned author, who before this night might have endured without understanding, ponders from various perspectives the consequences of fleeing and confronts his fears of exile and cowardice. He is no longer an unthinking soldier helplessly dragged along by Third Squad, the war, and his fears. During this night of observation, he journeys into his heart and mind attempting to explore and release the potential of what he might be. It is an example of Fussell's consideration stage in a soldier's evolution, and it is a journey that both Henry Fleming and Tim O'Brien the soldier, through their own consideration of courage, have also undertaken. Finally, it is an activity that Lieutenant Sidney Martin in *Going After Cacciato* believes is a soldier's most significant mission: "The overriding mission was the inner mission, the mission of every man to learn the important things about himself" (p. 201). True, Berlin does not achieve complete understanding, but through imagination he briefly establishes order in and control over his life. He also realizes the limits of this power: "The war was still a war, and he was still a soldier. He hadn't run. The issue was courage, and courage was will power, and this was his failing" (p. 379).

But does Berlin fail? True, his final assessment reveals his weakness. Yet at the same time it also highlights his newly found strength of character and the extent of his change from an unthinking soldier to one who has completed the metaphysical mission and momentarily controls his destiny. For some readers, the truly courageous act might have been for Berlin to follow the dictates of his heart and leave the war. But, despite doubting the war and acknowledging his physical embarrassment on the battlefield, Berlin refuses to flee. His courage to remain, affirmed in the imagination as well as in reality, does not translate into Henry Fleming's heroic actions on the battlefield. Nor does Berlin assume Caputo's romantic courage or the foolish courage of the quasi-soldier Herr. Instead, his is an ordinary but significant courage, one based upon a wise endurance in spite of fear and found among average, decent people. It is the common courage described earlier in *If I Die*: "You promise, almost moving your lips, to do better the next time; that by itself is a kind of courage" ([1973] 1979, 147).

At the thematic level, then, *Going After Cacciato* appears to be a straightforward novel. Just as Cacciato leads Berlin through a literal and figurative journey to partial understanding, O'Brien takes the reader on a journey exploring a soldier's fear. The portrait of fear is, however, part of a larger theme involving a soldier's, a character's, a quasi-author's, and even an author's pursuit of control to overcome the fear and to arrive at some degree of understanding in the midst of confusion and chaos. The setting for this quest, the disorder of the Vietnam War, complicates the novelist's task and turns the novel into a complex work. O'Brien faces the problem of capturing the special character of the Vietnam experience (episodic, confused, and illogical) within a fictional framework providing unity, coherence, perspective, and meaning. His solution to these artistic problems, a structure that counterpoints and mirrors the content, is an important feature of the book. Order opposes disorder. The disordered facts of the soldier's existence oppose the orderly progression of the tale about Cacciato, which – however – ends in confusion. On another level, the underlying unity and meaning of the novel counterbalance the surface disorder and multiple perspectives present in O'Brien's telling of Berlin's story. Unlike his quasi-author, O'Brien controls his material. Among the chapters, he carefully establishes structural, metaphorical, and thematic connections through a controlled juxtaposing or mixing of the three narrative strands, and he ties the multiple perspectives to one person.

Indeed, O'Brien's imagination and craftsmanship succeed in creating a complex, thoughtful novel. He achieves a formal completeness in this work missing in Berlin's tale, and he sustains a thematic depth and unity absent from *If I Die*. Moreover, the author reveals the value of imagination, his own and Berlin's, as a means of holding events in one's consciousness so they can be confronted, studied, and perhaps understood. He has followed Major Van Hgoc's advice to view things from many angles. The result is that, like Crane, O'Brien transcends the boundaries of time and place to consider once more central issues of traditional war stories – courage, fear, and manhood. Most important, *Going After Cacciato*, through its form and content, establishes art as a salvation in the midst of chaos: a source of order and truth in a study of the ambiguous human spirit. In the process, this novel becomes one of the most sophisticated war stories extending the form and content of this genre.

5

Aftermath

... he had realized he wanted to live. But how? How to
live with the legacies of war, with his loss of faith, his guilt
and nightmares?

Philip Caputo, *Indian Country*

Veterans living with the legacies of war, in particular the
aftermath of the Vietnam War, are the subjects of this chapter. Although not specifically mentioned by Fussell, this final
postwar stage (aftermath) logically extends his three stages
of a soldier's evolution. It combines considering one's war
experiences, the heart of the third stage, with struggling to
live in a civilian world, a new element. Having lost their innocence on the battlefield in a heart-of-darkness experience, and
having acquired an apocalyptic understanding of war, returning
American soldier-authors and their characters complete their
literal and spiritual journeys as they and their country grapple
with the consequences of Vietnam. It's a final stage that James
Jones labels the "DE-EVOLUTION OF A SOLDIER": "As the old
combat numbness disappeared, and the frozen feet of the soul
began to thaw, the pain of the cure became evident" (1975, 256).
Bearing physical and psychological scars, exhilaration mixed
with guilt at surviving the war, and memories of their war
experiences, these Vietnam survivors quickly exit the Vietnam
battlefields only to return alone to the United States and
another battleground. Once home they often encounter a hostile
or indifferent public; endure media images of veterans who
are drug-crazed, ticking time-bombs; feel alienated from the
civilian world; and inexplicably may long to return to the war.

167

Previously discussed Vietnam soldier-authors have briefly touched upon these difficult homecomings: Caputo in *A Rumor of War* describes his isolation in an alien civilian world after his military discharge; Herr describes his post-Vietnam malaise as the "Survivor Shuffle"; and Dosier in *Close Quarters* refers to his adjustment period in the States as a "Climbing Down." Webb's returning veteran, Goodrich, feels out of place on a college campus, and Staff Sergeant Gilliland in his Marine uniform endures a hurled bottle and taunts of "Fascist" as he hitchhikes home in California. Finally, Del Vecchio's Lieutenant Brooks has an inkling of this difficult "return to the World" as he and his wife suffer through a strained seven-day R & R in Hawaii where they discover that "they were both from different worlds" (1982, 380). In three recently published novels, two soldier-authors and a civilian survivor of the Vietnam era draw upon some of these feelings and incidents as they deal exclusively with the aftermath of Vietnam. One book, Heinemann's *Paco's Story*, examines the returning veteran's and society's adjustment trauma; the other two, Caputo's *Indian Country* and Mason's *In Country*, chronicle the struggles of veterans and their families in dealing with the war's aftereffects. All three novelists forgo lengthy anti- or pro-war messages to focus on human relationships shadowed by the Vietnam experience.

For these three authors, writing about this post-Vietnam stage is to enter a realm of controversial views, conflicting statistics, myths, misinformation, politics, bitterness, sympathy, poignant stories, self-aggrandizement, and media-perpetuated stereotypes such as the one suggested in the following newspaper headline: "Vietnam vet goes on rampage in Chicago; 5 dead (*Indianapolis Star*, 16 May 1988).[1] In reality, like veterans from other wars, the majority of American Vietnam veterans, men and women, have adjusted quietly and smoothly to their postwar life. Their undramatic stories remain, for the most part, untold.[2] But for other Vietnam veterans the future is bleaker: unemployment, drug use, criminal activity, marital difficulties, government apathy, and possible physical side-effects of exposure to Agent Orange. In fact some studies suggest that approximately half a million combat veterans (half of the soldiers who saw combat in Vietnam), as well as a significant number of nurses and support personnel, suffer from some lasting degree of psychological reaction to their war experiences.[3] This condition, which since 1980 the American Psychiatric Association has labeled Post-Traumatic Stress Disorder (PTSD), is characterized by spontaneous flashbacks to events in Vietnam; recurring nightmares; emotional numbness; guilt; a craving for isolation; and periods of panic, depression, malaise, and rage.[4] Yet in ways these reactions are similar to those associated with "shell shock" exhibited by World War I veterans, the "battle fatigue" of World War II soldiers, or the "operational exhaustion" diagnosed among Korean veterans.[5] In fact Willard Waller documents feelings of alienation, depression, and numbness in returning World War II veterans, as well as their bitter resentment of civilians" complacency toward their plight. He refers to these combatants as "immigrants in [their] native land" (1944, 93–110), a label that seems equally appropriate for many Vietnam veterans. Vietnam PTSD is, perhaps, a severer form of battle-related stress occasioned by a few special features of the Vietnam War: the young age of American soldiers, the seemingly inconclusive nature of the war and the battles, the brutality of combat emerging from a body-count strategy, a soldier's individual entrance into and exit from the war, and the limited tour of duty. Or, as Larry Heinemann suggests, the severity of the psychological reactions may simply result from the distinct difference from previous wars in "how society has chosen to deal with the Vietnam veteran" (1985, 62). Veterans, researchers, historians, and authors continue to debate these issues, and the various points of view influence the three Vietnam narratives in this chapter.

Unquestionably, significant portions of post-Vietnam American society and the military, unlike in previous postwar periods, felt uncomfortable with the war and its participants. Some segments upset with the country's involvement in Vietnam transferred their abhorrence for the war to the American soldiers who fought there, tagging the combatants "baby killers" involved in an immoral war. On the other side, another segment of Americans, angered with the negative media images of American troops in Vietnam and the disappointing results of the war effort, characterized these same soldiers as "losers." A majority of Americans simply wanted to engage in collective amnesia about the war and the veterans. Frederick Downs in *Aftermath*, a nonfictional account of his recovery from serious battle wounds received in Vietnam, comments on the absence of welcome-home rituals for the returning veterans. In particular, he wonders why there were no bands or parades. Conditioned by newsreels and Hollywood's scenes of wildly enthusiastic greetings for returning World War II "heroes," Downs, at each stage of his re-entry, expected some public recognition of his sacrifices:

> As I was loaded onto the Medivac flight the next morning for the final leg to Denver, I resolved to be conscious when we arrived so I wouldn't miss the band and welcoming committee. I had expected it at each stop and there had been none. But I had rationalized each disappointment. Since Denver would be my final stop, I knew they would be waiting for us – just like movies and books had always portrayed. ([1984] 1985, 95)

But at each stage Downs was disappointed. Perhaps as the ultimate personal symbol of America's confusion and unconcern for Vietnam veterans, this soldier-author relates that after months of recuperating from his wounds in a military hospital in Denver he returned to Terre Haute, Indiana, only to find that his soon-to-be ex-wife had *forgotten* to meet him at the airport.

Similar episodes of rejection and alienation confront the central characters in Caputo's, Heinemann's, and Mason's books, as soldiers turned civilians grapple with their emotional, spiritual, and physical scars carried from the battlefield, a postwar version of O'Brien's short story "The Things They Carried." Consequently, the brotherhood of soldiers extending across wars and formed by similar battlefield experiences and feelings is once more affirmed in these war stories about Vietnam homecomings. For example, like many of his Vietnam counterparts, "The Veteran" Henry Fleming in *The Red Badge of Courage* simply and honestly relates his unromantic story years later about his fear on the battlefield. And in Remarque's *All Quiet on the Western Front* Paul Baumer's reflections on his battlefield change and expected difficult adjustment to civilian life anticipate similar concerns of some Vietnam veterans:

> [H]ad we returned home in 1916, out of the suffering and the strength of our experience we might have unleashed a storm. Now if we go back we will be weary, broken, burnt out, rootless, and without hope. We will not be able to find our way any more. ([1929] 1987, 294)

Two other World War I soldier-authors adept at examining veterans' psychological scars, disillusionment, and efforts to control their emotions and lives are Wilfred Owen and Ernest Hemingway. Their portrayals of these physical, psychological, and spiritual struggles are particularly helpful entries into the three Vietnam texts.

Owen's fame as one of the best English soldier-poets of World War I emerges from his poems written between January 1917, when he first entered combat in the Battle of the Somme in northern France, and 4 November 1918 (one week before the Armistice ending the war), when he died from machine-gun fire as his men were attempting to cross the Sambre Canal. In between, he spent fifteen months recuperating from shell shock, or "Neurasthenia" as he labels it in one of his letters; voluntarily returned to his unit at the front line in September 1918; and received the Military Cross for bravery in late October.[6] Responding to these extensive war experiences, he wrote his poems to protest the war; to articulate the plight, misery, and fears of the common soldiers; to describe realistically the sights and sounds of trench warfare; and through imagination and a tightly controlled poetic structure to establish order and control in his own chaotic life as an infantry officer on the Western Front.

Owen's war poems contain graphic realism, such as found in "Dulce Et Decorum Est," biting attacks on the war-making establishment at home appearing in "The Parable of the Old Man and the Young," praise of the common soldier in "Greater Love," or the unacknowledged return of the veteran ("creep back, silent") in "The Send-Off." But drawing upon his observations during his own lengthy recuperation from a battle-related concussion and "nerves" at field-hospitals and at the Craiglockhart War Hospital in Edinburgh, Owen also wrote about war's aftermath.[7] For example, two poems deal with veterans" physical and psychological scars. "Disabled," the first of these, portrays the plight of a wheelchair-bound veteran. In this rhymed, iambic-pentameter poem, developed around the typical ironic loss-of-innocence theme, the persona recounts an underage soldier's naïveté about war and his irrational reasons for joining the Army: "He thought he'd better join. – He wonders why./Someone had said he'd look a god in kilts,/That's why; and may be, too, to please his Meg." Later, in this aftermath stage, "he is old," having lost his youth, his legs, and his self-respect on the battlefield, and he is reduced to living in "institutes" and accepting the rules and pity of others. The poem's theme, bitterness, and brooding tone anticipate Dalton Trumbo's *Johnny Got His Gun* and Ron Kovic's *Born on the Fourth of July*, both dealing with the severely wounded veteran. But the poem also poignantly addresses the veteran's feelings of isolation and psychological impotence symbolized by his physical relationship with women: "Now he will never feel again how slim/Girls' waists are, or how warm their subtle hands;/All of them touch him like some queer disease." With an adept bit of irony, Owen conveys the soldier's loss of self-respect as the former football hero finds that "To-night he noticed how the women's eyes/Passed from him to the strong men that were whole." Such a subtle and haunting insight about human nature and relationships reappears in Heinemann's *Paco's Story* and in Mason's *In Country*.

Another Owen poem examining the legacies of war and veterans' miseries is "Mental Cases," which graphically portrays British soldiers suffering from shell shock. Nothing is subtle about this poem filled with Owen's distinctive discordant half-rhymes and his arresting images of the afflicted residing in the living hell of a mental institution: "Drooping tongues from jaws that slop their relish,/Baring teeth that leer like skulls' teeth wicked?/Stroke on stroke of pain." The veterans' shocking outward appearances reflect their inner turmoil occasioned by the involuntary flashbacks to battlefield events and to "murders they once witnessed":

Always they must see these things and hear them
Batter of guns and shatter of flying muscles,

172

Carnage incomparable, and human squander
Rucked too thick for these men's extrication.

These war survivors live in a world without relief, since
every daily event, from breaking dawn to approaching night,
reminds them of their war experiences and heightens their
mental anguish. Owen ends the poem in a customary accu-
satory fashion as he describes the inmates' hands "plucking
at each other": "Snatching after us who smote them, brother,/
Pawing us who dealt them war and madness." Owen's indictment of the speaker and the questioner in the poem also
becomes a savage attack on society by a poet who characterized himself as a "conscientious objector with a very
seared conscience" (Blunden 1965, 167). Characters in the three
Vietnam aftermath novels also suffer from some of the same
inner turmoil and anger as Owen's veterans in "Mental Cases"
and echo the poet's own confusion and bitterness about war.

Another author writing extensively about the destructive
personal consequences of World War I is Ernest Hemingway. Of
course, in portions of his novel *A Farewell to Arms*, Hemingway
examines the results of Frederic Henry's decision to flee the
war and live in Switzerland with Catherine. His short stories,
however, more poignantly portray soldiers living with the
legacies of combat. Specifically, Hemingway's own World War
I tour of duty in 1918 as an ambulance-driver serving in an
American Field Service Unit attached to the Italian army and his
recovery from serious wounds in both legs inspired five short
stories masterfully portraying soldiers in this aftermath stage.[8]
In "Soldier's Home" (1925), Krebs, the disillusioned veteran,
has returned to the States ironically to find himself without a
spiritual home. Doing his own version of the "Survivor Shuffle,"
he is out of place, alienated from his family, religion, and society.
Hemingway also examines the soldier's plight in four of his
Nick Adams short stories, which Joseph M. Flora links through
their "potential" autobiographical connections and their thematic treatment of Nick's various stages of recovery from his
physical and psychological war wounds. Among its prominent
themes, "In Another Country" (1927) promotes the common
perception that people who have fought in war are inevitably

changed by their experience and are different from people who have not. In "Now I Lay Me" (1927) and "A Way You'll Never Be" (1933), Hemingway explores the traumatic psychological consequences of Nick's wounding. The young soldier still in the war zone suffers from hallucinations, insomnia, flashbacks to his wounding, and fears of death. He frequently loses control of his thoughts as well as his words. Furthermore, in "Now I Lay Me," Nick, similar to Paul Berlin in *Going After Cacciato*, engages in a soldier's familiar trick of the mind to occupy his thoughts and to control his fears. In this particular case, Nick's efforts to establish order in his life involve recalling "everything that had ever happened to [him]" (Hemingway 1987, 277)[9] or all the girls he had ever known. But perhaps his best trick to forget the war is to daydream of a "trout stream I had fished along when I was a boy and fish its whole length very carefully in my mind" (p. 276).

In the two-part "Big Two-Hearted River" (1925), the earliest of these four Nick Adams war stories, readers find another trout stream and Hemingway's most intriguing and focused view of the war survivor's efforts to recover from his psychic and physical wounds. This longest Adams story, with its fictitious Big Two-Hearted River and ominous swamp in the Michigan Upper Peninsula, can be read as a simple fishing story without any overt mention of Nick's war experiences.[10] Most critics, however, agree with Carlos Baker's comment that "Nick is a returned veteran seeking some natural therapy" ([1952] 1972, 125–7). Supporting such a view is Hemingway's comment that "the story was about coming back from the war but there was no mention of the war in it" (1964, 76). Still unresolved are questions about the severity of Nick's reactions to his war experiences (a shell-shocked veteran?) and the extent of his difficulty in adjusting to a postwar existence.

But as a literary context for this chapter on the Vietnam aftermath, this symbol-laden short story becomes a parable of a veteran's coming home. In this war story, Hemingway explores how a soldier returning home after the war strives to restore order, comfortable feelings, and psychological well-being in his life and how he cautiously responds to haunting memories of the war and troubling fears of the future. Through Nick's return to a familiar place connected to his prewar life, the "islands of dark pine," the trout "holding steady" in the stream, and the comfortable fishing become natural healers and contrast with the burned-over town of Seney, Michigan (symbol of the war he has left behind), where he begins his literal and psychological journey into the countryside. Nick has arrived at this familiar place having left "everything behind, the need for thinking, the need to write, other needs. It was all back of him" (Hemingway 1987, 164). Also, he has left behind people, preferring instead a therapy of isolation. Recovering from the war and attempting to avoid painful memories, Nick consciously tries to recapture slowly the primitive, pleasant feelings of his prewar existence. Hemingway's simple language ("good," "knew," "felt"), short sentences, and focus on basic positive sensations ("hot," "tired," "happy," "hungry") in the third-person narrative support the underlying theme of Nick's physical and spiritual recovery and renewal. In this comfortable place, described as "homelike," Nick, like soldiers in combat areas, engages in the familiar mind-numbing routines of making camp, cooking meals, and preparing his equipment. Similar to Conrad's Marlow, and characteristic of someone avoiding painful memories and seeking psychic renewal, Nick throws himself into the ritual of these surface actions as he firmly controls his feelings and his thoughts: "His mind was starting to work. He knew he could choke it because he was tired enough" (p. 169).

Nick, the only character in this short story, focuses on present activities and pleasant sensations. Momentarily, the past intrudes as Nick thinks about a previous fishing trip on the Black River and a friend's way of making coffee. Sporadically thoughts of the future emerge as Nick stares at the symbolic swamp – "In the swamp fishing was a tragic adventure" (p. 180). And occasionally Nick's emotions are out of control: "The thrill [hooking and then losing a big trout] had been too much. He felt vaguely, a little sick, as though it would be better to sit down" (p. 177). Nick, however, quickly chokes off these thoughts and feelings, and he concentrates on temporarily establishing a physical and spiritual home, one devoid of complexity, helplessness, randomness, fear, pain, and death – all characteristics of a war environment. The natural setting becomes a haven from his past unpleasant experiences and future obligations. Nick's familiarity with this comfortable home, his surrender to the rituals of camping and fishing, and his consummate skill in these activities allow him to control his thoughts and feelings and for the most part avoid the unexpected. Nick's temporary world is one of concreteness ("solid" tent pegs and "solid" and "steady" trout) and one in which the most often repeated phrase is Nick "knew."

Admittedly Nick is escaping, another trick to forget the war, but his fishing trip is a starting-point for his spiritual and psychological homecoming and an opportunity for a gradual climbing down that will enable him to begin recovering from the war and to acknowledge what lies behind and ahead: "He looked back. The river just showed through the trees. There were plenty of days coming when he could fish the swamp" (p. 180). Left unresolved are the length, difficulty, and outcome of this veteran's journey home from his own heart-of-darkness experience. In the three Vietnam narratives about homecomings, we encounter other veterans engaged in similar quests for spiritual recovery and a comfortable home – physical and emotional. They share Nick's desire for isolation, his fears of the past and future, and his struggle to establish order and meaning in his life. Unlike Nick, however, they exist in the midst of complex relationships and an often inhospitable environment.

Like "Big Two-Hearted River," Philip Caputo's *Indian Country*, published in 1987, emerges from the axiom that "wars don't end when the shooting stops and the treaties are signed. They go on and on in the wounded minds of those who did the fighting" ([1987] 1988, 395). Caputo's third novel takes readers to the American home front where, long after the fall of South Vietnam, the war still affects combatants and noncombatants. In moving from the battlefield to the "real world," Caputo and the other two novelists examining war's legacies develop different conflicts, themes, and character relationships related to the overall Vietnam experience. The battlefield is no longer the only prominent setting in these novels, and the central relationship of a soldier with the war is coupled with important domestic relationships. Within this framework, Caputo takes readers back to the Hemingway country of "Big Two-Hearted River" – the trout streams, forests, and physical isolation of the Michigan Upper Peninsula. He also includes echoes of Hemingway's initiation stories involving a young Nick Adams and Native Americans – specifically "Indian Camp" and "The Doctor and the Doctor's Wife." An additional coincidental (?) Hemingway connection is the central character's birthplace – Oak Park, Illinois, Hemingway's own hometown. Caputo's traditional novel emphasizes realism (at times a clinical study of psychological disorders) and conflicting human relationships. It also exhibits other thematic trappings of Hemingway's short stories: boyhood hunting and fishing trips, father–son relationships, and a soldier's struggle to live with the legacies of combat. In fact the book often appears to be a contemporary "Big Two-Hearted River" with the opening flashback scene set on a trout stream in the Michigan Upper Peninsula and the central character, Christian (Chris) Starkmann, seeking relief from the mental anguish of war's aftereffects through the psychotherapy of nature.

However, in this psychological case-study of a Vietnam veteran suffering from Post-Traumatic Stress Disorder, instead of ending the story with the ominous word "swamp," Caputo ends his narrative with the equally symbolic word "home." Significantly, this book is indeed about characters" quests to find physical and spiritual homes as they struggle to survive the aftermath of the Vietnam War. The title *Indian Country* refers literally to the setting of the book but also to American soldiers' use of the term in Vietnam to designate hostile territory. It also suggests the hostile psychological landscape that Vietnam veteran Chris Starkmann spends several years traversing. His goal, like Nick Adams's, is the ever-elusive control and order in his life. On this psychological journey he carries with him considerable psychic baggage: guilt at having enlisted in the military against his father's wishes, horror at having watched his boyhood friend die in Vietnam, tensions from a marriage wrecked by his unwillingness to share his Vietnam experiences with a sympathetic wife, and his inability to forgive himself for events occurring during his tour of duty. The war's legacies threaten all the relationships in this novel.

At the narrative and psychological core of this work is Starkmann's friendship with the Ojibwa Indian Bonniface (Bonny) George. As young boys, their relationship began when

Chris's father hired Bonny's grandfather, an Indian medicine man and hunting guide, during one of the Starkmanns' annual summer trips to the Upper Peninsula. Over ten years the friendship grew, culminating in an incident on a fishing trip when Bonny saved Chris from drowning. Caputo uses this relationship to highlight documented racial and social inequities in the Vietnam draft: a rich man's war; a poor man's fight. The poor, proud Native American, raised by his grandfather, is drafted into the Army, while Chris, a middle-class white kid with a deferment to attend divinity school, can ignore military obligations: "That men like Bonny George had no real choices, while men like himself could live their lives as they pleased, offended his sense of fairness" (p. 46). When Chris's attempts at draft counseling fail (urging Bonny to flee to Canada), Chris, out of loyalty to his friend, his own desire for adventure, and rebellion against his anti-war activist father, also enlists in the Army. In a situation right out of the Vietnam film *The Deer Hunter*, these two friends end up in the same military unit in Vietnam.

Aided by clues and lengthy narrative flashbacks, readers must play detective to figure out the traumatic event at the core of Chris's and Bonny's Vietnam experiences. Eventually we learn that Chris is responsible for Bonny's death from friendly fire (napalm). Panicking during an enemy attack, Chris gave the wrong coordinates to the fighter pilots attempting to save his company during this attack. Haunted by Bonny's dying words to Chris – "I saved you from the water, but you killed me with the fire" (p. 70) – he spends most of the book alternately denying and grappling with this war legacy. This contrived thematic thread ties together the novel's diverse plot lines and character interaction. Chris's survival guilt becomes one more part of the complex psychological puzzle of the scarred veteran that Caputo creates.

Two key father–son relationships shaped by the war establish interesting parallels and contrasts in the novel and contribute to the psychological study. In both relationships, sons are lost – physically and spiritually – to the war, but the fathers react in markedly different ways. After the death of his parents, Bonny is raised by his grandfather Louis St Germaine, who as Wawiekumig (an Ojibwa medicine man and mystic) teaches his grandson about Indian fatalism, tribal lore, and the beauty and mystical powers of nature. When Bonny faces his difficult decision about entering the military, he turns to his grandfather for advice and receives the counsel to fight not flee the war. Thus, after his grandson's death in Vietnam, Louis spends fourteen years grieving for his grandson, experiencing a form of survivor guilt for his advice, and seeking through mystical vision quests the reason why his grandson died. Unlike Bonny, Christian (note the symbolic name) returns to his father after his tour in Vietnam, but the elder Starkmann believes he has lost his son spiritually to the war: "My son left a long time ago. . . . He never came back" (p. 105). This Lutheran minister, who was a conscientious objector in World War II, a civil rights activist, and an outspoken critic of the Vietnam War, still cannot accept his son's voluntary enlistment in the military – "it was the obligation of all young Americans to refuse service" (p. 29). A fervent liberal in public, Lucius Starkmann is a cold, autocratic, unforgiving father at home. Caputo's sketchy portrait of this anti-war activist turns the father into the novel's villain and through guilt by association unfairly creates a negative image of the anti-war movement. Reverend Starkmann represents the people at home incapable of separating their political feelings about the Vietnam War from their attitudes about those who participated in it. The father also represents one side in Chris's spiritual conflict between his religion and his actions on the battlefield. Thus, exiled from his home, his father, and his religion, Chris lives with the guilt of having ignored his father's commands and longs for forgiveness and acceptance – something denied him even as his father lies dying in a hospital. On a symbolic level, Chris's plea to his father fourteen years after returning from Vietnam – "Hold me and say it ['Welcome home, son']" (p. 263) – becomes the quest of many Vietnam veterans for their country's acceptance.

In many ways all these relationships are Caputo's vehicles for developing mystery and melodramatic conflict in the novel, and they contribute additional psychological baggage for Chris to carry with him. But in Chris's relationship with his wife, June, Caputo develops an in-depth, gripping account of two people trapped in the psychological aftermath of the war. The depiction of their stormy marriage generates the book's emotional intensity and its literary merit. More so than Sarkin Aung Wan in *Going After Cacciato*, June is the first female character in the seven Vietnam narratives discussed so far who is presented with a depth, sensitivity, and appeal worthy of a central character. Furthermore, she may be the hero in the novel. The often violent conflicts occasioned by misunderstandings in Chris and June's nine-year marriage illustrate the timeless adage that it's difficult, if not impossible, for veterans to explain war and their feelings to people who have never had similar experiences. June represents the noncombatants on the home front desperately seeking to understand the Vietnam experience and the soldiers who returned from the conflict. Her contact with Vietnam veterans prior to meeting Chris was limited to stereotyped newspaper accounts of how Vietnam had "weirded-out a lot of guys" (p. 119). Yet, despite this unfamiliarity with the war and veterans, she is in many ways best-equipped to deal with Chris's invisible wounds, and as she learns more about her husband's problems, she undergoes her own loss of innocence related to the war and its aftermath.

In several ways, this husband and wife are kindred spirits, both suffering from alienation and psychic turmoil. Like Chris, June perceives herself as an outcast – born into Appalachian-style poverty in the Upper Peninsula, abandoned by her first husband, and obsessed with a need for respectability and stability in her life. A strong-willed individual and social worker in a child-support bureau, she is an advocate for women and families abandoned by men. She carries her own fears of abandonment, along with mental flashbacks of domestic violence, loneliness, transience, and the impermanence of love in her own life. Her fears, tenacious spirit, and love for her husband won't allow her to abandon Chris, despite his psychological turmoil, moroseness, and subjection of the family to an isolated and barren existence. She senses that he is "imprisoned" by the war and that the war is her rival in the struggle for her husband's attention. But in spite of June's best intentions Chris is incapable of responding to her sincere efforts to understand. Instead, he lashes out in anger or physical abuse to her pleas for communication. For both, their marriage appears to be nothing more than opportunities for sexual release from their psychological devils; neither can break through the barriers of silence:

> She knew the signs of a deteriorating marriage. . . . She wanted to fight to save it . . . but she didn't know what she was fighting against. Her adversary seemed . . . a menace without face, form, or name. (p. 134)

How can veterans receive sympathy and understanding if they are unwilling to share their feelings and stories with others and instead respond with silence or even violence to sincere offers of help? On the other hand, how can veterans be expected to articulate the horrors, the guilt, the nightmares, the disgust – the unspeakable – to people whose only contact with war has been through war stories or the media? Overcoming these seemingly insurmountable barriers between people becomes the central issue in this marriage. Caputo unties this Gordian knot in an undramatic but plausible fashion. June doesn't suddenly become Chris's confidante. Rather, she is unsuccessful in alternately bullying and cajoling Chris into responding to her. And finally, after Chris's brutal sexual attack on her, she leaves their remote home, taking their two children. But June does love Chris, and she realizes that Chris is psychologically consumed by his Vietnam experiences. His bizarre actions aren't a conscious attack on her, but an outward manifestation of the war's inner hold on him. Because of June's tenacity and support, Chris is eventually able to admit that he does love his kids and wife, wants to save his marriage, and must turn to someone to find help.

Starkmann's lengthy struggle to suppress this psychological turmoil forms the basis of the other central relationship in the novel, the Vietnam veteran's relationship with the self. Caputo's message about a soldier's deliverance from the war's psychological demons is pointed if not overly simplistic – "Heal Thyself." June's support provides impetus for Chris's quest; and a Vietnam veteran working as a clinical psychologist with a veterans outreach program guides Chris on his journey toward self-discovery. Nevertheless, Chris must, on his own, arrive at insights, forgive himself, and feel comfortable away from the battlefield. In sections of the novel dealing with this self-relationship, Caputo often reverts to his nonfictional narrative style and journalistic detail of *A Rumor of War*. The novelist disappears, replaced by the reporter doing a feature story on Post-Traumatic Stress Disorder among Vietnam veterans. Often the psychologist, Dr Eckhardt, speaks to the readers – not to the other characters – as he clinically explains what Chris is experiencing, or he becomes the mouthpiece for veterans' complaints about their treatment after the war:

> "That's Ulysses [*The Odyssey*] speaking," the psychologist said, resuming his seat. "Wishing he'd died with his comrades instead of being cast adrift by Poseidon. 'I should have had a soldier's burial and praise from the Achaians.' We didn't get either, did we, Chris? We survived the war, and instead of being praised, we got cursed. We were treated like shit, weren't we?" (p. 335)

As further evidence of this journalistic approach, Chris seems patterned after the real "tripwire" veterans living in isolation in the deep woods of Washington's Olympic Peninsula, whom Larry Heinemann profiles in his *Harper's* article.[11] As a result, Chris frequently appears to be a composite, for he displays most of the classic symptoms of PTSD – everything from his fear of going to sleep to his brooding silence, paranoia, acute depressive reactions, guilt, violence, spontaneous flashbacks, and obsessive desire to be alone. But Caputo the novelist creates the situations where these symptoms surface, portrays the conflicts they create, and imagines their resolution.

Certainly, Chris Starkmann is a tortured veteran: guilt-ridden, paranoid, grief-stricken, depressed, and uncommunicative. He is torn between two worlds. Seeking a haven in the past through memory and imagination, he finds that part of him is still in Vietnam and that the other part tries to find a comfortable spiritual home in an inhospitable civilian world. As he notes in an imaginary conversation with his father, "See, all of me never came home. . . . I've been here in the States, what is it now? Thirteen years. But part of me is still *there*. I don't know why, but it is" (p. 261). When life in the States becomes particularly threatening, Chris, nicknamed "Preacher" because he read the Bible in Vietnam, mentally returns to Vietnam as he displays the characteristic nostalgia for the battlefield and his friends – "He belonged there. The bush was his true home, and his nostalgia for it was so strong that, when he closed his eyes, his mind seemed to leave his body, entering another dimension in which it traveled backward in time" (p. 100). On these occasions he escapes through his imagination by conversing with three of his fellow-soldiers – DJ, Hutch, and Ramos – to overcome the loneliness of his postwar existence. They seem to be the only people who can possibly understand Chris's inner turmoil. But even this re-created Vietnam with its "musk of brotherhood" also turns into a frightening place. As was true for Paul Berlin, disturbing memories occasionally intrude upon imagination. Involuntary flashbacks take Chris back to the scenes of the enemy attack on his unit, Bonny George's death, or Chris's mental breakdown four days after these events. Unlike Nick Adams, he is incapable of choking off these unpleasant memories. Reality also intrudes upon his imaginary conversations as he acknowledges that his three war friends died, killed by a booby-trapped bomb while Chris was in the hospital suffering from acute depressive reaction. Thus, the resulting uncontrollable feelings of guilt, horror, and shame, along with fear that he is still crazy, make unsatisfying Chris's escape to this battlefield home.

What can he do, then, without seeking help or without confiding in June or Dr Eckhardt? For Chris, another option, one often embraced by soldiers suffering from PTSD, is to isolate himself from people as much as possible, to seek comfort in nature (a natural therapy), and, like combat soldiers, to immerse himself in routine tasks. The inhospitable reception Chris was given by his family after he returned from Vietnam, a physical attack soon after by a war protestor, and a constant barrage of media stories about Vietnam veterans as drug addicts and incompetent soldiers continue to haunt Chris thirteen years later and drive him further into a self-imposed exile. He distrusts people and avoids them as often as possible: "He was living in a dangerous land, where he was hated, and attacks were to be expected" (p. 102). Such fears evolve into classic paranoia as he believes most people, including co-workers, know about his Vietnam experiences, including the crack-up, and are trying to have him committed to a mental institution. Responding to these unfounded worries, this tripwire veteran fantasizes about living in anonymity with the highway as his home:

> . . . he could escape society as completely as any hermit in the mountains. He could move from one town to the next, eating in fast-food restaurants, sleeping in chain motels, an Interstate nomad, a citizen of the fringes, unnoticed, unremembered, unknown. (p. 87)

Significantly, other authors borrow Caputo's image of Vietnam veterans as "Interstate nomads" to emphasize their isolation and rootlessness. Chris's job as a timber cruiser for a large lumber company, which he has held for seven years, allows for some of this anonymity and freedom. The job also enables Chris to escape temporarily his anxieties and unpleasant thoughts about Vietnam. Like a battlefield soldier easing into combat numbness, or like Nick Adams preoccupied with decisions about camping and fishing, Chris suppresses his disturbing thoughts by immersing himself in the ritual of work: "Starkmann reveled in his work because its technicalities demanded a concentration that would not allow him to think about anything else, like going crazy" (p. 96). Furthermore, the job takes him into the forests of the Upper Peninsula where he temporarily feels at home. Here, he also senses an order and control in his life, confident that literally and figuratively he can never lose his way and that the unexpected will not happen.

Nevertheless, as is true with his imaginary escape to Vietnam, reality and the unforeseen intrude upon his job and this natural sanctuary. Despite his efforts to control them, Chris is unable to keep unpleasant Vietnam flashbacks at bay; his paranoia undermines occasional required contacts with people; and his environmentalist views eventually conflict with the economics of his job. Above all, nature ceases to be a haven: "The woods in whose fastness he had always experienced a sense of belonging and of sanctuary from the world would from now on deny him their refuge" (p. 316). Once more cast adrift without purpose and direction, fired from his job because of his unexplained bizarre and violent behavior, and mired in an alcoholic stupor, Chris isolates himself and his family even more from society. Acting in utter desperation, he merges the two worlds – Vietnam and his forty acres of secluded woods – into an isolated "base-camp." To accomplish this, he brings the Vietnam landscape to the Upper Peninsula as he erects physical and psychological barriers between himself and the hostile civilian world. Once more he attempts to establish order and control in his life and to withdraw further within himself by constructing elaborate barbed-wire fences around the perimeter of his property, digging foxholes, building an imposing gate for this fortress, fashioning a command bunker in the woods, and conducting regular security patrols. Eventually, when his family leaves him and he realizes that even this physically protected space cannot save him from his inner torment, he plots a fiery suicide, one worthy of a combat veteran, to end the "nightmares and pointless sufferings."

The suicide, however, does not occur; and, helped by June's encouragement and Eckhardt's efforts to get him to talk, Chris, unlike many troubled Vietnam veterans, heals himself – at least temporarily – as Caputo ends his novel on a hopeful note. The process begins appropriately with Chris's return to nature, his own "Big Two-Hearted River" episode taking place where his and Bonny George's last fishing trip occurred years earlier. Here Chris seeks Bonny's grandfather so that he can relate the story of his friend's death and confess that the whole episode was "a mistake I made. The accident was my fault" (p. 418). While confessing his sin to Louis St Germaine, Chris acquires important insights about himself. He acknowledges that he had enlisted in the Army not only out of love for his friend but also because of his hatred for his father. He had also gone to war seeking "an experience so awful there could be no coming back from it, one that would cut him off completely from Lucius" (p. 432). Unfortunately, that experience turned out to be Bonny's death, and at that moment Chris had discovered what Conrad had written about years earlier – the "fascination of the abomination." For a brief moment, he had inexplicably enjoyed watching "napalm boiling like a solar storm while men burning to death screamed in the jungle" (p. 432). This secret delight in this horror has given rise to the guilt and nightmares plaguing him ever since. Chris acknowledges that this guilt and self-condemnation became so overwhelming after his return to the States because he wanted them to be – a punishment for his involvement in his friend's death and a psychological barrier between Chris and people. Now, to survive, he must learn to live with himself and to forgive himself. From the wise Indian medicine man, Chris receives the absolution and comfort he seeks. Furthermore, both men find salvation in a new father–son relationship forged by the war. Chris receives a father's forgiveness, and Louis finds a son sent to him to be healed: "They'd adopted each other, each finding in the other what each had lost" (p. 431). After his symbolic immersion in the trout stream and a water burial of his military uniform, Chris realizes that by acting to control his psychological turmoil he has introduced order and symmetry into his life and that he has merged the two halves of his divided self, as well as the worlds of Vietnam and the home front:

> When the echoes died away, he dressed, hoisted his pack, and started walking, though not toward home; he was already there, returned to himself. Home, the place he had not seen or been these many years. *Home.* (p. 433)

Compared to Nick Adams, Chris does not appear to have any psychological swamps nearby. Perhaps Caputo is overly optimistic in suggesting such a successful and permanent end to Chris's quest for an emotional and spiritual home.

Despite the traditional literary symbolism of this cathartic concluding scene, Caputo's extensive use of fictional techniques throughout the novel, and a psychological depth of characterization missing in *A Rumor of War*, *Indian Country* is not far removed from Caputo's nonfictional first book in its realism, overt messages, and narrative style. In fact one might speculate that in contrast to *A Rumor of War*, begun as a novel and turned into nonfiction, this book may have started as a nonfictional account of PTSD but evolved into a novel. In any case, Caputo's exhaustive clinical treatment of PTSD, his portrait of a soldier's uneasy homecoming, and his convincing depiction of the soldier–civilian relationship between Chris and June are the novel's strengths. Equally important, this book straightforwardly presents key literary and socio-cultural themes of isolation and control associated with war's aftermath. Caputo suggests that, with support from others, Vietnam veterans must assume responsibility for controlling their own lives in grappling with the aftermath of war. This is an idea that many Americans, including some Vietnam veterans, would embrace, but one that others may dismiss as too simplistic. Finally, with his theme of a war-weary veteran attempting to recover from physical and psychological wounds, Caputo also connects this book with modern war literature portraying a veteran's search for a spiritual home. Thus, *Indian Country* becomes an appropriate starting-point for examining two other aftermath novels, which are more unconventional in their narrative style and more creative in treating characters, themes, and symbols.

Two contrasting adjectives fittingly describe Larry Heinemann's novel *Paco's Story* (1986), "explosive" and "haunting." Awarded the 1987 National Book Award for fiction, this work, along with O'Brien's *Going After Cacciato*, is significant literature transcending the war genre. In his second novel about the Vietnam War, Heinemann moves adeptly from the journal-like narrative of *Close Quarters* to a tightly crafted complex narrative. He also seems comfortable leaving the highly charged environment and frenetic pace of the Vietnam battlefield for the subdued atmosphere and slow pace of small-town America, which, as was true in *Indian Country*, turns out to be a threatening environment for returning veterans. Heinemann in his first novel overwhelms readers with the unrelenting description of the violence, profanity, and heart-of-darkness horror of the war as he examines combat numbness and the evils of war and human nature. In *Paco's Story*, however, he relies less on the obscenity of war to carry the narrative and more on an intriguing narrator and an ironic and often cynical commentary on American values and culture. But the book never strays too far from the battlefield as the author jolts readers with occasional snatches of gruesome war stories, including one particularly disturbing heart-of-darkness episode. Similar to Michael Herr's illumination rounds, these passages explode on unsuspecting readers who follow the struggle of Paco Sullivan to "discover a livable peace" (Heinemann [1986] 1987, 174) upon his return from Vietnam. In its haunting quality, brooding tone, cynicism, and subtlety interrupted by explosive graphic detail, this novel parallels Wilfred Owen's poetry, particularly his aftermath poem "Disabled." The book also illustrates Fussell's ironic vision of war, in this case the irony of war's aftermath as Paco anticipates "The Thanks of a Grateful Nation" (p. 34) but is left thinking "imagine breaking your balls for these people" (p. 66).

With *Paco's Story*, Heinemann returns to the theme of a war veteran "climbing down," a stage of adjustment he briefly introduces at the end of *Close Quarters* as Dosier returns to the Midwest after his Vietnam tour. Sergeant Paco Sullivan, the lone survivor from an Army unit of ninety-three soldiers overrun by the Vietcong at the "holocaust massacre at Fire Base Harriette," carries the memories of Vietnam and the physical pain of his own wounds. Viewed as a loser by most civilians he encounters, this Vietnam veteran is Caputo's "Interstate nomad" travelling west to find acceptance and a home. But, compared to Chris Starkmann's severe case of PTSD, Paco's problems in adjusting to a postwar existence seem less a result of his own devils and more related to the apathy of an ungrateful nation. The setting for this interaction of American society and Vietnam veteran is the small town of Boone, to which Heinemann never assigns a precise geographical location, thus suggesting its "anytown, USA," role. Readers and Paco expect this place to be a hotbed of patriotism and compassion for war veterans. At least for Vietnam veterans, however, the opposite is true. The town, a few miles from the interstate and described as a "haven and a conundrum" (p. 68), is one more inhospitable stop on Paco's odyssey. Added to this riddle are Paco's contacts with the local townspeople, mostly limited to the patrons of its greasy spoon restaurant (the Texas Lunch), residents of the Geronimo Hotel where Paco lives, and the clientele of Rita's Tender Tap and the local barber shop. Sprinkled among the inhabitants of this workers' town are "County maintenance-department rednecks," racists, and insensitive college students from the nearby Wyandotte Teachers College. Their attitudes toward Vietnam veterans in general and Paco in particular range from ignorance ("What war was that?": p. 75) to distrust ("a body hears too many stories as to how they got acting so peculiar": p. 84) to derision ("gimpy deadbeat": p. 65) to downright contempt: "Them

Vietnam boys sure do think you owe them something, don't they?" (p. 85).

The novel portrays Paco's efforts to live within this environ-ment and with his memories of combat. Anticipating the reactions of "people with the purse strings" who claim that war stories "put *other* folks to sleep where they sit," the unusual narrator of *Paco's Story* quickly alerts readers that "This ain't no war story" (p. 3); nevertheless, despite this disclaimer, the novel is one extended war story about the aftermath of war, with sev-eral battlefield stories included. Yet distinguishing this tale from so many other Vietnam narratives is Heinemann's imaginative way of telling it. Like O'Brien in *Going After Cacciato*, he cre-ates a sophisticated narrative structure by deftly interweaving past, present, and future through flashbacks, foreshadowings, digressions, asides, dreams, and multiple perspectives. But, unlike O'Brien, he doesn't mix fantasy and fact. This is a book firmly rooted in the realism of *Close Quarters* – except for the narrator who happens to be a ghost. This nameless, disembodied omniscient narrator assumes the collective identity of all the Alpha Company grunts killed in the massacre at Fire Base Harriette. While relating Paco's story in the form of a dramatic monologue directed to a woefully uninformed listener addressed as "James," this storyteller becomes one of Heinemann's cen-tral characters, artfully staging scenes and mixing helpful information with cynical commentary about human nature.[12]

In the traditions of intrusive narrators created by such eighteenth- and nineteenth-century British novelists as Fielding, Dickens, George Eliot, and Thackeray, Heinemann's narrator assumes many voices and many roles as he comments on the action and comprehensively describes places, events, and people. Often, the ghost assumes the dialect of a street-wise hipster revealing to his readers the secrets of the schemers and freeloaders in this world: "Yes, sir, James, plenty of good brothers and sisters got right and righteous *that* night. And Brother Doo-dah was left ... pondering – wondering – just exactly how did he do that marvelous thing" (p. 17). Occasionally, his language is that of an urbane traveller cataloging the ambience of restaurants in America or that of a naturalist with an eye for detail describing a rural scene: "Upstream to the right as far as he can see is the deep and broad backwater, still and shimmery as a warm horizon" (p. 67). And frequently, the familiar battlefield argot – sights, sounds, obscenities, gruesome details – from *Close Quarters* appears:

> and everything was transformed into Crispy Critters for half a dozen clicks in any direction you would have cared to point; everything smelling of ash and marrow and spontaneous combustion; everything – dog tags, slivers of meat, letters from home, scraps of sandbags and rucksacks and MPC scrip, jungle shit and human shit – *everything* hanging out of the woodline looking like so much rust-colored puke. (pp. 15–16)

Through asides to his audience (usually marked by parentheses), digressions, background information, and stage directions (three pages on how Paco washes dishes), the narrator carefully controls the narrative and various characters and manipulates his listener. Along the way, the ghost acts as historian (both local and world), psychologist probing Paco's psyche, teacher (defining words, explaining concepts), dramatist hinting of events to come, and social commentator describing life in small-town America. But the voice also constantly reminds his audience that he was a grunt in Alpha Company and is, therefore, obligated to relate some of the unit's war stories, portray a few of its prominent members, and educate James about the combat soldier's life in Vietnam.

In addition, the ghost of Alpha Company's most important role is to tell a war story – Paco's story, a seemingly simple task that becomes complicated as Paco's quest for a livable peace leads to stories about other soldiers. Thus, the narrative is occasionally interrupted by what might best be described as interpolated tales – brief war stories told by the narrator or stories related by other characters in the book. For example, Old Man Elliot, an immigrant Russian antique dealer, became disillusioned with war and deserted the Tzar's army in 1917 during the Russian Revolution. Ernie Monroe, owner of the Texas Lunch, narrates his horrible experiences as a Marine on Guadalcanal and Iwo Jima during World War II. A brief anecdote surfaces about a local Korean veteran who upon his return to the States "lapsed into a deep and permanent melancholy" (p. 42). And Jesse, a bitter Vietnam vet, uses the John Wayne theme to undercut the romance of war, cynically assessing his own tour in Vietnam as well as a proposed "Vietnam Monument" in Washington:

"And you know that statue will be some dipped-in-shit, John Wayne crapola. . . . They'll mount that John Wayne-looking thing on a high pedestal and set it out by the road so the lifers and gun nuts can cruise by in their Jeep campers and Caddies and see it good and plain." (p. 157)

Finally, the Bravo Company medic who found Paco after the massacre of Alpha Company narrates his own version of the events surrounding Paco's miraculous survival.

Uniting these soldiers and their tales are the inevitable changes they have undergone in war and their inability to escape the resulting memories, pain, and bitterness. Specifically, the memories of war atrocities occurring fifty years earlier in Russia continue to haunt Old Man Elliott: "all those memories alive in him still, twitching" (p. 75). Ernest relives the horror of seeing the people of Hiroshima soon after the atomic bomb was dropped. This event, coupled with his own battlefield experiences, has shaped his contempt for war and blind patriotism: "but I'll be fucked if you'll see me fly the flag. Not Flag Day or the Fourth of July. Not Memorial Day or Veterans Day – which *used* to be called Armistice Day, see? – no kind of goddamned day" (p. 126). Such cynicism connects him to the bitter Vietnam veteran Jesse who ironically proposes a Vietnam memorial composed of a marble wall, with the names of all Vietnam war dead, surrounding a granite bowl filled with money and "every 'egregious' excretion that can be transported across state lines from far and wide" (p. 158). Finally, the Bravo Company medic, who has never escaped his war-related feelings of frustration and hopelessness and the scenes of horror associated with the massacre and Paco's rescue, survives the war's aftermath in an alcoholic stupor. He is doomed to tell year after year the patrons of a local bar his abbreviated version of Paco's story and its traumatic effect on his own life:

Almost any night of the week he will sit there and brag

that he could have made something of himself. "Would have been a goddamn *good* doctor, hear? . . . Except for this one guy, this *geek*," the guy not dead, but should have been. (p. 33)

The "guy not dead, but should have been" of course refers to Paco, whom Heinemann intentionally fashions into the most enigmatic and disturbing figure in the tale. What readers don't know about Paco is just as significant as what they do know. The ghost of Alpha Company, so capable and eager to comment on most people and events, appears reticent to share with James too much information about Paco. Readers do not receive as complete a portrait of the prewar Paco as they might expect or even his reactions to several crucial events during and after the war. Such a narrative strategy heightens the mystery surrounding Paco and purposely creates potential conflicting perspectives of this character.

This classic silent drifter, right out of a Hollywood western movie, arrives in Boone because he doesn't have any money to go farther. Paco is just as much a riddle for the towns-people as they are for him. His appearance is marked by his slight build, numerous physical scars, a pronounced limp, an ever-present black hickory cane, and the familiar 1,000-meter stare of someone who has seen a lot of combat. Responding to the wearisome question "Why do you have that cane?" he grudgingly gives his stock reply, "wounded in the war." Once, while talking with Jesse, he expands this response as he tersely summarizes the Alpha Company massacre and his subsequent recovery:

"Got fucked up at a place called Fire Base Harriette near Phuc Luc," and he stretches his arm and turns his head to the side to show off the scars. "Been in the hospital. Got out of the Army. Convalesced in one VA hospital after another. Cane's to help with the walking." (p. 152)

Such a cryptic explanation glosses over the cataclysmic nature of this battle, the torture of Paco's two days of exposure awaiting rescue, and the agonizing recovery from his horrific wounds. Also absent from this response is any reference to his unacknowledged homecoming after the war and his life on the road working day labor and sleeping in barns, hospitals, and bunkhouse hostels. Readers learn from the narrator and Paco's reply to another one of Jesse's questions that despite this bleak existence Paco is stoical about his fate. Never asking "Why me?" in considering his misfortunes, he tells Jesse that he is bitter about the events during and after the massacre but that he tries to put them in a proper perspective: "I'm just glad to be here" (p. 163). Such a response seems appropriate in a world created by Heinemann where irony abounds (Harriette was supposed to be a "piece of cake") and chance (note the irony of the pronunciation of Phuc Luc) rather than a divine hand governs events: ". . . an abundance of sheer luck, against which nothing can prevail" (p. 68).

It's left to the ghost to relate a few additional details for readers about Paco's war experiences and current dreary existence. For example, in one digression the narrator tells James about Paco's job in Alpha Company as the fearless and expert "booby-trap" man who after going off alone to set up his various booby-traps could return to the base able to "kill another man, unseen, and still sleep soundly" (p. 194). Within the same war story, the narrator also describes Paco's face-to-face encounter with an enemy soldier and their subsequent hand-to-hand combat. The scene contains the gruesome details and psychological tension of Dosier's similar confrontation in *Close Quarters* and parallels Paul Baumer's experience with the dying French soldier in a bomb crater. Readers also learn that, as Paco wanders the United States, he carries important war mementos. Packed in his AWOL bag is a ghastly reminder of the massacre, a petri dish containing the shrapnel and bone fragments removed from Paco's body. Also in this bag is a sentimental memento of his war experience – two medals, a Purple Heart and a Bronze Star, presented to him in the hospital by a sympathetic colonel who reminded Paco of his dead father: "That was the reason Paco never threw away the medals, or pawned them, as many times as he was tempted and as stone total worthless as the medals were. . . . It is the kiss he cherishes [the colonel's] and the memory of the whispered word" (p. 59). Paco also bears war-related scars covering his body and permanent pain from his wounds – "his whole body tingles and thrums with glowing, suffocating uncomfortability that is more or less the permanent condition of his waking life" (p. 36). Such a condition requires an endless cycle of muscle relaxants and anti-depressants to aid him in enduring his waking hours and in sleeping at night. Typical of Heinemann's subtle approach to characterization, neither Paco nor the narrator ponders at length the significance of these events or their impact on Paco's psyche.

Like many combat veterans, Paco also carries with him his dreams, waking and sleeping, that haunt his existence. Unlike the welcome battlefield daydreams soldiers indulge to control their lives and to escape their surroundings, these are unwelcome aftermath dreams significantly increasing Paco's mental anguish. If Chris Starkmann displays most of the classic symptoms of PTSD, then the one Paco most shares with him is this unexpected occurrence of dreamlike flashbacks and forebodings. Some contain the surrealistic elements characterizing a few of Dosier's dreams in Heinemann's first novel. All, as the narrator informs James, are courtesy of the ghosts of the dead Alpha Company soldiers who hover around Paco nightly while he lies in a drug-induced stupor from his medication:

> And when Paco is most beguiled, most rested and trusting, at that moment of most luxurious rest, when Paco is all but asleep, *that* is the moment we whisper in his ear, and give him something to think about – a dream or a reverie. (p. 138)

These disquieting whispers are very unlike the consoling words of the colonel or his father from a time past. The dreams, ranging from menacing chase scenarios to those of waiting-rooms, executions, and out-processing centers, mix the confusion, events, bitterness, horror, fears, tensions, guilt, pain, and unrealized possibilities from his Vietnam tour. The dreams remain as much a part of his life as the physical pains.

However, one dream, more meaningful than the others, Paco wishes to avoid but cannot. Late in the novel, Heinemann and his narrator drop this dream on readers and James like an unexpected mortar round. It contains an apocalyptic heart-of-darkness experience involving Paco's participation in the rape and brutalization of a "hardcore" VC girl who had ambushed an American night listening-post. As described by the ghost, also a participant, this episode is the conventional atrocity scene found in various forms in so many Vietnam narratives. For example, its elements appear in Groom's *Better Times than These* where American soldiers rape two captured VC nurses, and similar brutalization and humiliation occur in *Close Quarters* in the treatment of the Vietnamese prostitute. But the ghost's narrative, shockingly detailed and matter-of-factly related, is one of the most disturbing and frightening in all the Vietnam narratives. It fits O'Brien's requirement for a true war story – one that makes the reader's "stomach believe." The litany of unrelenting violence, sadism, and degradation dramatically reveals the evil side of humans out of control and sinking into a brutish state. As James and readers become Marlows glimpsing Kurtz's depravity for the first time, the scene once more gives meaning to Caputo's words in *A Rumor of War* that in some soldiers' moral descent they discover "in their bottommost depths a capacity for malice they probably never suspected was there" (Caputo [1977] 1978, xx). Unlike atrocity episodes in previous books, such as *A Rumor of War* or *If I Die*, where narrators attempt to moderate the soldiers' actions by citing extenuating circumstances or blaming the act on US military policies, the ghost of Alpha Company zeroes in on the rape, not on the events leading up to it. "Wiseacre" Gallagher, with his symbolic dragon tattoo on his forearm, is the ringleader and eventually shoots the young girl after the brutalization. But most company members, including Paco, are consumed by an animal frenzy and participate in the abhorrent acts:

> Paco remembers feeling her whole body pucker down; feels her bowels, right here and now, squeezing as tight as if you were ringing out a rag, James; can see the huge red mark in the middle of her back. (Heinemann [1986] 1987, 181)

At the end of this narrative sequence, the narrator typically avoids a psychoanalytical discussion of the event's impact on Paco's psyche or an analysis of its moral implications. Perhaps all that is needed is the ghost's succinct judgement of the incident – his own version of "The horror! the horror!": "We looked at her and at ourselves, drawing breath again and again, and knew that this was a moment of evil, that we would never live the same" (p. 184).

Without question this event and Paco's subsequent survival of the massacre insure that this soldier will never live the same. He grapples with the aftermath of his Vietnam experiences in the best way he can. He seeks a type of inner peace the narrator metaphorically compares to that which a weary traveller would have upon being welcomed to a "comfortable cabin as solid as a castle keep" (p. 174) and invited for dinner and a night's rest. Paco's isolation and stoicism drive his quest for order, control, and this spiritual haven. Unlike Chris Starkmann, who is much more out of control and unable to manage the psychological stress of the war's aftermath, Paco seems to keep a tight rein on his feelings. He accepts the humiliation of working for $2.25 an hour as a dishwasher at the Texas Lunch, avoids emotional highs and lows, and does not indulge the bitterness and cynicism present in Jesse's diatribes against the war, the military, and American society. Also, the medicines keep the physical pain at a manageable level; and, like Nick Adams, Paco focuses on order and pattern in his life to manage the psychological pain. Like so many other fictional soldiers, including Chris Starkmann, suffering from war-related stress, he busies himself with work and routines: six days a week at the Texas Lunch he works from eleven in the morning until midnight washing dishes by hand and occasionally waiting tables. As he loses himself in a mind-numbing world of glasses, dishes, and cutlery, his place of employment becomes a haven where the work is "straightforward and mechanical" and where the daily events and people are familiar and controllable. This monotonous existence helps dull the mental pain, and his self-imposed isolation enables him to control his feelings. The narrator, however, never articulates the frustrations and difficulty involved in Paco's efforts to remain in control.

In a town where Paco's opportunities for a meaningful relationship are rare, even with Ernest and other war veterans, Paco comes closest to an emotional involvement with Cathy, a student at the Teachers College, who has the room next to Paco's at the Geronimo Hotel. Theirs is an unsatisfactory connection built on sexual tension created by distance rather than by physical contact. It is a relationship mirroring the one described in Owen's "Disabled" as the veteran longs to touch a woman but notes that "the women's eyes/Passed from him to the strong men that were whole." Paco is sexually aroused by the young woman; Cathy seems more fascinated with the mystery surrounding this war veteran and his titillating scars. He becomes part of her sexual fantasies. At night from the stoop in back of the Texas Lunch, Paco stares up at her room, glimpsing her in various stages of undress. She, on occasion, turns off all the lights in her room, watching him while he works or spying on him in the adjoining hotel room. Each onlooker eventually becomes aware of the other's interest, thus heightening the sexual fantasies and game-playing. But the sexual games are one-sided. Cathy becomes one more mental torment for Paco as she teases him ("I get a nice kick from teasing that gimp"; p. 173) to the point of having intercourse with her boyfriend, knowing that Paco is next door listening to their lovemaking. This perverse relationship of distance is one aspect of Paco's minimalist existence that he has difficulty controlling as his frustrations grow and his anger toward Cathy and her boyfriend increases.

This relationship is also the occasion for a second unexpected narrative illumination round. Heinemann shakes his readers' views of Paco by introducing a narrative twist – a character sketch of Paco from someone other than the ghost. Is Paco an admirable character stoically attempting to live with his mental and physical wounds from the war? Or is he merely a pathetic figure – a physical and social oddity whose 1,000-meter stare, drug use, anti-social behavior, and Vietnam experiences make him an object of ridicule? Until the final pages of the novel, the ghost of Alpha Company has been doing his best to present Paco in a sympathetic light. Granted the narrator is biased by the brotherhood of the bush he shares with Paco; and, yes, Paco's participation in the rape of the VC girl and his cold, calculating approach to his job as the booby-trap man are disturbing. Despite this, he appears to be a survivor whose attempts at coping with the war's aftermath should elicit sympathy from readers and suggest that he is unfairly treated by an ungrateful American society. But is this the view that Heinemann wants to leave with his readers? Just when readers feel comfortable in assessing Paco's character, "Paco the

Sneak" (title for chapter 7) surreptitiously enters Cathy's room, rifles through her clothes, and leisurely reads her diary found under the mattress – all part of a symbolic sexual violation. What he and readers discover is a description of Paco much different from the narrator's characterization. In her diary, Cathy reveals her sexual immaturity and sexual fantasies, but she also portrays Paco in an unflattering light as she relates his nightly rituals of cheap booze, pills, and erratic behavior:

> Getting more and more drunk, holding his head with both hands. Slapping the flat of his belly with cupped hands, making a POP POP POP sound. Hoarsely whispering, "Come on, hit me! Hit me! Hit me!" and taking time out to wave that bottle around, drinking and splashing booze and slurring, "Bang! Bang! Bang-bang-bang!" Flicking his wrist and sprinkling booze in all corners of his room . . . and he's a dingy, dreary, smelly, shabby, *shabby* little man. (p. 205)

She also describes his drinking habits during the day, his moaning and weeping at night (which in an aside the narrator informs James are his reactions to his execution dreams), and his physical ugliness. The diary ends with Cathy's narration of her recent dream mixing sexual fantasy with a surrealistic horror scene in which Paco torments her by removing his scars and laying them on her body: "And then I woke up. I just shuddered. . . . It made my skin crawl" (p. 209).

These unexpected revelations, especially the phrase a "shabby little man," startle Paco, James, and the reader. Whose portrait of Paco – the ghost's or Cathy's – is accurate? No doubt the diary details of Paco's strange behavior are factual, the actions of a soldier desperately grappling with his inner devils and his outer physical pain. Obviously, Paco isn't as adept at controlling his emotions, fears, and flashbacks as the narrator leads James and the reader to believe. Paco is engaged in a challenging and perhaps impossible struggle. What is so disturbing about the young woman's character sketch, however, is that, unlike the ghost's portrait, hers lacks any hint of sympathy or understanding for the subject. In *Indian Country*, although June is an outsider to the Vietnam experience and has difficulty comprehending what her husband is striving to overcome, she sympathizes with him, tries to communicate with him, and attempts to understand the causes of his PTSD. Cathy's inconsiderate attitude toward Paco is exactly the opposite, yet it is consistent with the views of Boone's other residents who label this Vietnam veteran a curiosity, "gimp" and "creep." As Cathy records in her diary, "Unc says that creeps like him are best got rid of, and is going to start working on him" (p. 206). Understanding, sympathy, and support for Paco are missing. The stereotype of the dangerous and bizarre Vietnam veteran seems firmly entrenched in these people's minds. As a result, after reading the diary, this veteran has his own revelation: "Whatever it is I want, it ain't in this town. . . . Man, you ain't just a brick in the fucking wall, you're just a piece of meat on the slab" (p. 209).

At the end of this war story, the ghost and Heinemann bring James and the reader full circle. This unsatisfactory stop on Paco's quest for a home concludes the way it began with this disillusioned nomad again boarding the interstate bus for a destination farther west (a symbolic death of the spirit?). In a book where overt messages from the author are deliberately avoided and where the focus is on characters and their interaction, or lack of interaction, rather than on political issues, Heinemann's understated point still seems to be clear. The Vietnam War, like other wars, has created turmoil within its participants and barriers between those who fought and those who did not. As deftly and sympathetically portrayed by Heinemann, Paco becomes a tragic figure – a victim of the war and society's indifference as well as an unwilling agent of his own turmoil. The image of the Vietnam veteran as the anonymous interstate nomad, briefly introduced in *Indian Country*, is fully realized in *Paco's Story*. Yet, to his credit, Heinemann's novel is not a mawkish portrait of the veteran, a strident attack on America's treatment of the veteran, or a simple resolution of complex human problems. Instead, the work is an imaginative, moving, and thought-provoking war story of people who years later remain affected and unaffected by the Vietnam War and its ironies.

Bobbie Ann Mason's *In Country* appropriately concludes this critical introduction to modern war literature in general and

Vietnam narratives in particular. This intriguing novel recapitulates themes and characters previously encountered in this
study, but from a different perspective – a woman's view.
As such the novel takes us backward and forward in our
literary journey: backward to the themes of innocence lost and
experience gained found in *All Quiet on the Western Front, A
Rumor of War*, and *Dispatches*; forward to the home front where
the daughter of an American soldier killed in Vietnam in 1966,
one month before his daughter's birth, seeks information about
her father and the war. On one level, the book is a conventional
coming-of-age story unrelated to Vietnam: a 17-year-old girl,
Samantha Hughes (Sam), gains insights about responsibility,
identity, adult relationships, and decision-making. On another
level, this novel realistically portrays Vietnam veterans and
civilians living with the war's legacies. Mason, whose most
notable other fiction includes a novel, *Spence and Lila* (1988),
and two collections of short stories, *Shiloh and Other Stories*
(1982) and *Love Life* (1989), is not a soldier-author, nor did she
ever spend time in Vietnam as a journalist. But she notes in an
interview that after visiting the Vietnam Veterans Memorial in
Washington, DC, in 1983 and accidentally seeing a version of her
name on the wall (Bobby G. Mason) "I knew then that Vietnam
was my story too, and it was every American's story."[13] As a
result, her novel, like *Indian Country*, probes the war's effects
on a family several years after the fighting ended. As evidence
of her success in capturing the feelings and struggles of all
involved, the Vietnam Veterans of America honored Mason
with a "President's Citation" given to non-veterans in the arts
who significantly contribute to the public's understanding of
the Vietnam War and its aftermath.

Unlike Caputo and Heinemann in their postwar novels,
Mason, for the most part, moves well beyond the battlefield.
In comparison, the two-soldier authors never stray too far
from combat realism as their central characters relive their
battlefield experiences through memories and dreams. Mason's
novel, however, is more concerned with another perspective
– an innocent youth's imagined view of the war, which in
some ways is where we began this critical study with the
John Wayne Syndrome in *A Rumor of War*. In broader terms,
Sam's curiosity and fantasies about the war ("Sam's got Nam

on the brain": Mason [1985] 1986, 48) reflect the current interest among America's youth about more than just the war's history. Her innocent questions, including those about Agent Orange, soldiers' drug use, Vietnam's climate and landscape, and the attraction of combat, become the questions of a new generation fascinated with the Vietnam experience: "I want to know what it was really like. What was in that jungle" (p. 189). Furthermore, her sometimes painful movement from innocence though experience to consideration within the context of this war parallels several soldiers' tripartite battlefield journeys portrayed in the Vietnam narratives.

To tell her war story, Mason, Like O'Brien in *Going After Cacciato*, emphasizes the intersection of past, present, and future in her central character's life, as well as the power and limitations of imagination to transform memory and facts into fiction. Specifically, Sam transmutes textbook facts and veterans' memories of Vietnam into an imaginative re-creation of her father's Vietnam tour of duty. And like Heinemann's second novel, this war story stresses the effects of war on people living in small-town America. But, compared to *Paco's Story*, this novel has a simpler narrative structure. The complex multi-layered narrative and intrusive narrator-character of Heinemann's novel are missing, replaced by a relatively straightforward third-person limited narrator. The story unfolds through Sam's eyes, thoughts, imagination, and teenage language. The narrative frame (the present) is an interstate odyssey much different from Paco's quest. Instead of traveling west, three "Interstate nomads" are on a purposeful journey east. Sam, her uncle Emmett Smith (a Vietnam veteran), and her paternal grandmother (Mawmaw, who is carrying a pot of geraniums) depart in Sam's 1973 VW on a pilgrimage to visit the Vietnam Veterans Memorial and find the name of Dwayne Hughes, Sam's father, inscribed on "The Wall." In between two frame sections describing the trip, the narrator extensively chronicles the previous few months of Sam's summer of 1984, a pivotal time in her life following high school graduation. Locked into a crucial period of consideration, she, like Paul Berlin, looks forward and backward, worrying about her future and hoping to learn the truth about her father and the Vietnam War from the residents of her hometown of Hopewell, Kentucky.

Her hometown displays a familiar apathy toward the war and its combatants. Unlike Boone's treatment of Paco, however, this small town has, as one Vietnam veteran notes, "treated the vets OK, because the anti-war feeling never got stirred up good around here. But that means they've got a notion in their heads of who we are, and that image just don't fit all of us" (p. 79). Within this community, two Vietnam veterans, who don't fit the townspeople's image of well-adjusted, patriotic veterans, and other members of a local Vietnam veterans organization figure prominently in Sam's journey into the past. Through these characters, Mason pointedly catalogs many of the legacies of war related in the previous two aftermath novels. For example, several of the veterans suffer from typical survival guilt as they mourn the deaths of friends in Vietnam and question their own safe return from the war. Others, feeling out of place in the civilian world, display familiar nostalgia for the intensity, camaraderie, and individual power associated with Vietnam: "It was the best life I ever knew, in a way. It was really something" (p. 134). A few express their frustration that American soldiers were not given a chance to win the war, and others articulate their sense that Vietnam, compared to other wars, was different: "Nam was different, though. Take my daddy [Second World War veteran]. . . . He knew who the enemy was. He knew what he was fighting for" (p. 124). Another veteran, claiming to have adjusted easily to his postwar existence, berates his fellow-veterans for wallowing in self-pity. And other Hopewell veterans experience marital problems, isolation from the community, and physical disabilities they believe are directly related to their exposure to Agent Orange in Vietnam. The controversy in the book involving the conflicting attitudes toward the treatment of these Agent Orange victims emerges as an important issue and evolves into a metaphor for America's callousness toward Vietnam veterans in general. Hopewell's veterans bitterly complain about the Veterans Administration's and the general medical community's failure to treat this problem seriously – a dispute still raging today.[14]

But the two veterans whose difficulties most affect Sam's life are Tom Hudson and Emmett. "Her whole life centered on two men at the mercy of the VA" (p. 129). Both men, spouting a version of the ironic phrase from *The 13th Valley*, "Don't Mean

Nothing," have been psychologically emasculated by the war. (Such sexual impotence, both physical and psychological, has become a recurring symbol within the war genre – Owen's disabled soldier, Hemingway's Jake Barnes in *The Sun Also Rises* – of war's debilitating aftermath.) Interestingly, like Heinemann, Mason fashions a relationship between a young woman and a much older Vietnam veteran. Paralleling Cathy's relationship with Paco, Sam is sexually attracted to Tom (seventeen years older than she) and his Vietnam connection. But, unlike Cathy, she is not interested in playing psychological games with a tormented veteran. Instead, Sam is sincerely interested in the war and sympathizes with Tom's plight. As a result Sam's naïve compassion replaces the perverse sexual tensions that Cathy encourages in her relationship with Paco. Thus after learning about Tom's impotence as they attempt to have sexual relations, Sam comforts him and wants to continue seeing him, a gesture that Tom is too embarrassed to accept.

Emmett, the novel's other prominent veteran and a central character, is in his behavior and torment closely allied with Chris Starkmann and Paco Sullivan. Like these two combat veterans, he suffers from the physical and psychological aftereffects of the war. But, unlike Starkmann, he doesn't succumb to violent rages; and, compared to Paco, he is not a silent drifter. In fact he has roots and a sardonic humor. Yet Emmett is controversial; Mason intentionally or unintentionally has created a character who evokes either sympathy or disgust from certain segments of readers. Unquestionably, he is the atypical veteran; he is eccentric or, as one character notes, downright "weird." Living with his niece in a rundown home purchased by his sister (Sam's mother), Emmett survives on money provided by his sister and on a small income from fixing toasters and hairdryers. Hounded by the Veterans Administration to repay a college loan, he steadfastly resists all encouragement to get a regular job. Instead, like Starkmann and Paco, he immerses himself in comfortable daily routines. He spends his mornings at the local McDonald's, where he meets a few fellow-veterans, and passes the rest of the day at home where he divides his time between watching television, particularly reruns of *M*A*S*H*; playing video games; taking care of his cat, Moon Pie; and preparing junkfood meals for Sam and him. In honor of his favorite television show, he frequently wears a skirt, *à la* Corporal Klinger. Occasionally, he can be found outside the home: digging a trench around the house to repair a leaky foundation or visiting Cawood Pond to look for an egret, a beautiful bird he saw in Vietnam. Emmett fits the stereotype of the bizarre war veteran or an irresponsible adult living off other people's generosity and indulgence. Furthermore, in his quasi-father relationship with Sam, where he is supposed to guide his niece, he turns into Sam's best friend, occasionally supplying her with marijuana and alcohol. Worse, this 35-year-old is frequently an immature adult requiring Sam's direction and prodding.

Clearly, despite this maddening behavior, Mason wants readers to respond sympathetically to Emmett, who exhibits several obvious symptoms of PTSD. In describing the condition of his decaying home, he is also describing his own physical and psychological state: "'My basement's flooded and my foundation's weak,'" Emmett said with a grin. "And my house might fall down while I'm here'" (p. 110). And, in digging a trench around his house, he, like Starkmann, erects physical and psychological barriers around himself. His chain smoking, gastrointestinal disorders, severe acne, and constant headaches outwardly signal internal distress caused by war memories and secrets he carries with him. Since returning from Vietnam, Emmett, as readers learn late in the novel, has been "grieving for fourteen years" (p. 241) – grieving for the past and fearing an unfulfilled future. This innocent young soldier, like so many others, went to war with romantic notions to avenge his brother-in-law's death and to protect his sister and her daughter. His battlefield experience, like Chris's and Paco's, included the by now familiar traumatic incident; he was the only survivor of an NVA ambush. Later, he returned to Hopewell a cynical veteran who, along with some hippie friends, protested the war, even flying a Vietcong flag from the town's clock tower. Having passed through this protest stage, he, like Paco, has turned inward, concentrating his energy on simply surviving each day and living in the present: "This is what I *do*. I work on staying together, one day at a time. There's no room for anything else. It takes all my energy" (p. 225). Like other veterans, he is preoccupied with order and control in his life to "keep memories from intruding." Thus, his seemingly eccentric behavior is a carefully designed routine allowing him to choke off unpleasant thoughts, to escape into television's comfortable version of the Korean War in *M*A*S*H*, or to prevent outsiders from intruding upon his life. Even his birdwatching becomes a way to distance himself from flashbacks and grief associated with Vietnam, as well as thoughts about his depressing future: "I *want* to be a father. But I can't. The closest I can come is with you [Sam]. And I failed" (p. 225). His assessment of his birdwatching as a metaphysical experience echoes Marlow's comment about working as a way to escape truth:

"If you can think about something like birds, you can get outside of yourself, and it doesn't hurt as much. That's the whole idea. That's the whole challenge for the human race." (p. 226)

In marked contrast to Emmett's efforts to avoid the past and escape the memories of Vietnam (Emmett believes that "[y]ou can't learn from the past": p. 226), Sam is obsessed with resurrecting the past, particularly the Vietnam War and stories about her father. Uncle and niece, therefore, have an unusual co-dependent relationship. Sam's presence provides Emmett with an emotional anchor in his life and a stable relationship. In addition, her concern for Emmett's welfare allows him to live securely in his eccentric world. For Sam, her uncle, who genuinely cares about his niece, is a link to the past, a flesh-and-blood contact to the Vietnam War and a source of occasional war stories. Such an unusual living arrangement and Sam's preoccupation with Vietnam separate her from her peers.

Yet in many ways, she is a typical teenager undergoing a conventional rite of passage into adulthood. Her world is one of fast-food restaurants, shopping malls, MTV, HBO, rock music, and teenage romances. Like many of her peers, Sam anticipates leaving the dull life of a small town and doing something exciting. She also eagerly wants to buy her own car, a step towards independence and an important stage in her rite of passage. And Irene, her mother living in Lexington, Kentucky, with her new husband and baby, offers Sam an entry into this future. Weary of looking after Emmett for thirteen years, Irene left Hopewell and the past behind to start a new life; now, she encourages Sam to do the same by living with her in Lexington and enrolling at the university. But, if Sam's mother is beckoning her into the future, the ghost of Sam's father, the mysteries of the Vietnam War, and her romantic conceptions of life in America during the late 1960s and early 1970s draw her attention backward. This tension between past and future underlies Sam's journey from innocence through experience to consideration and aftermath during her summer of 1984.

Along the way, Sam is a naïve but persistent historian encountering obstacles in her quest for a "fresh message from the past" (p. 125) and in her efforts to transport herself through her imagination "in country" (the soldier's term for being in Vietnam). Armed with a picture of her father at age 19, a few of Emmett's war stories, information from books about Vietnam, HBO war movies, and images from *M*A*S*H*, she wants to know more about her father and Vietnam. She wants to care about him, establish a father–daughter relationship, and vicariously experience his tour of duty. Not so different from Caputo years earlier, her quest also feeds fantasies about adventure and daydreams about being a combat soldier, a role denied American women. But barriers appear at every step. Her father has died with his war stories, and Irene, who married Dwayne one month before he left for Vietnam, did not know her husband well and has put this marriage and the whole Vietnam experience behind her. Her well-intentioned response to Sam's questions about the war and Dwayne is blunt: "Don't fret too much over this Vietnam thing, Sam. You shouldn't feel bad about any of it. It had nothing to do with you" (p. 57).

Because Sam has never participated in a war, and because she is a female, the Vietnam veterans in Hopewell also hesitate to share information with her. They admire her perseverance but consider her efforts futile as she enters a male-dominated arena. Traditionally, fathers tell war stories to their sons, not to their daughters; men protect women from the horrors of war; and books and films portray wars in male terms – John Wayne figures or male sexual imagery (Herr's comparing the exhilaration of war to "undressing a girl for the first time"). Her uncle's chauvinistic admonition that Sam forget her quest to understand the war suggests this skewed male perspective, one that critic Susan Jeffords sees as an outgrowth in this novel of men's efforts to restore male bonding, power, and war as an exclusive male domain: "'Women weren't over there [Vietnam],' Emmett snapped. 'So they can't really understand'" (p. 107). And another of Emmett's comments, one reiterated by veterans in several novels, emphasizes the barrier between combatants and civilians, both male and female:

"Stop thinking about Vietnam, Sambo. You don't know how it was, and you never will. There is no way you can ever understand. So just forget it. Unless you've been humping the boonies, you don't know." (p. 136)

Despite such discouragements, Sam presses the issue by asking more questions about the people, events, and landscape in Vietnam: "'I want to know what it was like over there. I can't really imagine it. Can you tell me what it was like?'" (p. 94). She is gathering raw material for her imagination so that, like Paul Berlin, she can explore possibilities as well as create an imaginary tour of duty. Her gender is not an issue here. For in this respect she is no different from innocent soldiers going off to war. They, without the benefit of experience, have also fed their youthful imaginations with bits of information culled from books, the media, and war stories to create romantic war scenarios. On the other hand, denied an opportunity to act out her fantasies on real battlefields, Sam must substitute connecting her life in Hopewell with the images, people, and places of the Vietnam War stored in her mind. Thus, a trip to a gas station triggers an imaginary scene of a "sky-high explosion, like an ammunitions dump blowing up" rushing through Sam's mind (p. 5); Sam compares her discomfort during a bouncy ride in a van to "feeling like a soldier in an armored personnel carrier" (p. 34); or a walk with Tom becomes a dangerous combat patrol – "He was following her, his keys jangling. She was walking point now" (p. 125). And once, when seeing Emmett in front of the television intently playing video games, she "had a picture of him with an M-16, in a tropical jungle, firing at hidden faces in the banana leaves" (p. 89). Occasionally, however, these imaginary scenes and thoughts of her father's death mix with paranoia about Agent Orange affecting Emmett, her naïve musings about penile implants for Tom and Emmett, and images of an odd assortment of characters and episodes from *M*A*S*H*. For Sam, the results are dissatisfying, often a hodgepodge of unrelated facts, fears, fiction, and absurd fantasy and at other times an artificial view of Vietnam: "'I can't really see it,'" Sam said. 'All I can see in my mind is picture postcards. It doesn't seem real. I can't believe it was really real'" (p. 95).

Gradually, reality intrudes upon Sam's imaginative re-creation of Vietnam, especially during this summer after her high school graduation, and Fussell's notion of war being worse than expected proves true, even for noncombatants. On one occasion, reality assumes the form of a gruesome anecdote about American soldiers cutting off the ears of dead Vietcong soldiers – a story that Sam does not want to hear. Most often, these glimpses of war's realities emerge through her relationships with Hopewell's Vietnam veterans. In living with Emmett for several years, she has confronted war's social, physical, and psychological legacies for veterans. Despite her uncle's outwardly lackadaisical approach to life, Sam realizes he is battling his inner war devils. He had a nervous breakdown a few years earlier; and a more recent episode at Cawood Pond, when an approaching thunderstorm and a war flashback unsettled him, suggests to Sam the depth of Emmett's psychological torment. She also perceptively notes that Emmett's digging a trench around the home becomes more than an effort at home repair: "'You know what you're doing? You're just digging yourself a foxhole to hide in. Like the enemy was all around us. But it's not'" (p.189). Even more disconcerting for Sam is the shock of Tom's war-related impotence. Suddenly, a young girl's romantic fantasy of being with an older man turns into an unexpected insight about war's hidden toll on lives:

> The sadness of his affliction hit her then like a truck. She thought of all the lives wasted by the war. She wanted to cry, but then she wanted to yell and scream and kick. She could imagine fighting but only against war. (p. 140)

Notwithstanding this partial education about the real Vietnam and its aftermath, as opposed to Sam's imaginary version, the most significant and unexpected dose of reality comes

ironically from Sam's father. His war diary, written at Quang
Ngai (the setting for Paul Berlin's imaginary journey), contains
the "fresh message from the past" that Sam has been seeking
and that no-one else in his family has bothered to read. Unlike
Dwayne's war letters to his family, which Sam characterizes as
"strangely frivolous, as if he were on a vacation" (p. 182), the
diary contains a few graphic war stories undermining Sam's
romantic illusions about the war and her father. The content
from a combat soldier's perspective is a commonplace narrative
of a patrol, an encounter with a rotting "gook" body, the bloody
death of a platoon member, and Dwayne's first kill: "Face to
face with a VC and I won. Easier than I though. . . . At last"
(p. 204). For Sam, such details presented matter-of-factly and
the surprise revelation of her father's "insensitive curiosity" and
"murderous" instincts shock her the way Cathy's diary shocks
readers and Paco or the way that Kurtz's behavior shocks
Marlow. She becomes physically ill. As she experiences disgust
mingled with self-recognition and insight, her reading the diary
becomes a revelatory heart-of-darkness experience. She, like so
many people before her, suddenly recognizes the dark side of
human nature in a combat environment and acknowledges the
limitations of her imagination as an adequate substitute for
experience:

> She had a morbid imagination, but it had always been like a
> horror movie, not something real. Now everything seemed
> suddenly so real it enveloped her, like something rotten she
> had fallen into, like a skunk smell, but she felt she had to
> live with it for a long time before she could take a bath.
> (p. 206).

Despite this loss of innocence, Sam's education is still
incomplete and her imagination still active. Confused and
angry at men, especially her father and uncle, for what she
concludes is their innate desire to kill, "their basic profession"
(p. 209), she resolves to actualize what is in her imagination. She
resolves to find out, once and for all, what soldiers in Vietnam
encountered. Her efforts are laudable but unfortunately ineffectual, more like those of a kid playing at war. Armed with a
space blanket, Emmett's Vietnam poncho, her backpack, and a

picnic cooler she goes off to "hump the boonies" at Cawood Pond, the nearby snake-infested swamp which is "the last place in western Kentucky where a person could really face the wild" (p. 208). During her night in the swamp, somewhat similar to Paul Berlin's six hours of guard duty, she pretends to walk point, hide from snipers, and establish a routine for a base-camp. Once again, she gives free rein to her imagination as music from the Doors, images from *Apocalypse Now*, and facts about Vietnam merge in her mind. Again reality intrudes, this time in the form of her worried uncle who has followed her to the swamp. He lectures her about the artificiality of this war experience:

> "You think you can go through what we went through out
> in the jungle, but you can't. This place is scary, and things
> can happen to you, but it's not the same as having snipers
> and mortar fire and shells and people shooting at you from
> behind bushes." (p. 220).

He also assails her childish motives for hiding out in the swamp and forces Sam to admit that her trip is an act of revenge against her uncle and father because of the disturbing facts she has learned about war and human nature: "'The way he (Dawyne) talked about gooks and killing – I(Sam) hated it. . . . I hate him'" (p. 221).

On a rational level, Sam's actions are indeed those of an immature teenager reacting with anger and spite when her imaginary war story and its characters are undercut by unsettling facts. Nevertheless, on an emotional level, Sam's trip to the swamp is also understandable. She is motivated by her overwhelming desire to make Vietnam her war and by her frustration at not being able to satisfy her curiosity and fulfill this inner need for a father and adventure. Moreover, as Sam forces Emmett to admit, her actions of hiding in the symbolic swamp are no different from Emmett's efforts to escape his own swamp (reality) by hiding in his eccentric world: "'Don't you think it's childish to do what yo do, the way you hide and won't get a job, and won't have a girlfriend?'" (p. 223). As a result, this episode at Cawood Pond becomes a catharsis for both Emmett and Sam, and it abruptly changes their relationship and the novel's tone. Soon after, Sam, Emmett, and Mamaw depart for Washington. Emmett rightfully assumes his role of surrogate parent, getting a job, urging Sam to live with Irene in the fall, and arranging the trip to Washington, DC. Moving into a combination consideration-aftermath stage in her Vietnam experience, Sam suffers from her own form of "post-Vietnam stress syndrome" (p. 229). She allows Emmett to control her life as she realizes that she has just passed through an important period of experience and enlightenment. Her rite of passage is almost complete.

With the final scene at the Vietnam Veterans Memorial, Mason transforms into fiction her own experience at the Memorial, along with the feelings of anyone who has visited this moving monument. Mason's depiction of the wall with its 58,175 names etched in the polished black granite incorporates what semiotician Harry Haines labels the monument's function as a "therapeutic place of healing and accord," "a sign signifying both a sense of loss for the dead and a sense of reincorporation of the survivors. . . . It is the sign of community refound" (1986, 4). Thus, the mother, daughter, and soldier-friend of Dwayne E. Hughes, killed eighteen years earlier in Vietnam, collectively mourn his loss, but each gains much more from the experience. For Emmett, this moment at the Memorial ends years of grieving and begins his healing. As was true with Chris Starkmann's symbolic immersion at the conclusion of *Indian Country*, so Emmett's success in finding the names of comrades killed in Vietnam enables him to end his self-imposed isolation (a return to the community) and to commence the purging of his war devils: "He is sitting there cross-legged in front of the wall, and slowly his face bursts into a smile like flames" ([1985] 1986, p. 245). For Mamaw, this pilgrimage and opportunity to touch her son's name on the wall allow a mother to affirm her son's sacrifice and to rekindle his memory.

Still, Sam's pilgrimage is the most meaningful in terms of Mason's overarching theme. Ironies abound as this daughter of a dead Vietnam veteran approaches a war monument designed by another young woman – Maya Ying Lin, a 21-year-old student of architecture at Yale University. Neither has experienced the war firsthand, but in unique ways both are veterans of the war. As quoted in *US News & World Report* soon after the selection of her design, Lin noted that "I don't think you have to live through a trauma to understand it" (6 November,

1989, p. 18). As for Sam, her act of touching her father's name and the subsequent tears cement the emotional connection with her father that she has been seeking. Equally important, as she is flipping through the directory listing names on the wall, she finds her own name "Sam Alan Hughes PFC AR" and touches it on the wall: "How odd it feels as though all the names in America have been used to decorate this wall" (p. 245). This moment symbolically affirms her earlier words that the war had "*everything* to do with with me'" (p. 71). Sam's past, present, and future have merged. Her quest for a father and truths about the war, her journey from innocence through experience to a consideration of Vietnam, and her own rite of passage are complete. She realizes that she is just beginning to understand the war and that "she will never really know what happened to all these men in the war" (p. 240). More important for Mason and readers, Sam senses that she is indeed part of a community of survivors – soldiers and civilians, men and women, sons and daughters – who live with the memories and legacies of this war but who can come to terms with them and proceed with their lives. Out of the tragic legacies of Vietnam, Mason's message is one of healing, promise, and affirmation – for Americans, the Vietnam War is everyone's experience, but in different ways.

Afterword

An important message emerging from Mason's *In Country* (1985) is that Americans did not have to experience firsthand the Vietnam War nor even to have lived during the historical period for it to be their war. All Americans are affected by ambiguous legacies of the Vietnam experience – from foreign policy to the national conscience to continuing military and political debates. This critical study of Vietnam narratives reinforces this notion, taking readers on their own literary journey from innocence, through literary experience, to consideration of war and its aftermath. Within such a context, these books by Caputo, Herr, Heinemann, Webb, Del Vecchio, O'Brien, and Mason are important on two levels. First, they extended their authors' third and fourth stages of change. These writers, through memoirs or fiction, persisted in pondering their involvement with the war and its aftermath and in struggling with the memories, feelings, and images they carried with them. Several of these books, published in the late 1970s, appeared when Americans wanted to forget Vietnam and authors faced frustrating obstacles in publishing their war stories. These books, therefore, were not written to satisfy sympathetic readers' demands, nor were they written to defend America's involvement in Vietnam. Instead, these and later books emerged as confessionals – an individual and national purging of heart and mind – as authors, through memory and imagination, answered why American soldiers fought in an unpopular war, how they survived, how the experience changed them, and how they and their families live with the war's aftermath.

On another level, readers' enthusiastic responses to these

books suggested a shift in America's attitude toward the war and its participants. Such reactions also signaled the nation's movement into a final stage of its own relationship with the war, a period of consideration and healing that continues. As suggested in recent articles noting the twenty-fifth anniversary of the war's first major battle in the Ia Drang Valley (November 1965), Vietnam ended American innocence about the politics of war, the role of political dissent, the effectiveness of technology, and battlefield brutality. Media myths about war and Hollywood's early view of Vietnam in *The Green Berets* proved false. Even John Wayne could not change the outcome in Vietnam. From the resulting blows to America's pride and spirit arose profound disillusionment throughout all segments of American society during the war's final years. Consequently, after the war ended, much of the country rejected the war and, most tragically, rejected the combatants. Postponed was the country's final step in confronting the Vietnam experience. Authors of Vietnam narratives discussed in this book are a few of the writers whose works enabled America to move from this period of denial into one of reconstructing and considering the "splendid little war" that turned into an ugly war and a national trauma.

This literary consideration has not ended political debate about Vietnam. Through the literature, however, readers can appreciate the changes soldiers undergo on the battlefield and recognize the variety, power, mystery, evil, and commonality of the human spirit. Specifically, they discover how average people face war's horrors, occasionally succumb to them, and live with the aftermath. As this critical study stresses, these responses and the attendant issues of fear, courage, and character transcend individuals and wars. Also, in the best war stories the individuality, honesty, and truth of the experiences shine through the conventions of their description as authors present insights about the self, others, and war. The selected authors in this book describe many of the same experiences but view them from different angles. Therefore, they often arrive at different understandings, images, metaphors, and kernels of human emotions ranging from Herr's fascination with war, to Webb's battlefield valor and sacrifice, to Heinemann's unspeakable evils. Aided by this literature, America has almost completed its own rite of passage as it contends with the lessons and aftermath of the Vietnam War.

Perhaps America's recent military success in the Gulf War has, temporarily, diminished the so-called "Vietnam Syndrome" by restoring self-esteem and self-confidence to the country and to the soldiers. But the demons of the Vietnam experience will not so easily be exorcised from the American psyche. The war simply has too many living reminders of the trauma. Furthermore, like Caputo, one wonders, if a new generation of American men and women influenced by an updated John Wayne figure – John Rambo and his romantic battlefield exploits – or the deadly "Star Wars" military hardware – dazzlingly displayed on television during the Gulf War – is ready to start the cycle over again and take its own heavy heart-of-darkness journey out of innocence: "every generation is doomed to fight its war . . . and learn the same old lessons on its own." All that the Vietnam narratives can do is warn, but as Hemingway observed: "No catalogue of horrors ever kept men from war. Before the war you always think that it's not you that dies" (*Esquire*, September 1935).

Notes

Introduction

1 As evidence of this profusion of literature about the Vietnam experience, two annotated bibliographies provide extensive citations (novels, short stories, poetry, drama, and miscellaneous materials): Sandra M. Wittman's *Writing about Vietnam: a Bibliography of the Literature of the Vietnam Conflict* (Boston, Mass: G. K. Hall, 1989), which also includes entries on literary criticism, periodicals, and teaching materials; John Newman's *Vietnam War Literature: an Annotated Bibliography of Imaginative Works, about Americans Fighting in Vietnam*, 2nd edn (Metuchen, NJ: Scarecrow Press, 1988).

2 Two books are particularly helpful in providing a literary and historical perspective of American women's roles in Vietnam: Deborah Butler's *American Women Writers on Vietnam, Unheard*

Voices: a Selected Annotated Bibliography (New York: Garland, 1990) is an annotated bibliography with 781 entries devoted to women's writing (several genres) published between 1954 and 1987 about Vietnam and the war's aftermath. Major General Jeanne Holm's *Women in the Military: an Unfinished Revolution* (Novato, Calif.: Presidio, 1982) chronicles American women's service in wartime, including their roles in Vietnam.

1 Thematic Contexts

1 See also Cornelius A. Cronin's "From the DMZ to No Man's Land: Philip Caputo's *A Rumor of War* and Its Antecedents," in William J. Searle (ed.), *Search and Clear: Critical Responses to Selected Literature and Films of the Vietnam War* (Bowling Green OH: Bowling Green State University Popular Press, 1988), pp. 74–86, for more analysis of the tripartite structure of *A Rumor of War*.

2 For an extensive account of the corruption, political pressures, unpreparedness, and inefficiency plaguing the South Vietnamese Military (ARVN), see Neil Sheehan's *A Bright Shining Lie: John Paul Vann and America in Vietnam* (New York: Random House, 1988). In this nonfiction book (National Book Award for 1989), Sheehan, among other issues, describes the ARVN's war efforts from 1962 through 1972.

3 Conrad's "An Outpost of Progress," published in *Tales of Unrest* (New York: Gordon 1974), is the precursor to *Heart of Darkness*. The short story deals with two Europeans physically and psychologically destroyed by their tour of duty as the only two white men in a remote ivory-trading post in Africa.

4 In discussing this film, director Francis Coppola notes that Milius' script for *Apocalypse Now* made only superficial use of *Heart of Darkness*. But Coppola decided "to take the script much more strongly in the direction of *Heart of Darkness* – which was opening a Pandora's box" (Francis Coppola and Greil Marcus, "Journey Up the River: an Interview with Francis Coppola," *Rolling Stone*, 1 November 1979, p. 53).

5 In commenting about his own experiences in the Congo (1890) as an officer on river steamboats, Conrad noted to Edward Garnett that in his early years at sea he had "not a thought in his head." "I was a perfect animal." But the Congo experiences developed in him a somber moral mission changing his attitude toward men and society: quoted in Robert Kimbrough (ed.), *Heart of Darkness*, Norton Critical Edition (New York: Norton, 1988), p. 195. Such a spiritual change is, of course, similar to Marlow's own heart-of-darkness experience and establishes a significant archetype for characters in war literature facing moral dilemmas.

6 One interesting visual example of imperialism and a startling

parallel between European technology described in *Heart of Darkness* and American technology in Vietnam emerges in the novel. Marlow describes a French man-of-war anchored off the African coast "incomprehensibly" lobbing shells "into a continent" at an unseen enemy with no appreciable effect (p. 20).

7 The parallel passage in *Heart of Darkness* reads: "How can you imagine what particular region of the first ages a man's untrammeled feet may take him into by the way of solitude – utter solitude without a policeman – by the way of silence – utter silence, where no warning voice of a kind neighbor can be heard whispering of public opinion? These little things make all the great difference. When they are gone you must fall back on your own innate strength, upon your own capacity for faithfulness" (p. 70).

8 A reference to the early influence of silent movies on the attitudes of American soldiers entering combat appears in Dos Passos' *Three Soldiers* (Boston: Houghton Mifflin, 1949) as characters in this World War I novel anticipate what combat will be like – "Memories of movies flickered in his mind" (p. 35) – and assess the realities of combat: "Hell, but I thought it'd be excitin' like in the movies" (p. 62).

9 Since Crane had no military experience when he wrote this novel, the book's realism is remarkable. Despite the realistic details and psychology of this scene, according to Edwin Cady, "There is no evidence that he [Crane] had read any book about war other than *Battles and Leaders* [of the Civil War] before he wrote *The Red Badge*": *Stephen Crane* (Boston: Twayne, 1980), p. 118. Cady notes, however, that as a youth Crane knew several Civil War combat veterans with whom he could talk. Later, after writing *The Red Badge of Courage*, he experienced war firsthand when he reported on the Greco-Turkish War in 1897 and traveled to Cuba in 1898 as a reporter for the *New York World* covering the Spanish–American War.

10 Paul Fussell describes this recurring scene as one in which "a terribly injured man is 'comforted' by a friend unaware of the real ghastliness of the friend's wounds": *The Great War and Modern Memory* (New York: Oxford University Press, 1981), p. 34. In Remarque's *All Quiet on the Western Front* a similar event occurs as Paul Baumer carries the mortally wounded Kat to an aid station.

11 In "The Postwar War," *Journal of Social Issues*, 31.4 (1975), Robert J. Lifton defines desensitization as "loss of feeling in order to escape the impact of unacceptable images." Furthermore, "this numbing, psychologically necessary at the time, can later give rise to despair, depression, and withdrawal" (p. 182). Lifton discusses this phenomenon further in *Home from the War: Vietnam Veterans, Neither Victims Nor Executioners* (New York: Basic Books, 1985), pp. 108–12.

12 Much of this book examines the similarities of war experiences across time and place, but obviously differences do exist. Whether such dissimilarities significantly change from war to war soldiers'

battlefield experiences is open to debate. Nevertheless, the fact that soldiers, often without the benefit of a historical perspective, believe these significant differences exist unquestionably influences the ways in which they talk and write about their war experiences.

13 Max Hastings finds that American responses to an unpopular government of South Korea, as well as US reliance on technology and firepower in the Korean War, taught the wrong lessons to the American military as it developed strategy for waging war in Vietnam: *The Korean War* (New York: Simon & Schuster, 1988), pp. 333–4. Neil Sheehan also notes the Korean War set a precedent for the American military to ignore reality. He writes of John Paul Vann's belief that Korea was "a lesson in why it made no sense to attempt to fight a war of attrition on the Asian mainland with American soldiers" (*Bright Shining Lie*, 452), a lesson that went unheeded in Vietnam.

14 Marshall McLuhan's terms "hot" and "cool" describing a medium's degree of involvement for its audience suggest such a controversial war (hot content) on such an involving medium (cool television) was bound to create passionate responses among American television audiences, particularly from 1968 onward when the war became more controversial at home. Recent communications research, however, convincingly shows that television had less of an effect on shaping the public's perceptions of the Vietnam War than originally believed. In many ways, the so-called negative television reporting mirrored middle Americans' growing dissatisfaction with the war. For further discussion of this, see Daniel C. Hallin's *The "Uncensored War": the Media and Vietnam* (New York: Oxford University Press, 1986).

15 George C. Herring quotes Ho Chi Minh from Jean Lacouture's *Ho Chi Minh*: "If ever the tiger [Viet Minh] pauses . . . the elephant [France] will impale him on his mighty tusks. But the tiger will not pause, and the elephant will die of exhaustion and loss of blood" (*America's Longest War: the United States and Vietnam, 1950–1975*, New York: Wiley, 1979,) p. 9.

16 See Loren Baritz, *Backfire: a History of How American Culture Led Us into Vietnam and Made Us Fight the Way We Did* (New York: Ballantine, 1986), pp. 239, 290–1; Thomas D. Boettcher, *Vietnam: the Valor and the Sorrow* (Boston: Little, Brown, 1985), p. 398; Al Santoli, *Everything We Had: an Oral History of the American War by Thirty-Three American Soldiers Who Fought It* (New York: Random House, 1981), pp. 85–6; and Sheehan, *Bright Shining Lie*, 339–40, for discussions of body-counts as ambiguous measures of combat performance in Vietnam.

17 British correspondent Richard West in *Victory in Vietnam* (London: Private Eye/André Deutsch, 1974), pp. 20–2, discusses the "progress of demoralization" among American soldiers in Vietnam. To support his views, he uses information from the *Overseas Weekly*.

The Pacific edition of this underground military newspaper first appeared in 1966 and was sold through street sales or subscriptions. Its news stories, described by West as "factual and stark," regularly contained accounts of court-martials, drug use, and fraggings among the American troops.

18 In Korea a soldier was awarded four points for each month served at the front and two points for each month served elsewhere in Korea. Thirty-six points meant rotation home: Donald Knox and Alfred Coppel, *The Korean War: Uncertain Victory* (New York: Harcourt, Brace, Jovanovich, 1988), pp. 346–7. This policy of individual rotation differed from Second World War policy of unit rotation and service for the duration of the war.

19 Regarding this policy, Sheehan (*Bright Shining Lie*) notes:

> The army personnel bureaucracy tended to view Vietnam as an educational exercise and rationalized the six-month rule as a way of seasoning more officers for the "big war" yet to come with the Soviets in Europe and for more of these "brushfire wars." The real reason ... which explained why the practice was derisively called "ticket-punching" was a mechanistic promotion process and the bureaucratic impetus this created. ... To keep an officer in a battalion or brigade or regimental command longer than six months was regarded as unfair to his contemporaries. (pp. 650–1)

20 In commenting on this debriefing opportunity for Korean veterans, Knox and Coppel (*Korean War*) note: "If there were any positive aspects of being confined aboard ship for three weeks after nine months in a combat area, it was the almost unlimited opportunity to ventilate one's experiences with one's peers. It was sort of forced emotional catharsis" (p. 352).

21 As evidence of this skewed racial and class mix of American combat troops, Baritz describes the war as one fought by "the poor man's son." "Poor young Americans, white as well as black and Hispanic, were twice as likely to be drafted and twice as likely to be assigned to combat as wealthier draft-aged youth" (*Backfire*, 278). Boettcher notes that African-Americans "constituted one-ninth of the US forces in Vietnam but one-fifth of combat troops" (*Vietnam*, 401).

2 Innocence

1 Ronald Weber in *The Literature of Fact: Literary Non-Fiction in American Writing* (Athens, OH: Ohio University Press, 1980) and Robert Smart in *The Nonfiction Novel* (New York: University Press of

America, 1985) discuss this category of modern literature positioned between fiction and historical nonfiction.

2 For a revealing account of international press coverage of the Vietnam War within the context of modern war reporting, see Phillip Knightley's *The First Casualty – from the Crimea to the Falklands: the War Correspondent as Hero, Propagandist and Myth Maker* (London: Pan Books, 1989), pp. 373–426.

3 Nancy Anisfield comments that this dislocated narrative style represents well the "American soldiers' feeling of confusion and alienation in a war that lacked definite objectives." She notes that such a style appears in prominent Vietnam novels, such as Tim O'Brien's *Going After Cacciato*, Stephen Wright's *Meditations in Green*, Nicholas Proffitt's *Gardens of Stone*, and Rob Riggan's *Free Fire Zone*: "Words and Fragment: Narrative Style in Vietnam War Novels," in William J. Searle (ed.), *Search and Clear: Critical Responses to Selected Literature and Films of the Vietnam War* (Bowling Green, OH: Bowling Green State University Popular Press, 1988), pp. 56–7.

4 In his article "Reporters of the Lost War," *Esquire*, July 1984, Thomas Morgan describes Herr's bout with depression and his subsequent period of analysis. Upon completing *Dispatches*, Herr vowed never to write another book about war or cover another war (p. 52). He has, however, worked on two screenplays about Vietnam: *Apocalypse Now* and *Full Metal Jacket*. Moving away from the war, he wrote the text for Guy Peellaert's celebrity album of portraits, *The Big Room*, and he recently published *Winchell* (1990), a fictional look at American gossip-reporter Walter Winchell.

5 Gordon O. Taylor compares Greene's novel to *Dispatches*, in the process labeling the latter a "novel with an autobiographical core" and the "auto-erotic experience of a war-freak"; "American Personal Narrative of the War in Vietnam," *American Literature* 52 (1980): 306.

6 Herr, in the "Foreword" to the screenplay for Stanley Kubrick's *Full Metal Jacket*, referred to his 1979 pledge to stay away from Vietnam material: Stanley Kubrick, Michael Herr, and Gustav Hasford, *Full Metal Jacket* (New York: Knopf, 1987). He claimed that this opportunity to work with Kubrick and his admiration for Hasford's book *The Short-Timers* led him to agree to co-write the screenplay. *Full Metal Jacket*, adapted from Hasford's novel, also contains brief episodes, images, and bits of dialogue from *Dispatches*.

3 Experience

1 In discussing the graphic realism of contemporary war literature, Paul Fussell notes: "As we perceive in the work of Mailer, Pynchon,

and James Jones, it is the virtual disappearance during the sixties and seventies of the concept of prohibitive obscenity, a concept which has acted as a censor on earlier memories of 'war,' that has given the ritual of military memory a new dimension. And that new dimension is capable of revealing for the first time the full obscenity of the Great War" (*The Great War and Modern Memory*, New York: Oxford University Press, 1981, p. 334).

2 "Being drafted [in 1943] suited [Mailer's] plans exactly, because, as he told his bride of two months, after that he intended to write THE War Novel": Michael Lennon (ed.), *Conversations with Norman Mailer* (Jackson, MS: University of Mississippi Press, 1988), p. 3.

3 In describing his guidelines for the style and content of *The Thin Red Line*, Jones notes that he used a "completely objective style" and dealt with "only those things I have experienced myself, and those told me by men in my old company": Frank MacShane, *Into Eternity: the Life of James Jones, American Writer* (Boston: Houghton Mifflin, 1985), p. 197.

4 James R. Giles suggests that *From Here to Eternity* introduces Jones's basic theme of the soldier's evolution, which continues in *The Thin Red Line*: *James Jones* (Boston: Twayne, 1981), p. 36. The soldier's acceptance of death and anonymity, as displayed by Sergeant Welsh in this latter novel, characterizes the last stage of the soldier's evolution and "is the one Jones said he could never quite himself attain" (ibid., 126).

5 Fife's exit from combat is similar to Jones's own experience. He reported that he was talked into a medical discharge after receiving a head wound and an ankle injury (ibid., 21).

6 This episode of hand-to-hand combat with the Japanese soldier is autobiographical (MacShane, *Into Eternity* 56). "When it came time to write the scene based on his [Jones's] killing of the Japanese soldier, he suffered, especially because he not only had to relive the experience emotionally, he also had to be accurate in order to get it right" (ibid., 200).

7 In the same article, Cornelius A. Cronin attributes this shift in guilt among Vietnam soldier-authors to the moral ambiguities of the Vietnam War: "Historical Background in Larry Heinemann's *Close Quarters*," *Critique: Studies in Modern Fiction* 24 (1983): p. 122.

8 Heinemann repeats this image later in the novel: "You keep greasing this one and that and lob grenades, and the bodies pile up and still they keep trotting out of the woods and you grease them by the squad and they pile higher until you reach up with your arms – as though you're looking for a hand up and *scream* your lungs flat" (p. 279).

9 Webb's other books are *Micronesia and US Pacific Strategy* (nonfiction); *A Sense of Honor* (fiction), set at Annapolis; and the Vietnam-related *A Country Such as This* (fiction), portraying the careers from 1951 to 1978 of three Naval Academy graduates.

10 For another example of a "first novel" by an inexperienced Vietnam

soldier-author, see Winston Groom's *Better Times than These* (New York: Berkley, 1979). To satisfy reader expectations and to develop his multiple plots, Groom resorts to extensive telling rather than showing. He does not disappear from the work; he is busy in it, telling about characters, abruptly moving the plot along, and hyping the emerging conflicts. As a result, many of the characters are straw figures, and Groom is hard pressed to explore the soldier's relationship to his environment or to deal, in depth, with the conundrums of the Vietnam War.

11 In Washington, Webb served as assistant to the US House of Representatives' Committee on Veterans' Affairs. Under President Reagan, he became Assistant Secretary of Defense for Reserves and finally Secretary of the Navy in April 1987, a position he held for less than a year. (Incidentally, one of Webb's classmates at Annapolis was Colonel Oliver North of Iran–Contra fame who also chose to enter the Marines instead of the Navy upon graduation.)

12 Loren Baritz notes that "the Vietnam draft was an ideal of discriminatory social policy": *Backfire: a History of How American Culture Led Us into Vietnam and Made Us Fight the Way We Did* (New York: Ballantine, 1986). The poor (all races) were twice as likely to be drafted and twice as likely to be in combat units, since draftees represented 88 percent of infantry riflemen in 1970. Of 27 million draft-age men during this era, 16 million were deferred, exempt, or disqualified; 8,700,000 enlisted and 2,215,000 were drafted; 500,000 were draft-evaders or -resisters. Of those serving in the armed forces during the Vietnam conflict, approximately half were stationed in Vietnam (ibid., 276–81).

13 In this scathing attack on "draft avoiders," the narrator describes the tactics of several other fictional Harvard students who developed ingenious ways of flunking their induction physicals: going temporarily berserk during the exam, taking a pill that raised their blood pressure to an unacceptable level, feigning an overly aggressive personality, or manifesting suicidal tendencies. The narrator sarcastically notes that all of these young men received deferments and will become prominent doctors, lawyers, professors, or politicians (p. 89).

14 Continuing the John Wayne comparisons, we find parallels between Senator and the cynical reporter in *The Green Berets* (played by David Jannsen). The latter initially questions American involvement in Vietnam, but after spending time with the Green Berets in Vietnam he becomes a vocal supporter of the war.

15 Del Vecchio's second novel, *For the Sake of All Living Things* (New York: Bantam, 1990), is a thoroughly researched historical novel about America's involvement in the political turmoil, civil war, and holocaust occurring in Cambodia since 1967.

16 In a footnote, Del Vecchio tells readers that the "Significant Activities" have been taken from a real document: "Defense Documentation Center Document AD 515195: *101st Airborne Division*,

Operations Report – Lessons Learned for the Period ending 31 October 1970; declassified 11 November 1977" (p. 122).

4 Consideration

1 O'Brien is, perhaps, the most prolific and most critically acclaimed of the soldier-authors emerging from the Vietnam War. In addition to *If I Die in a Combat Zone: Box Me Up and Ship Me Home* and *Going After Cacciato*, he has written three other novels: *Northern Lights* (1975), *The Nuclear Age* (1985), and *The Things They Carried* (1990). In the 1975 novel, O'Brien deals peripherally with the Vietnam War as he explores the relationship of a Vietnam veteran with his brother, and in *The Nuclear Age* he portrays a man's obsessive fear of a nuclear attack. The book's only connection to the Vietnam era is the main character's past as a sixties radical. With his latest novel, O'Brien returns to the Vietnam battlefield, specifically the Quang Ngai Province of *Going After Cacciato*, as a middle-aged narrator named Tim recalls the Vietnam experiences and stories of a rifle platoon by relating twenty-two self-contained but interlocking war stories, essays, and sketches.

2 In an interesting comment on writing about the emotions of war secondhand, Crane observes that "I have never been in a battle, but I believe that I got my sense of rage, of conflict, on the football field, or else fighting is a hereditary instinct and I wrote intuitively": J. C. Levenson, Foreword to *The Works of Stephen Crane*, Vol. 2 (Charlottesville, VA: University of Virginia Press, 1975), p. lxx. Crane's reference to sport, particularly the physical and mental aspects of football, as a preparation for war is a common theme in war literature and a frequent analogy in American sports culture.

3 For a detailed account of events surrounding the My Lai Massacre (16 March 1968) and the subsequent cover-up and press investigation, see Seymour Hersh's *My Lai 4: a Report on the Massacre and Its Aftermath* (New York: Random House, 1970) and *Cover-up: the Army's Secret Investigation of the Massacre at My Lai 4* (New York: Random House, 1972). Hersh, later a reporter for the *New York Times*, was a freelance writer at the time he filed the first story about My Lai on 13 November 1969.

4 John G. Leland suggests formal inspiration for the novel comes from William Golding's *Pincher Martin* (1956) and Ambrose Bierce's "An Incident at Owl Creek Bridge" (1890): "Writing about Vietnam," *College English* 43 (1981): 739–41.

5 For an interesting discussion of this interplay between imagination and memory, fact and fiction in O'Brien's books, see Eric Schroeder's "The Past and the Possible: Tim O'Brien's Dialectic of Memory and Imagination," in William J. Searle (ed.), *Search and Clear: Critical Responses to Selected Literature and Films of the Vietnam*

War (Bowling Green, OH: Bowling Green State University Popular Press, 1988), pp. 116–34.

6 Of course, the film making the most literal and figurative use of Russian roulette is *The Deer Hunter* (1978) directed by Michael Cimino. The recurring image first appears when the Vietcong torture American prisoners by making them play the game. Next, it is shown as a sport waged in the back rooms of gambling-houses in Saigon. A much earlier literary allusion to this theme of gambling with one's life occurs in Hemingway's *A Farewell to Arms* (New York: Scribner's, 1957) as Frederic Henry explains his view of life: "They threw you in and told you the rules and the first time they caught you off base they killed you. Or they killed you gratuitously.... But they killed you in the end" (p. 327).

7 In *Wartime: Understanding and Behavior in the Second World War* (New York: Oxford University Press, 1989), Paul Fussell notes that in the Second World War soldiers were asked to describe the physical signs of their fear during combat. "Over one-quarter of the soldiers in one division admitted they'd been so scared they'd vomited, and almost a quarter said that at terrifying moments they'd lost control of their bowels. Ten per cent had urinated in their pants" (p. 277). Fussell goes on to say that one of the common fears among these soldiers was "the very fear of wetting oneself and betraying one's fear for all to see by the most childish symptom" (p. 277).

8 Philip D. Beidler in "Truth-Telling and Literary Values in the Vietnam Novel," *South Atlantic Quarterly* 78 (1979): 141–56, discusses the soldier-narrator in Durden's *No Bugles, No Drums* (1976), who in his sense of artistic creation and concern with the relationship of art and life parallels Paul Berlin the author.

5 Aftermath

1 For a survey of the content and cause of these media images, including that of the "psychotic Vietnam combat veteran," see William J. Searle's "Walking Wounded: Vietnam War Novels of Return,", in William J. Searle (ed.), *Search and Clear: Critical Responses to Selected Literature and Films of the Vietnam War* (Bowling Green, OH: Bowling Green State University Popular Press, 1988), pp. 147–59, and see Charles Figley and Seymour Leventman's "Introduction: Estrangement and Victimization," in Charles Figley and Seymour Leventman (eds), *Strangers at Home: Vietnam Veterans Since the War* (New York: Praeger, 1980), pp. xxi–xxxi.

2 William K. Lane, Jr, a Special Forces veteran of the Vietnam War, writes in "Vietnam Vets without Hollywood, without Tears," *The Wall Street Journal*, 26 July 1988, p. 24, about the distorted media view of Vietnam veterans as "a legion of losers" and emotional

and psychological basket-cases unable to live with the horror of the war. In his commentary, he counters that the majority of Vietnam veterans don't fit this fictional stereotype, are no different from veterans of other wars or civilians who have experienced "bad things," and have adjusted normally to their postwar life "without whining, acting nutty or looking for a free ride."

3 For a discussion of these statistics, see Herbert Hendin and Ann Pollinger Haas's, *Wounds of War: the Psychological Aftermath of Combat in Vietnam* (New York: Basic Books, 1984), p. 7.

4 The subject of PTSD, as well as other sociological and psychological studies of returning Vietnam veterans, is thoroughly examined in Figley and Leventman's *Stranger's at Home.*

5 Paul Fussell notes in *Wartime: Understanding and Behavior in the Second World War* (New York Oxford University Press, 1989), p. 273, that the term "shell shock" originated in World War I as a convenient euphemistic label for bizarre behavior exhibited by combat soldiers on the battlefield or in the rear areas. According to Fussell, such behavior was not attributed to the real causes – stress and fear resulting from the physical and psychological horror and "madness" of war – but was attributed to soldiers' adverse reactions to repeated exposure to the concussion of exploding artillery shells.

6 Edmund Blunden's "Memoir" (1931) about Wilfred Owen is an excellent source of information about this soldier-poet's war experiences and includes excerpts from his letters: *The Collected Poems of Wilfred Owen,* ed. C. Day Lewis (New York: New Directions Books, 1965), pp. 147–80.

7 At this hospital facility specializing in treating officers with mental disorders, Owen met a fellow soldier-poet, Captain Siegfried Sassoon, who quickly became Owen's poetry critic and mentor. By this date (June 1917) Sassoon had already published poetry and sketches based on his war experiences.

8 For a helpful introduction to Hemingway's short stories, specifically publication history, sources-influences, and a survey of scholarship, see Paul Smith's *A Reader's Guide to the Short Stories of Ernest Hemingway* (Boston: G.K. Hall, 1989).

9 All quotations from Hemingway's short stories are taken from the Finca Vigia Edition (1987).

10 As Paul Smith notes, critics disagree whether the story should be read as a literal narrative of a fishing trip or an extended "waking dream" similar to Nick's nocturnal imaginings in "Now I Lay Me" (*Reader's Guide*, 90). The latter possibility raises some interesting parallels to Paul Berlin's own "waking dream" to escape the war and establish control over his battlefield existence.

11 In his article, Larry Heinemann notes that in Vietnam, tripwires (pieces of blackened wire about as thick as fishing-line) were attached to booby-traps and noisemakers and used as early-warning devices. According to Heinemann and psychologists

working with Vietnam veterans, tripwire veterans suffering from PTSD, have chosen to withdraw physically from society, usually to remote rural locations, and are constantly alert (early warning) to maintaining their distance from other people. A VA official quoted in this article defines these veterans as "combat veterans who have forsaken the comforts of society to disappear into the backwoods": "'Just Don't Fit': Stalking the Elusive "Tripwire" Veteran," *Harper's*, April 1985, p. 56. An unusually high percentage of veterans fitting this definition reside in the state of Washington, particularly in the Olympic Peninsula.

12 For an explanation of the origin of this term "James," see Heinemann's "Foreword" to the Penguin edition in which he explains that the name is a formal version of the "Jim" or "Jack" used by street folks to address total strangers and engage them in conversation.

13 This quote, along with Mason's description of her trip to the Vietnam Veterans Memorial, appears in "A Film Guide to *In Country*" compiled by the Cultural Information Service and funded by Warner Brothers, distributor of the film. Mason notes that "Sam's questions were my questions" as the author tried to educate herself about the Vietnam War. Mason also states that after visiting the Memorial she felt that she "had a right to tell a small part of that story [Vietnam]. Seeing the mothers, the fathers, the brothers, sisters, wives, children – the families – there that rainy day, I knew we were all in it together."

14 Agent Orange (named for the orange stripes painted on the storage-barrels) was a herbicide sprayed in Vietnam by the US Air Force ("Ranch Hands") to remove jungle cover and crops. It contained dioxin, a highly toxic chemical that some studies have found increases cancer risks. On one side in the controversy are the US government, chemical companies, and the CDC (Center for Disease Control) claiming that "exposure to Agent Orange did not pose a health risk." On the other side are veterans groups arguing that Americans in Vietnam exposed to this chemical, as well as their children born after their return, have suffered side-effects including cancer, skin disease, and physical deformities. In 1979 there was an out-of-court settlement with chemical companies that manufactured Agent Orange, and more recently the US government allocated $8 million a year to Vietnam veterans and their children suffering from certain cancers they claim resulted from the herbicide.

Bibliography

Aichinger, Peter. *The American Soldier in Fiction, 1880–1963: a History of Attitudes toward Warfare and the Military Establishment.* Ames, IA: Iowa State University Press, 1975.

Anisfield, Nancy. "Words and Fragment: Narrative Style in Vietnam War Novels." In *Search and Clear: Critical Responses to Selected Literature and Films of the Vietnam War,* edited by William J. Searle, 56–61. Bowling Green, OH: Bowling Green State University Popular Press, 1988.

Baker, Carlos. *Hemingway: the Writer as Artist.* 1952. Reprint. Princeton, NJ: Princeton University Press, 1972.

Baritz, Loren. *Backfire: a History of How American Culture Led Us into Vietnam and Made Us Fight the Way We Did.* 1985. Reprint. New York: Ballantine, 1986.

Bates, Milton J. "Tim O'Brien's Myth of Courage." *Modern Fiction Studies* 33 (1987): 263–79.

Beidler, Philip D. "Truth-Telling and Literary Values in the Vietnam Novel." *South Atlantic Quarterly* 78 (1979): 141–56.

Beidler, Philip D. *American Literature and the Experience of Vietnam.* Athens, GA: University of Georgia Press, 1982.

Berger, Peter L. *et al. Facing Up to Modernity: Excursions in Society, Politics and Religion.* New York: Basic Books, 1977.

Blunden, Edmund. "Memoir (1931)." In *The Collected Poems of Wilfred Owen,* edited by C. Day Lewis, 147–80. New York: New Directions Books, 1965.

Boettcher, Thomas D. *Vietnam: the Valor and the Sorrow.* Boston: Little, Brown, 1985.

Bryan, C. D. B. *Friendly Fire.* New York: G. P. Putnam's Sons, 1976.

Butler, Deborah. *American Women Writers on Vietnam, Unheard Voices: a Selected Annotated Bibliography.* New York: Garland, 1990.

Cady, Edwin H. *Stephen Crane.* Boston: Twayne, 1980.

Capps, Walter. "The War's Transformation." *The Center Magazine* 11.4 (1978): 18–21.

Caputo, Philip. *A Rumor of War*. 1977. Reprint. New York: Ballantine, 1978.

Caputo, Philip. *Indian Country*. 1987. Reprint. New York: Bantam, 1988.

Conrad, Joseph. "An Outpost of Progress." *Tales of Unrest*. 1898. Reprint. New York: Gordon, 1974.

Conrad, Joseph. *Heart of Darkness*. 1902. Reprint. New York: Penguin, 1975.

Coppola, Francis, and Greil Marcus. "Journey up the River: an Interview with Francis Coppola." *Rolling Stone*, 1 November 1979, 51–7.

Crane, Stephen. *The Red Badge of Courage*. 1895. Reprint. New York: Puffin, 1986.

Cronin, Cornelius A. "Historical Background in Larry Heinemann's *Close Quarters*." *Critique: Studies in Modern Fiction* 24 (1983): 119–29.

Cronin, Cornelius A. "From the DMZ to No Man's Land: Philip Caputo's *A Rumor of War* and Its Antecedents." In *Search and Clear: Critical Responses to Selected Literature and Films of the Vietnam War*, edited by William J. Searle, 74–86. Bowling Green, OH: Bowling Green State University Popular Press, 1988.

Del Vecchio, John M. *The 13th Valley*. New York: Bantam, 1982.

Del Vecchio, John M. *For the Sake of All Living Things*. New York: Bantam, 1990.

Dos Passos, John. *Three Soldiers*. 1921. Reprint. Boston: Houghton Mifflin, 1949.

Downs, Frederick. *Aftermath*. 1984. Reprint. New York: Berkley, 1985.

Durden, Charles. *No Bugles, No Drums*. New York: Viking, 1976.

Dyson, Freeman. *Disturbing the Universe*. New York: Harper & Row, 1979.

Ehrhart, W. D. "Why I Did It." *Virginia Quarterly Review* 56 (1980): 19–31.

Ehrhart, W. D. (ed.). *Carrying the Darkness: American Indochina – the Poetry of the Vietnam War*. New York: Avon, 1985.

Eisinger, Chester E. *Fiction of the Forties*. Chicago: University of Chicago Press, 1963.

Fenton, James. "Nostalgie de la guerre." *New Statesman*, 7 April 1978, 464.

Figley, Charles, and Seymour Leventman. "Introduction: Estrangement and Victimization." In *Strangers at Home: Vietnam Veterans Since the War*, edited by Charles Figley and Seymour Leventman, xxi–xxxi. New York: Praeger, 1980.

Flora, Joseph M. *Hemingway's Nick Adams*. Baton Rouge, LA: Louisiana State University Press, 1982.

Fussell, Paul. *The Great War and Modern Memory*. 1975. Reprint. New York: Oxford University Press, 1981.

Fussell, Paul. *Wartime: Understanding and Behavior in the Second World War*. New York: Oxford University Press, 1989.

Giles, James R. *James Jones*. Boston: Twayne, 1981.

Gray, Paul. "Secret History." *Time*, 7 November 1977, 119–20.

Greene, Graham. *The Quiet American*. 1955. Reprint. New York: Penguin, 1980.

Groom, Winston. *Better Times than These*. 1978. Reprint. New York: Berkley, 1979.

Haines, Henry W. "'What Kind of War?'": an Analysis of the Vietnam Veterans Memorial." *Critical Studies in Mass Communication* 3 (1986): 1–20.

Halberstam, David. *One Very Hot Day*. 1967. Reprint. New York: Warner, 1984.

Hallin, Daniel C. *The "Uncensored War": the Media and Vietnam*. New York: Oxford University Press, 1986.

Hasford, Gustav. *The Short-Timers*. 1979. Reprint. New York: Bantam, 1983.

Hastings, Max. *The Korean War*. New York: Simon & Schuster, 1988.

Heinemann, Larry. *Close Quarters*. 1977. Reprint. New York: Penguin, 1986.

Heinemann, Larry. "'Just Don't Fit': Stalking the Elusive 'Tripwire' Veteran." *Harper's*, April 1985, 55–63.

Heinemann, Larry. *Paco's Story*. 1986. Reprint. New York: Penguin, 1987.

Heller, Joseph. *Catch-22*. 1961. Reprint. New York: Dell, 1979.

Hellmann, John. "The New Journalism and Vietnam: Memory as Structure in Michael Herr's *Dispatches*." *South Atlantic Quarterly* 79 (1980): 141–51.

Hellmann, John. *American Myth and the Legacy of Vietnam*. New York: Columbia University Press, 1986.

Hemingway, Ernest. *A Farewell to Arms*. 1929. Reprint. New York: Scribner's, 1957.

Hemingway, Ernest. *A Moveable Feast*. New York: Scribner's, 1964.

Hemingway, Ernest. *The Complete Short Stories of Ernest Hemingway*. The Finca Vigia Edition. New York: Scribner's, 1987.

Hendin, Herbert, and Ann Pollinger Haas. *Wounds of War: the Psychological Aftermath of Combat in Vietnam*. New York: Basic Books, 1984.

Herr, Michael. *Dispatches*. New York: Knopf, 1977.

Herring, George C. *America's Longest War: the United States and Vietnam, 1950–1975*. New York: Wiley, 1979.

Hersh, Seymour M. *My Lai 4: a Report on the Massacre and Its Aftermath*. New York: Random House, 1970.

Hersh, Seymour M. *Cover-Up: the Army's Secret Investigation of the Massacre at My Lai 4*. New York: Random House, 1972.

Holm, Jeanne. *Women in the Military: an Unfinished Revolution*. Novato, CA: Presidio, 1982.

Jeffords, Susan. *The Remasculization of America: Gender and the Vietnam War*. Bloomington, IN: Indiana University Press, 1989.

Jones, James. *From Here to Eternity*. New York: Scribner's, 1951.

Jones, James. *The Thin Red Line*. New York: Scribner's, 1962.

Jones, James. *Viet Journal*. New York: Delacorte, 1974.

Jones, James. *WWII*. New York: Grosset & Dunlap, 1975.

Jones, Peter G. *War and the Novelist: Appraising the American War Novel*. Columbia, MO: University of Missouri Press, 1976.

Just, Ward. "Vietnam: the Camera Lies." *Atlantic*, December 1979, 63–5.

Karnow, Stanley. *Vietnam: a History*. New York: Viking, 1983.

Kazin, Alfred. *Bright Book of Life*. Boston: Little Brown, 1973.

Kimbrough, Robert. "Conrad's *Youth* (1902): an Introduction." *Heart of Darkness*. Norton Critical Edition, edited by Robert Kimbrough, 408–18. New York: Norton, 1988.

Knightley, Phillip. *The First Casualty – from the Crimea to the Falklands: the War Correspondent as Hero, Propagandist and Myth Maker*. 1975. Reprint. London: Pan Books, 1989.

Knox, Donald, and Alfred Coppel. *The Korean War: Uncertain Victory*. New York: Harcourt, Brace, Jovanovich, 1988.

Kovic, Ron. *Born on the Fourth of July*. 1976. Reprint. New York: Pocket Books, 1977.

Kubrick, Stanley, Michael Herr, and Gustav Hasford. *Full Metal Jacket* (screenplay). New York: Knopf, 1987.

Lane, William K., Jr. "Vietnam Vets without Hollywood, without Tears." *The Wall Street Journal*, 26 July 1988, 24.

Leland, John G. "Writing about Vietnam." *College English* 43 (1981): 739–41.

Lennon, Michael (ed.). *Conversations with Norman Mailer*. Jackson, MS: University of Mississippi Press, 1988.

Levenson, J. C. Foreword. *The Works of Stephen Crane*. Vol. 2, xiii–xcii. Charlottesville, VA: University of Virginia Press, 1975.

Lewis, Lloyd B. *The Tainted War: Culture and Identity in Vietnam War Narratives*. Westport, CT: Greenwood, 1985.

Lifton, Robert Jay. "The Postwar War." *Journal of Social Issues* 31.4 (1975): 181–94.

Lifton, Robert Jay. *Home from the War: Vietnam Veterans, Neither Victims Nor Executioners*. 1973. Reprint. New York: Basic Books, 1985.

McNeill, William H. *The Pursuit of Power: Technology, Armed Force, and Society since AD 1000*. Chicago: University of Chicago Press, 1982.

MacShane, Frank. *Into Eternity: the Life of James Jones, American Writer*. Boston: Houghton Mifflin, 1985.

Mailer, Norman. *The Naked and the Dead*. 1948. Reprint. New York: Henry Holt, 1981.

Mailer, Norman. *Cannibals and Christians*. New York: Dial, 1966.

Mailer, Norman. *Why Are We in Vietnam?* New York: Putnam, 1967.

Mailer, Norman. *The Armies of the Night*. New York: New American Library, 1968.

Mason, Bobbie Ann. *In Country*. 1985. Reprint. New York: Harper Row, 1986.

Mason, Bobbie Ann. Interview. "A Film Guide to *In Country*." New York: Cultural Information Service (Warner Brothers), 1989.

Moore, Robin, *The Green Berets*. New York: Coward, 1965.

Morgan, Thomas B. "Reporters of the Lost War." *Esquire*, July 1984, 49–60.

Myers, Thomas. *Walking Point: American Narratives of Vietnam*. New York: Oxford University Press, 1988.

Newman, John. *Vietnam War Literature: an Annotated Bibliography of Imaginative Works about Americans Fighting in Vietnam*. 2nd edn. Metuchen, NJ: Scarecrow Press, 1988.

O'Brien, Tim. *If I Die in a Combat Zone: Box Me Up and Ship Me Home*. 1973. Reprint. New York: Dell, 1979.

O'Brien, Tim. *Northern Lights*. New York: Delacorte, 1975.

O'Brien, Tim. *Going After Cacciato*. 1978. Reprint. New York: Dell, 1979.

O'Brien, Tim. *The Nuclear Age*. New York: Knopf, 1985.

O'Brien, Tim. *The Things They Carried*. Boston: Houghton Mifflin, 1990.

Owen, Wilfred. *The Collected Poems of Wilfred Owen*, edited by C. Day Lewis. New York: New Directions Books, 1965.

Palm, Edward F. "James Webb's *Fields of Fire*: the Melting Pot Platoon Revisited." *Critique: Studies in Modern Fiction* 24 (1983): 105–18.

Pochoda, Elizabeth. "Vietnam, We've All Been There." *The Nation*, 25 March 1978, 344–6.

Proffitt, Nicholas. *Gardens of Stone*. New York: Carroll & Graf, 1983.

Remarque, Erich Maria. *All Quiet on the Western Front*. 1928. Trans. A.W. Wheen. Reprint. New York: Fawcett, 1987.

Remarque, Erich Maria. *The Road Back*. Trans. A. W. Wheen. New York: Grosset & Dunlap, 1930

Riggan, Bob. *Free Fire Zone*. New York: Norton, 1984.

Saltzman, Arthur M. "The Betrayal of the Imagination: Paul Brodeur's *The Stunt Man* and Tim O'Brien's *Going After Cacciato*." *Critique* 22.1 (1980): 32–8.

Santoli, Al. *Everything We Had: an Oral History of the American War by Thirty-Three American Soldiers Who Fought It*. New York: Random House, 1981.

Schroeder, Eric. "Two Interviews: Talks with Tim O'Brien and Robert Stone." *Modern Fiction Studies* 30 (1984): 135–64.

Schroeder, Eric. "The Past and the Possible: Tim O'Brien's Dialectic of Memory and Imagination." In *Search and Clear: Critical Responses to Selected Literature and Films of the Vietnam War*, edited by William J. Searle, 116–34. Bowling Green, OH: Bowling Green State University Popular Press, 1988.

Searle, William J. "Walking Wounded: Vietnam War Novels of Return." In *Search and Clear: Critical Responses to Selected Literature and Films of the Vietnam War*, edited by William J. Searle, 147–59. Bowling Green, OH: Bowling Green State University Popular Press, 1988.

Sheehan, Neil. *A Bright Shining Lie: John Paul Vann and America in Vietnam*. New York: Random House, 1988.

Smart, Robert A. *The Nonfiction Novel*. New York: University Press of America, 1985.

Smith, Julian. *Looking Away: Hollywood and Vietnam*. New York: Scribner's, 1975.

Smith, Paul. *A Reader's Guide to the Short Stories of Ernest Hemingway*. Boston: G.K. Hall, 1989.

Steel, Danielle. *Message from Nam*. New York: Delacorte, 1990.

Taylor, Gordon O. "American Personal Narrative of the War in Vietnam." *American Literature* 52 (1980): 294–308.

Terry, Wallace. *Bloods: an Oral History of the Vietnam War by Black Veterans*. 1984. Reprint. New York: Ballantine, 1985.

Trumbo, Dalton. *Johnny Got His Gun*. 1939. Reprint. Secaucus, NJ: Lyle Stuart, 1970.

Waller, Willard. *The Veteran Comes Back*. New York: Dryden, 1944.

Walsh, Jeffrey. *American War Literature: 1914 to Vietnam*. London: Macmillan, 1982.

Watt, Ian. *Conrad in the Nineteenth Century*. Berkeley, CA: University of California Press, 1979.

Webb, James. *Fields of Fire*. Englewood Cliffs, NJ: Prentice-Hall, 1978.

Webb, James. *A Country Such as This*. New York: Doubleday, 1983.

Weber, Ronald. *The Literature of Fact: Literary Non-fiction in American Writing*. Athens, OH: Ohio University Press, 1980.

West, Richard. *Victory in Vietnam*. London: Private Eye/André Deutsch, 1974.

Wilson, James C. *Vietnam in Prose and Film*. Jefferson, NC: McFarland, 1982.

Wittman, Sandra M. *Writing about Vietnam: a Bibliography of the Literature of the Vietnam Conflict*. Boston: G.K. Hall, 1989.

Wright, Stephen. *Meditations in Green*. 1983. Reprint. New York: Bantam, 1984.

INDEX

Numbers in bold indicate major discussions of entries

233